1995

RESEARCH PERSPECTIVES IN ADULT EDUCATION

RESEARCH PERSPECTIVES IN ADULT EDUCATION

Edited by
D. Randy Garrison

KRIEGER PUBLISHING COMPANY
MALABAR, FLORIDA
1994

Original Edition 1994

Printed and Published by
KRIEGER PUBLISHING COMPANY
KRIEGER DRIVE
MALABAR, FLORIDA 32950

Copyright © 1994 by Krieger Publishing Company

Library of Congress Cataloging-In-Publication Data
Research perspectives in adult education / edited by D. Randy
  Garrison.
      p. cm.
    ISBN 0-89464-716-4 (alk. paper)
    1. Adult education—Research. 2. Adult education—Research—
  Methodology. I. Garrison, D. R. (D. Randy), 1950–
  LC5225.R47R47   1994
  374′.0072—dc20   93-32730
                                                                        CIP

10 9 8 7 6 5 4 3 2

CONTENTS

CONTRIBUTORS

ADRIAN BLUNT is an associate professor in the College of Education at the University of Saskatchewan where he teaches courses in adult, continuing and post-secondary education. Currently he serves as coeditor of *The Canadian Journal for the Study of Adult Education* and is a member of the editorial boards of *Adult Education Quarterly* and *Adult Basic Education.*

ROGER BOSHIER is a professor of adult education at the University of British Columbia, Vancouver, Canada. He was born in Hastings, New Zealand, and studied psychology at Victoria University of Wellington. An active member of the movement to oppose the testing of nuclear weapons in the South Pacific, he moved to Canada in 1974.

RALPH G. BROCKETT is an associate professor in the Department of Educational Leadership, University of Tennessee, Knoxville. Previously he had faculty positions at Montana State University and Syracuse University. He currently serves as editor-in-chief of *New Directions for Adult and Continuing Education.*

D. RANDY GARRISON is a professor and currently holds the position of Associate Dean (Research and Development) in the Faculty of Continuing Education at The University of Calgary.

WILLIAM S. "BILL" GRIFFITH has been a professor of adult education for over 30 years, having been a tenured member of the adult education special field at the University of Chicago before moving to the University of British Columbia where he has been a professor since 1977. He and Howard McClusky served as series editors for the eight-volume 1980–81 Handbook Series of the Adult Education Association of the United States.

ROGER HIEMSTRA served as professor of adult education at the University of Nebraska (1970–1976), as professor and chair of adult education at Iowa State University (1976–1980), and as professor and chair of adult education at Syracuse University from 1980–1992. Currently he is professor of adult learning and instructional technology at

Syracuse University. He has served as the editor for two national adult education journals.

SHARAN B. MERRIAM is a professor of adult and continuing education at the University of Georgia. She received her Ed.D. degree from Rutgers University in adult education. Before coming to the University of Georgia, she served on the faculties of Northern Illinois University and Virginia Polytechnic Institute and State University. She is a former coeditor of *Adult Education Quarterly*. She is also coeditor with Phyllis Cunningham of the 1990 *Handbook of Adult and Continuing Education*.

KJELL RUBENSON is the director of the Centre for Policy Studies in Education and professor of adult education at the University of British Columbia. Much of his research has addressed broader policy issues in Canadian and Swedish adult education.

DOUG SHALE is an analyst in the Office of Institutional Analysis at The University of Calgary. He has had extensive experience in and published widely on nontraditional educational delivery to adult learners.

THOMAS J. SORK is an associate professor and coordinator of the adult education program at the University of British Columbia. His recent research has focused on understanding the dynamics of program planning as it occurs in practice and developing a descriptive model of resource allocation processes in adult education.

ALLISON TOM is an assistant professor in the Department of Administrative, Adult and Higher Education at the University of British Columbia where she teaches women's studies and ethnographic research methods.

PREFACE

At the 1992 Adult Education Research Conference (AERC) a heated discussion erupted with regard to the book *Adult education: Evolution and achievements in a developing field of study*. This book was "intended to update the 1964 sacred scripture of adult education, the so-called black book" (Carlson, 1992, p. 4). It was suggested at the conference that the contributors to the above-mentioned book, although acting as adult education's gatekeepers and power brokers, no longer represent the field. Reflecting upon this situation, Thomas (1992) contends that *Adult education: Evolution and achievements in a developing field of study* does not reflect new directions of research and that it may best be described as "the end of the beginning" (p. 7). Other AERC partici- pants commented that there is a new sense of direction and the old guard has taken its last gasp (Carlson, 1992). In any case, it would seem that the adult education research community is, at a minimum, experiencing a challenge to the status quo. The question is whether this challenge will translate into a new and vital stage in the theoretical development of the field or be simply the replacement of one ideology for another.

Long (1992) goes further in describing the adult education research community in the United States as being in a state of disarray and at an important crossroad. While "hundreds of research reports are being published annually . . . too few of these reports add to our theoretical understanding of adult education phenomena or to adult education prac- tice" (Long, 1992, p. 67). However, the problem goes beyond political dissension. Adult education is at a crossroad because the field has not produced a coherent and distinctive body of knowledge. As we shall see in subsequent chapters, our research efforts have been too fragmented and we have not clearly identified what distinguishes the field of adult education from other educational endeavors. Or at least we have not shaped this perspective and theory in a recognizable framework. The need for theory to define adult education needs and to guide practice has never been greater. During times of fundamental social change tremen- dous opportunities exist, and adult education has never been more rele- vant as we face the need for education and training in the quest for personal meaning and economic competitiveness.

It has only been 30 years since adult education has taken a systematic approach to the study of the field and to the development of an epistemological foundation. However, adult education as a field of study currently appears to be on the verge of a major transition. While there have been minor shifts in the focus of study and the methodologies used, it is suggested here that fundamental changes are needed in the magnitude and direction of our research efforts. This transition is necessary to ensure the credibility and development of the field of adult education as a distinct area of research and graduate study.

With this in mind, the purpose of this book is to bring together a range of issues related to the conduct of research in adult education. These include identifying issues/problems in the study of adult education, describing research perspectives and practices, suggesting ways to encourage the development of research programs, and facilitating the publication of research findings. A basic premise is that the identity and viability of the field is dependent upon critically analyzing and explicating its theoretical base through systematic research. It is time that adult educators take a critical look at the state of research and knowledge development in their field. While this critical analysis may at times be painful, those who have the courage to critically assess the epistemological foundation of the field are its true benefactors.

Research Perspectives in Adult Education is intended for those who are concerned with or engaged in developing the knowledge base of adult education and thereby ensuring its continued development and acceptance as a legitimate field of study. While the primary audience for this book may be researchers, both established and novice, there is much that would interest the adult education practitioner. Especially those professional adult educators who consider themselves "reflective practitioners" and who may be involved in various forms of action or participatory research.

OVERVIEW OF CONTENTS

This book is essentially concerned with understanding the epistemological foundation of adult education, the research process, policy issues, and directions for the future. Chapter 1 provides an overview of adult education research. It briefly describes the historical development, identifies issues, addresses the scope of the knowledge base, and discusses approaches to developing the epistemological foundation of the field. Chapter 2 addresses the complex problem of research paradigms and methods. Historical philosophical positions are used as the backdrop for a discussion of complementary research methodologies, necessary research standards, and the need for adult education researchers to take an inclusive view of research paradigms.

Chapter 3 presents the background to collaboration between practitioners and academic researchers. Theoretical and practical issues are discussed with regard to planning and carrying out collaborative research. Chapter 4 takes a look at the potential as well as the limits of collaboration and networking in adult education research. Several strategies are discussed in promoting research collaboration along with a consideration of ethical issues.

Chapter 5 addresses the often neglected first stage of any research: originating an idea (identifying a problem) and developing a conceptual approach (research perspective). The chapter is constructed on the basic notion that research problems are found in the experiential (real) world most familiar to the researcher. Chapter 6 provides strategies and approaches to the writing process as well as procedures and expectations with regard to getting a manuscript published.

Chapter 7 outlines an historical and current perspective on graduate training and research in adult education. A discussion of approaches to improving research training as well as to the production and dissemination of research in adult education is also presented. Chapter 8 addresses the function of policy research, its role in the creation of knowledge, and the development of adult education as a field of study.

Chapter 9, in particular, extends the discussion in the first two chapters. The first part of this chapter discusses the process of research and, therefore, complements the methodology discussion in chapter 2. Although the terminology used to identify major paradigms in this chapter differ somewhat from that used in chapter 2, we are talking about similar paradigms. Such differences implicitly recognize the complexity and fragmentation of perspectives in the philosophy of science. The second part of chapter 9 focuses on the product of adult education research and extends the discussion initiated in chapter 1. Finally, chapter 10 identifies the central issues discussed in previous chapters.

REFERENCES

Carlson, R. A. (1992, Fall). Open season on gate keepers at the 1992 Adult Education Research Conference. *CPAE Newsletter,* p. 4–6.

Long, H. B. (1992). University adult education research in the United States. *International Journal of University Adult Education, 31*(3), 66–89.

Thomas, A. (1992). Response to "Open season on gate keepers". *CPAE Newsletter,* Fall, 7.

ACKNOWLEDGMENTS

The concept for this book has been with me for several years but, as the result of various contingencies, I was not able to proceed. In retrospect, this may have been fortuitous for I believe, as Huey Long suggests, that the study of adult education is currently at a crossroad. I hope that the book will stimulate interest and precipitate critical reflection and discourse with regard to the challenges of developing the epistemological foundation of the field of adult education.

Let me offer my sincere thanks to my colleagues who took the time to contribute so ably to this book. In my view, their insights will prove to be invaluable to the development of the field. I must also express my gratitude to Krieger Publishing Company for supporting this project.

CHAPTER 1

AN EPISTEMOLOGICAL OVERVIEW OF THE FIELD

D. Randy Garrison

The process of research is to formulate, analyze, and test theories in an open, critical, and systematic manner. The aim is to create order through the development of coherent theoretical frameworks. Theoretical frameworks provide the assumptions and foundation for knowledge development in all disciplines and fields of study. Adult education is no exception. If adult education is to be recognized as a worthwhile field of study it must generate relevant, distinctive, and coherent theoretical frameworks. The methods and issues used to investigate and describe adult education may be open to debate, but the necessity of distinct and coherent theoretical frameworks for its identity, vitality, and development should not be in question.

This chapter will provide an overview of epistemological issues that concern the field of adult education. That is, the chapter will describe and discuss the origin, nature, and methodology of the development of knowledge in adult education. This is accomplished by retrospectively describing the development of a research tradition in adult education, providing a discussion of what constitutes a knowledge base for a field of study, and finally, by describing approaches to the construction of theoretical frameworks for the development of adult education as a field of study.

ORIGIN OF THE FIELD

There is little question that the field of adult education has a rich history of practice (Selman & Dampiere, 1991; Stubblefield & Keane, 1989); however, as a field of study, adult education is a relative newcomer. The initial concern for research was perhaps to justify its professional status by delineating its foundational knowledge base (Jarvis,

1987). In the early 1960s, Verner, Liveright, and Jensen (1961), representing The Commission of the Professors of Adult Education (24 members), wrote that "the discipline of adult education is not yet much beyond the outline stage" and research "is still only a secondary interest of isolated social scientists and educators" (p. 11). However, with publication of the book *Adult Education: Outlines of an emerging field of university study* (Jensen et al., 1964), there appears to be a clear demarcation of the evolution of adult education as a field of study.

While *Adult education: Outlines of an emerging field of university study* may have marked the beginning of a systematic approach to the study of adult education, there existed a history of research before this publication. Graduate programs specializing in adult education emerged in the 1930s. In addition, organizations such as The American Association for Adult Education (AAAE), formed in 1926, stimulated the growth of adult education as a field of study. AAAE sponsored many publications including the *Handbook of adult education* published in 1934, 1936, and 1948 (Long, 1990). In 1950 the journal *Adult Education* was published as an "amalgamation of the AAAE's *Adult Education Journal* and the National Education Association Department's *Adult Education Bulletin*" (Knowles, 1962, p. 236). It is the journal *Adult Education* and its successor in 1983, the *Adult Education Quarterly* (AEQ), that perhaps best documents the development of adult education as a field of study.

Dickinson and Rusnell (1971), operating on the assumption that professional journals generally reflect the development of a field of study, analyzed volumes of *Adult Education* published between 1950 and 1970. They attempted "to identify trends and patterns in the content of the journal since those might be indicative of the development of the discipline of adult education" (Dickinson & Rusnell, 1971, p. 178). Several distinct trends were identified that indicated development in the study and practice of adult education. They noted that authors associated with a university doubled to 84.5% from the first 5-year period to the last 5-year period. The average number of references rose sharply from 0.7 per article to 13.2 per article when comparing the first and last 5-year intervals. Again, comparing the first and last 5-year periods, it was found that articles representing program descriptions and personal beliefs declined dramatically (36.0 to 5.1% and 44.3 to 12.8% respectively), while a significant increase in empirical research was reported (8.2 to 43.6%). Due to this growing sophistication in research methodology, Dickinson and Rusnell suggested that it reflects a "gradual emergence of a discipline of adult education" (p. 180).

Long and Agyekum (1974) conducted a similar meta-research analysis of *Adult Education* covering the period 1964–1973. This period marked the 10 years of research development from the publication of *Adult education: Outlines of an emerging field of university study*. Long and Agyekum (1974) stated that during "the early 1960's a chorus of voices challenged adult educators to increase their efforts in research and theory building" (p. 103). Of the 163 authors during this 10-year period, most only contributed once. Forty-three were members of the Commission of Professors. Eleven authors contributed three or more articles. However, in terms of research thrust, there was no definitive content area by authors affiliated with the most productive institutions. The conclusion of this study was consistent with the Dickinson and Rusnell study in that *Adult Education* "reflects an increasing quality and sophistication in research design and importance of research questions in adult education" (Long & Agyekum, 1974, p. 113).

Blunt and Lee (1994) recently completed a study that documented the contribution of articles by graduate students to *Adult Education/Adult Education Quarterly* (1969–1988) and thus their contribution to the epistemological base of adult education. From a survey of all contributors to the journal, it was found that research conducted by authors who were graduate students increased over the 20-year period and currently is estimated to represent nearly half (46%) of all research published in AEQ. The results of this survey also revealed that 60% of the articles were contributed by students from only nine of the 41 programs. Assuming fair access to AEQ, the low relative and absolute number of programs associated with student publication raises the question as to whether a sufficient number of graduate programs are adequately preparing adult educators to contribute to the epistemological foundation of the field, especially since graduate students play such a prominent role in AEQ published research.

A second established source that reflects the development of research and knowledge in the field is the proceedings of the Adult Education Research Conference (AERC). The AERC was inaugurated in 1959 and has since become an important forum for sharing ideas and research findings in their formative stages. The purpose of AERC is "to promote the improvement of research and evaluation in adult education, and to foster professional collaboration among scholars who promote research, conduct research, and utilize research findings in the field of adult education" (Boyd, Coggins, & Forest, 1989, p. iv). Long (1983) analyzed AERC abstracts from 1971–1980 and reported that from a quantitative perspective, AERC is a significant addition to the field given that 355 papers were presented at AERC in the 10-year period by 347 different individuals. Professors of adult education constituted 26% of the contributors and they were responsible for 33% of the papers. It is important to note that the length of the abstract/paper varied from one-half page in 1972 to seven pages in 1980. Long (1983) concluded that the "value of the AERC proceedings as a vehicle for disseminating research could be strengthened by addressing problems associated with the nature, structure and content of the abstracts" (p. 93).

The previous description has provided a sketch of the development of adult education's knowledge base. This development has been described in terms of three somewhat overlapping phases of research development (Deshler & Hagan, 1989). The phases are atheoretical program description, improvement of research methods and designs, and theory building and definition of research territory. Although no dates were attached, it is possible to extrapolate from the previously cited studies and provide an approximate chronology. The first phase appears to have ended in the mid-1960s while the second phase likely ended in the late 1970s. The third and current phase perhaps can be identified by the emergence of qualitative methodological approaches and an acceptance of both qualitative and quantitative research methodologies. In any case, adoption of qualitative research methodologies encouraged theory development and increased the focus on research as we approached the end of the 1980s.

DEFINING ISSUES

In moving toward a conceptualization of adult education as a field of study, adult educators first must address issues surrounding the interdisciplinary nature of adult education. Many authors have written about the study of adult education and referred to it as an emerging discipline (Boshier & Pickard, 1979; Boyd & Apps, 1980; Jensen, 1964; Long & Agyekum, 1974; Rubenson, 1982; Welton, 1987). However, the view of adult education as an emerging discipline may be based more on hope than on a critical understanding of what a discipline entails. Boshier & Pickard (1979), while acknowledging there is some disagreement whether education itself is a discipline, suggest that adult education is an emerging discipline by virtue of citation evidence that it is developing a unique body of knowledge. On the other hand, Bright (1985) and Plecas and Sork (1986) stand out because they are among the few who have questioned adult education's status as a discipline. Bright (1985) states unequivocally that "adult education can only, at best, be regarded as a 'field of knowledge' " (p. 170).

While adult education does have an identifiable body of knowledge, it does not necessarily follow that adult education qualifies as a discipline.

We need to be careful how we use the term *discipline* to refer to domains of knowledge. A discipline is dependent upon an autonomous and distinctive body of knowledge or established scientific principles (i.e., theories and laws) (Scheffler, 1973). According to Scheffler (1973), it is fallacious to suggest that every distinct realm or domain must be the object of some discipline or that disciplines can be created simply by producing new terms. Shulman (1988) states categorically that education is not a discipline but a field of study since it is interdisciplinary in the development of a body of knowledge. This seems to be the key criteria in rejecting adult education as a discipline. Due to its interdisciplinary nature, it would be difficult to describe its knowledge domain as autonomous. That is not to say, however, that adult education's knowledge domain should not be distinctive. Scheffler (1973) concluded that education would be advanced by being less concerned as to its disciplinary status and more concerned with "attempts to formulate principles relevant to our work, no matter what their disciplinary labels" (pp. 55–56). Relating this to adult education, adult educators might also be well advised to formulate concepts and theories distinctive to the phenomenon as it exists. This would suggest as well that adult education accept its interdisciplinary status and realize that it will not likely develop an autonomous body of knowledge.

Using an epistemological structure suggested by Hirst, Bright (1985) stated that "adult education would appear to be unavoidably categorized as a derived, composite body of knowledge utilizing knowledge generated from other and relatively more intrinsic sources" (p. 172). He suggested that not only has adult education not generated unique concepts that would qualify it as a discipline, much work needs to be done to reformulate borrowed concepts into an overall theoretical framework identifiable to adult education. In short, we do not have an easily identifiable subject matter central to adult education pursuits. Looking at this question from a practical or operational perspective, it has been argued "that adult education is involved in the same activity as education generally" (Bright, 1985, p. 180). This is consistent with Houle's (1972) view of adult education as being essentially the same process as education generally. Griffith (1987) stated that Houle's "basic assumption is that the essentials of the educative process remain the same for all ages of life" (p. 157). With regard to adult education, Peters (1991) also concluded that "the field should locate itself in the broader field of educational practice" (p. 432), but concedes that this view "is not as widely accepted as one might think" (p. 432). Therefore, adult education may be best described as a field of study and perhaps, more accurately, a subfield of educational study.

Adult education is at best an emerging field of study given the uncompleted task of achieving consensual agreement as to what constitutes the field and how this differentiates adult education from other fields of study and practice. Further, while adult education may appear to have a body of knowledge, there is little coherence or distinctiveness to its formulation. Plecas and Sork (1986) stated that there "is no evidence that adult educators have made a concerted effort on any sizeable scale to use theory and research arising from adult education and other relevant literature as building blocks in the creation of consolidated theoretical models" (p. 48). If this is the case, a serious challenge exists for adult education researchers to consolidate their efforts in the goal of developing distinctive and coherent theoretical frameworks and, thus, establishing the credibility of adult education as a field of study.

A FIELD OF STUDY

As a field of study, adult education is interdisciplinary in nature but obligated to delineate a coherent body of knowledge peculiar to its area of pursuit. A theoretical field of knowledge "involves organizing . . . and integrating that knowledge relative to the pursuit in question sufficient to enable a coherent and comprehensive description, specification and interpretive analysis of the activities involved" (Bright, 1985, p. 173). Furthermore, the body of knowledge cannot be an eclectic enumeration of theories but instead "must demonstrate the organisation of its derived knowledge in a manner which justifies and expresses the relevance of its focus of interest" (Bright, 1985, p. 173). While this represents an enormous challenge to the field of adult education, it also represents a necessary goal and standard to guide research that will allow adult education to fully emerge as a recognized field of study.

To say that adult education is interdisciplinary and requires coherent theoretical frameworks of its own raises questions about the role of borrowing theory from other fields and disciplines. When adult education as a field of study began to emerge in the mid-1960s, Jensen (1964) advocated borrowing and reformulating knowledge from other disciplines. More recently, however, Welton (1987) states that "Borrowing from the disciplines only makes sense if we know our own domain, and within the domain, the regions" (p. 58). This is essentially the position of Boyd and Apps (1980) who argue strongly against the free borrowing of concepts and theories from other disciplines "until we have clearly understood the structure, function, problems, and purposes of adult education itself" (p. 2).

Such arguments for understanding the adult education phenomena are important because the field is ultimately dependent upon coherent knowledge distinctive of the pursuits of the field. At the same time, however, it makes little sense to ignore related and relevant research findings. Surely both approaches should and must coexist. It may be that through familiarizing themselves with other fields and disciplines, adult education researchers will become more aware of the field's distinctiveness (or nondistinctiveness). That is, it is legitimate to borrow knowledge from other disciplines to inform research so long as it is reformulated to address or define the distinct contextual demands and phenomena of adult education. Such borrowing and reformulating must also be integrated into a coherent theoretical framework. If adult education is to rid itself of the charge of being atheoretical (Boshier, 1980; Rubenson, 1982) and establish itself as a field of study, then adult education researchers who borrow knowledge must reformulate that knowledge such that it is coherent and distinctive. Good research practice necessitates a building upon previous research and an interpretation and integration of previous findings within a coherent theoretical framework.

Deshler and Hagan (1989) suggest that borrowing and reformulating in itself is not particularly controversial. They believe that what is at issue is whether such borrowing might produce research that is narrow, incomplete, and discipline-bound. It would seem, however, that the real risk of producing narrow and incomplete research is to ignore the findings of other disciplines in the false assumption that this borrowing will preclude or thwart the efforts of adult education researchers to define and coherently conceptualize the distinctiveness of adult education. As a field of study, multidisciplinary and interdisciplinary research approaches are called for, not single discipline or exclusively inward-focusing research efforts. From a European perspective, Hake (1992) suggests that not seeking the help of recognized disciplines is a massive epistemological error. We need the help of all social scientists in understanding the complex and diffuse field of adult education. Therefore, the "more important question is how we can come to some understanding of adult educational phenomena in theoretical terms which can guide academically reputable research" (Hake, 1992, p. 70). The balance of internal and external focusing will vary according to the research question, but the goal remains coherent and distinctive theoretical frameworks central to the adult education phenomenon.

It is not sufficient for adult education to simply identify a relevant domain of knowledge, whether it is generic or borrowed. The knowledge must be integrated into a coherent theoretical framework that is distinctly adult education in orientation if it is to be identified as a field of study. There must also be a concerted effort to build on previous research that will lead to the systematic development of relevant and distinctive theory. At present, the development of adult education as a field of study is at risk due to the fragmentation of the field's goals and a lack of systematic research efforts. Plecas and Sork (1986) suggest that "the field has been moved to consider education not only as a tool to help individuals learn, but as a tool to affect economic, social, political, community, and societal living conditions" (p. 53). They also state that adult education has assumed within its purview all learning—planned and organized as well as chance learning in the natural societal setting. Given this proliferation of purposes and practices, it is difficult to focus research efforts in a systematic and sustained manner that will define the distinctiveness of the field. Some adult education researchers seem to accept the diffuse nature of adult education and believe "only a multitude of context and domain specific theories are likely to result" (Brookfield, 1992, p. 79). While a number of specific theories does not in itself exclude a coherent view of adult education phenomena, if adult education is to have any sense of identity it is necessary to define itself in a coherent manner.

The reality is that adult education has not in any way "achieved a masterful synthesis of what can confidently be said to be the central principles or the basic knowledge of the field" (Houle, 1991, p. xvii). Although we must encourage diversity of perspectives, research has generally been noncumulative, with the result that the knowledge base has broadened but appears not to have deepened (Long, 1991). Due largely to unsystematic and noncumulative research efforts, an integration and description of the distinctiveness of the field remains an elusive goal. Broadening the field may have served a useful purpose in the past, but efforts must now be directed to identifying the central principles and pursuits of adult education. To this end, Plecas and Sork (1986) suggested that "the primary phenomenon under study would be organized learning, with the goal of the discipline [field?] being to develop a body of disciplined knowledge relating to how learning can best be facilitated given various adult learner populations and various social and political conditions" (pp. 58–59). Similarly, Peters (1991) believed that adult education "should locate itself at the level of design of educational programs in terms of the subject matter to be emphasized" (p. 432). Notwithstanding minor differences in terms of scope regarding key words such as facilitating and design, these two views provide a focused vision of the field of adult education that should be debated.

There is, however, a major difficulty in attempting to focus research efforts, even if consensus can be achieved as to the central pursuit and phenomena of adult education. It may be somewhat naive to suggest that adult education researchers would suddenly shift their research interests to domains that may be of importance to the field but have little connection to their previous work. Even if adult education could identify these important research questions, it is not realistic and there is no evidence that researchers will follow any other lead than what interests them (Garrison & Baskett, 1987). Perhaps the only reasonable solution to address the problem of diversity of research interests and to focus on phenomena central to adult education is to train and socialize a new generation of researchers. In fact, this may be the only realistic strategy to ensure the continued development of concepts and theories distinctive to adult education. While training future adult education researchers is of primary importance, an understanding of the field's knowledge domains is also crucial.

Several knowledge domains in adult education show promise in terms of developing a distinctive theoretical framework. Examples of knowledge domains that reflect varying stages of development and distinctiveness are andragogy, self-directed learning, critical thinking/reflection, participation/dropout, program planning, and adult development. While these knowledge domains do have the potential to provide a theoretical basis to understand and describe the phenomena of adult education, they all require concerted and extensive research efforts to meet the requirement of a distinctive theoretical framework. The various knowledge domains themselves need to be interrelated to convey a coherence within the field of adult education. Such a model was provided by Boyd and Apps (1980) with the intention that it would contribute to a demarcation of the nature and parameters of adult education. They also state that it could be used as a framework within which the applicability of theories and concepts developed in other fields can be evaluated. A modest approach to integrating two knowledge domains (self-directed learning and critical thinking) was attempted by Garrison (1992).

APPROACHES TO DEFINING THE FIELD

Notwithstanding the need for frameworks that reflect the central focus and pursuits of the field of adult education, it is also important that more domain-specific research be conducted. Rubenson (1982) stated that since adult education is concerned not with natural but man-made phenomena, "we cannot look for general theories comparable to those in the natural sciences, but only search for theories which explain situationally-bound regularities determined by the social context" (p. 65). Many more researchers and much more effort needs to be devoted to understanding the previously mentioned concepts and theories and how they inform the distinctiveness of adult education pursuits. In the short term, progress will likely be greater in specific contexts and theoretical areas, although attempts should not be abandoned to define the essence and territory of the field. There will always be a need to provide overarching theoretical frameworks that reflect the field's coherence and distinctiveness.

Deshler and Hagan (1989), in discussing strategies for defining the research territory, suggested that one strategy would be to synthesize theory through meta-research. They suggested that general and critical reviews of research "can be an effective means for generating comprehensive, integrative maps of the territory of adult education research" (p. 160). The advantage of such reviews would be to identify worthwhile research questions not only in specific domains, but it would assist in conceptualizing a central view of the field. One of the goals might be to refine and relate the concepts that currently exist in the field of adult education. Critical reviews could perform the function of integrating concepts in a field that is characterized by considerable diffusion of research effort that seldom builds upon previous findings.

A much needed strategy is to have systematic research projects that build upon themselves as well as relate to previous knowledge. This strategy is particularly important considering the relatively few adult education researchers who are engaged in systematic research. Courtney (1986) made a crucial observation with regard to the cadre of researchers in adult education when he stated that for research to function successfully, there must exist a sufficient number of people engaged in the research enterprise. A significant subpopulation of researchers must be engaged in studying the same set of problems. In a survey of the membership of the Commission of Professors of Adult Education conducted by Willie, Copeland, and Williams (1985), it was reported that the professors spent "only one-tenth of their time in research and scholarly activities" (p. 66). Even more telling is that two thirds of the 215 active professors of adult education, on an average, published fewer than one article per year over a 5-year period preceding the study. Therefore, it might be argued on the basis of productivity that only one third (approximately 71) of adult education professors have any sort of sustained research program.

In a similar study, Garrison and Baskett (1989) reported on the extent and nature of adult education research activities in Canada. The study was based upon members of the Canadian Association for the Study of Adult Education. Of the 247 questionnaires mailed, 150 were returned. Forty-four percent of the respondents stated they were expected to publish. The findings revealed that only 4% of those expected to publish spent more than 40% of their time on research. Furthermore, there was a great diversity of research interests with at most four individuals identifying any one, broadly defined, common area of interest. It was concluded that adult education in Canada does not have a critical mass of researchers in any particular area of study and, therefore, the field is largely dependent upon creative individuals working in relative isolation.

This chronic lack of researchers combined with a diffusion of research effort appears to be one of the most serious limitations in the theoretical development of the field of adult education. It is not that we do not have sufficient graduates at the doctoral level or that this research is not being published. The issue is that too few pursue their research after graduation. Is it acceptable that nearly half of all research published in *Adult Education Quarterly* (AEQ) results primarily from graduate student research? To compound the problem, too few graduate programs and faculty contribute to *AEQ* (Blunt & Lee, 1994). Courtney (1986) suggests that "it is not in the nature of the adult education enterprise to socialize new generations of researchers" (p. 162). However, this will have to change if adult education is to develop into a fully recognized field of study.

It is not enough to say that we simply have to shift our limited resources to study the important questions. As noted previously, researchers do not respond well to being told what to research. The paradox is that quality of research depends on a certain quantity of output. No researcher sits down to produce a definitive piece of work that will change the understanding of adult education. Only through a sustained research program do researchers converge on an insight or new way of conceptualizing a central aspect of the field. Most researchers contribute small pieces of the puzzle while a very few are fortunate to provide larger chunks or a broader picture of the field. We therefore come back to the desperate need to socialize increasing numbers of researchers as well as encourage and support them in developing and sustaining research programs. Research programs that work within and build upon research paradigms are desperately needed in order to reduce atheoretical and disconnected studies.

Increased numbers of researchers are needed to conduct lines of inquiry at macro and microlevels as well as in terms of applied and basic research goals. In a field such as adult education, which has a rich history of practice but only a recent focus on the theoretical orientation of the field, it is natural that a tension would exist between basic and applied research. This tension exists in most adult educators' minds because research, while not being completely divorced from practice, is not concerned with immediate practical applications. Furthermore, the practical importance of basic research is not always apparent at the start (Rachel, 1986). However, as has been noted throughout, there is a need to conceptualize the distinctiveness of adult education. This conceptualization inherently goes beyond immediate practical application. Rubenson (1982) believes that unless we "try to develop a clearer view of adult education phenomena . . . the discipline will not advance, nor will it be able to serve the field of practice" (p. 66). More to the point, Rubenson goes on to say that the problem is atheoretical research that makes it difficult to convert findings into practical applications.

Practice without theory only supports and encourages mindless routine. Successful practice capable of addressing the unexpected and creating the novel will inevitably be embedded in some theoretical context or framework. While the degree of abstraction may vary, all rational action is theory based. These theories may be explicit or implicit, but they represent the accumulation and synthesis of experience. Theory and practice in adult education are inextricably linked. Complex fields of social practice such as adult education need theory to guide the pressing responsibility to make judgments and decisions in constantly changing and uncertain settings. Rubenson (1984) suggests there is a lack of balance between applied and basic research. Much greater status and emphasis needs to be placed upon basic research. Deshler and Hagan (1989) states that adult education is beginning to appreciate "that both deductive (beginning with theory and testing it) and inductive approaches (beginning with practice and building theory) are legitimate and required" (p. 152). Ideally, both theory generation and theory testing should be encouraged regardless of whether it is borrowed and reformulated or generated in a practical setting.

Clearly, the one thing that should not be tolerated in adult education research is the creation of misleading and artificial dualities. For example, we should not tolerate the wasted effort and restricted research approaches encouraged by ideological adherence to particular methodologies, narrow and autonomous disciplinary perspectives of the field, nor uncritical and mutually exclusive positions regarding basic and applied research.

CONCLUSION

The goal of research in adult education is to generate concepts and theories that reflect and explain the field's central focus and distinctiveness. Although there is a need to understand the central purpose of adult education and focus research effort toward developing concepts related to this purpose, a variety of approaches should be encouraged. However, if adult education is to make a concerted effort and progress toward the goal of establishing itself as a distinct field of study and practice, then it must concern itself with coherently describing its primary phenomena—facilitating adult learning. Given the limited resources in both the study and practice of adult education, it would make sense that the field should focus its activities to a greater extent on matters of educational concern. Adult educators must critically consider whether essentially noneducation activities and causes in political and social fields are central to the adult education phenomena and whether such activities further its development as a field. Adult education must distinguish itself from other related fields if it is to emerge as a recognized field of study and practice.

Defining and differentiating the field of adult education is the first step toward a full emergence and recognition as a distinct field of study. Assuming adult educators can agree on a manageable territory that is properly educational, the research agenda will still be complicated by a diversity of knowledge domains and insufficiently systematic research. As revealed in Long and Agyekum's (1974) meta-analysis of *Adult Education* articles over a 10-year period ending in 1973, only 11 authors contributed three or more articles. A cursory analysis of *Adult Education Quarterly* by the present author of a recent 10-year period (Volumes 32–41) revealed that 13 authors contributed three or more articles and 15 others contributed two articles. While caution must be exercised in interpreting these data, it would appear that the number of prolific authors has not increased from the previous period. If frequency of publication reflects sustained and systematic research programs, then we are no better off than we were 20 years ago. The question remains whether the necessary cadre of adult education researchers currently exists in order to reach that critical mass of researchers in knowledge domains central to the adult education phenomenon. The evidence seems to suggest that there are too few researchers with sustained and systematic research programs. If this is true, then a concerted effort needs to be made to attract and socialize new generations of researchers to the field.

REFERENCES

Blunt, A., & Lee, J. (1994). The contribution of graduate student research to *Adult Education Quarterly*, 1969–1988. *Adult Education Quarterly, 44*, 125–144.

Boshier, R. (1980). A perspective on theory and model development in adult education. In P. Cunningham (Ed.), *Yearbook of adult and continuing education* (pp. 20–31). Chicago: Marquis Academic Media.

Boshier, R., & Pickard, L. (1979). Citation patterns of articles published in *Adult Education* 1968–1977. *Adult Education, 30,* 34–51.

Boyd, R. D., & Apps, J. W. (1981). A conceptual model for adult education. In R. D. Boyd & J. W. Apps (Eds.), *Redefining the discipline of adult education.* San Francisco: Jossey-Bass.

Boyd, R. D., Coggins, C. C., & Forest, L. (1989). *Adult Education Research Conference Proceedings.* Madison: University of Wisconsin.

Bright, B. P. (1985). The content-method relationship in the study of adult education. *Studies in the Education of Adults, 17,* 168–183.

Brookfield, S. (1992). Developing criteria for formal theory building in adult education. *Adult Education Quarterly, 42,* 79–93.

Courtney, S. (1986). On derivation of the research question. *Adult Education Quarterly, 36,* 160–165.

Deshler, D., & Hagan, N. (1989). Adult education research: Issues and directions. In S. B. Merriam & P. M. Cunningham (Eds.), *Handbook of adult and continuing education* (pp. 147–167). San Francisco: Jossey-Bass.

Dickinson, G., & Rusnell, D. (1971). A content analysis of adult education. *Adult Education, 21,* 177–185.

Garrison, D. R. (1992). Critical thinking and self-directed learning in adult education: An analysis of responsibility and control issues. *Adult Education Quarterly, 42,* 136–148.

Garrison, D. R., & Baskett, H. K. (1987). Research and publishing in adult education. A study of the approaches and strategies of the field's most successful researchers. *Adult Education Research Conference Proceedings* (pp. 90–95). Laramie, WY: University of Wyoming.

Garrison, D. R., & Baskett, H. K. (1989). A survey of adult education research in Canada. *The Canadian Journal for the Study of Adult Education.* 3(2), 32–46.

Griffith, W. S. (1987). Cyril O. Houle. In P. Jarvis (Ed.), *Twentieth century thinkers in adult education* (pp. 147–168). London: Croom Helm.

Hake, B. J. (1992). Remaking the study of adult education: The relevance of recent developments in the Netherlands to the search for disciplinary identity. *Adult Education Quarterly, 42,* 63–78.

Houle, C. O. (1972). *The design of education.* San Franciso: Jossey-Bass.

Houle, C. O. (1991). Forward. In J. M. Peters & P. Jarvis (Eds.), *Adult Education: Evolution and achievements in a developing field of study* (pp. xiii–xvii). San Francisco: Jossey-Bass.

Jarvis, P. (1987). The development of adult educator knowledge. In P. Jarvis (Ed.), *Twentieth century thinkers in adult education* (pp. 3–13). London: Croom Helm.

Jensen, G. (1964). How adult education borrows and reformulates knowledge of other disciplines. In G. Jensen, A. A. Liveright, & W. Hallenbeck (Eds.)

Adult education: Outlines of an emerging field of university study (pp. 105–111). Washington, DC: Adult Education Association of the U.S.A.

Jensen, G., Liveright, A., & Hallenbeck, W. (Eds.). (1964). *Adult education: Outlines of an emerging field of university study.* Washington, D.C.: Adult Education Association of the U.S.A.

Knowles, M. S. (1977). *A history of the adult education movement in the United States* (rev. ed.). Malabar, FL: Krieger.

Long, H. B. (1983). Characteristics of adult education research reported at the Adult Education Research Conference, 1971–1980. *Adult Education, 33,* 79–96.

Long, H. B. (1990, March). *Twentieth century social and contextual factors contributing to the development of adult education knowledge.* Paper presented at the Syracuse University Kellogg Project's Second Visiting Scholar Conference in the History of Adult Education, Syracuse, NY.

Long, H. B. (1991). Evolution of a formal knowledge base. In J. M. Peters & P. Jarvis (Eds.), *Adult education: Evolution and achievement in a developing field of study* (pp. 66–96). San Francisco: Jossey-Bass.

Long, H. B., & Agyekum, S. K. (1974). Adult Education 1964–1973: Reflections of a changing discipline. *Adult Education, 24,* 99–120.

Peters, J. M. (1991). Advancing the study of adult education: A summary perspective. In J. M. Peters & P. Jarvis (Eds.), *Adult education: Evolution and achievements in a developing field of study* (pp. 421–445). San Francisco: Jossey-Bass.

Plecas, D. B., & Sork, T. J. (1986). Adult education: Curing the ills of an undisciplined discipline. *Adult Education Quarterly, 37,* 48–62.

Rachal, J. (1986). Assessing adult education research questions: Some preliminary criteria. *Adult Education Quarterly, 36,* 157–159.

Rubenson, K. (1982). Adult education research: In quest of a map of the territory. *Adult Education, 32,* 57–74.

Schefler, I. (1973). *Reason and teaching.* London: Routledge & Kegan Paul.

Selman, G., & Dampier, P. (1991). *The foundations of adult education in Canada.* Toronto: Thompson Educational Publishing.

Shulman, L. S. (1988). Disciplines of inquiry in education: An overview. In R. M. Jaeger (Ed.), *Complementary methods for research in education* (pp. 3–17). Washington, DC: American Educational Research Association.

Stubblefield, H. W., & Keane, P. (1989). The history of adult and continuing education. In S. B. Merriam & P. M. Cunningham (Eds.), *Handbook of adult and continuing education* (pp. 26–36). San Francisco: Jossey Bass.

Verner, C., Liveright, A. A., & Jensen, G. (1961). *Adult education: A new imperative for our times.* Washington DC: The Adult Education Association of the U.S.A.

Welton, M. R. (1987). "Vivisecting the nightingale": Reflections on adult education as an object of study. *Studies in the Education of Adults, 19,* 46–68.

Willie, R., Copeland, H., & Williams, H. (1985). The adult education professoriate of the United States and Canada. *International Journal of Lifelong Education, 4,* 55–67.

CHAPTER 2

METHODOLOGICAL ISSUES: PHILOSOPHICAL DIFFERENCES AND COMPLEMENTARY METHODOLOGIES

D. Randy Garrison and Doug Shale

Much debate and controversy has occurred over the merits of apparently conflicting research paradigms and methods used to generate fact and theory in adult education. Although the conflict between research methods in adult education has not been as acrimonious as in other areas of social science research, confrontational methodological positions do exist. However, rigid positions are unfounded and can only prove to be counterproductive. The adoption of one method while dismissing the validity of another can only perpetuate an unnecessarily narrow and prejudicial view of human phenomena and the world in which we live. We believe much of the disagreement around this issue arises from a misapprehension, and perhaps even a misrepresentation, of the intent behind research paradigms and methods. In order to clarify some of the confusion regarding research paradigms, this chapter examines the epistemological assumptions of two prominent paradigms and then explores the complementarity of research methodologies.

We also believe that part of the apparent disagreement behind the "methodology wars" results from an implicit sociopolitical agenda that has as a major effect a displacement of the argument from what is properly implied by research and scholarly inquiry to a competition for the "primacy of methods." We discuss this as a separate matter later in the chapter.

The chapter is not meant to be an epistemological debate as to the merits and limitations of research paradigms; however, for the purposes of providing an historical and philosophical context, we begin with a discussion of logical positivism and phenomenology. The phenomenological paradigm was selected since it is most frequently contrasted with logical positivism and is associated with qualitative approaches to research methods. However, this is not the only paradigm associated with naturalistic/interpretive methodologies. Other paradigms that have considerable overlap with phenomenology are hermeneutics, critical theory, and ethnography.

We explore some of the presuppositions and basic assumptions of logical positivism and phenomenology to provide a perspective on the research process. Although real and substantive differences exist in their basic assumptions, in practice research methodologies are complementary. The appropriateness of these methodologies is determined largely by the researcher's perspective and the nature of the research question; this appropriateness is, in turn, assessed by "the trustworthiness of inferences drawn from data" (Eisenhart and Howe 1992, p. 644)—that is, by validity considerations.

HISTORICAL AND PHILOSOPHICAL PERSPECTIVES

Logical positivism and phenomenonology are the two philosophical paradigms that have created much discussion and controversy regarding metaphysical and epistemological questions. It is an impossible task to give both a brief and accurate sketch of these philosophies within the limits of this chapter because of the general complexity of their philosophical positions. Moreover, recent thinking about research methods and disciplined inquiry has evolved toward less extreme and more compatible positions. However, a clearer contrast can be made between the two philosophies by analyzing their "original" assumptions. This may, in turn, result in a better understanding of the origins of the current methodological debate. The first philosophical position to be explored is that of logical positivism.

Logical Positivism

The antecedents of positivism can be found in Hume and Compte, although the logical (i.e., noncontradictory) connection of observables and ideas can be traced to Leibniz and Russell (Feigl, 1981, p. 21). The logical positivist position was developed during the 1920s and 1930s by Wittgenstein and Carnap, as members of the Vienna Circle. In essence, its "tenet was the verifiability principle of meaning, which stated that something is meaningful only if it is verifiable empirically" (Phillips, 1987, p. 204).

Logical positivism is concerned only with knowledge of the world that is open to observation. In this view, anything that transcends the objective (physical) world is not considered within the bounds of scientific investigation. This movement identified itself only with the properties and relations of the objectively observable world. The world of subjective reflection was considered in the realm of metaphysics and thus had no place in logical positivism.

For the logical positivist, meaning results only from the ability to verify a statement. More important, the method of verification is to ground a statement in observable or empirical reality. This represents a complete rejection of metaphysics or a priori knowledge. Metaphysics, according to positivism, says nothing about the physical world and can lead only to unanswerable (i.e., unverifiable) questions that are factually meaningless.

Due to this insistence on verification, a connection has to be made between direct observation and theoretical formulations. Within the early logical positivist paradigm, the truth of a theory can never be verified because it does "not have direct empirical reference" (Hesse, 1969, p. 91). Theory can, however, be "confirmable" by logical relations with direct observation. While there are observation statements and predicates related to sense objects whose confirmability or falsifiability is possible, science "also employs theoretical predicates, which do not have direct empirical reference" (Hesse, 1969, p. 88). Furthermore, "science employs theoretical statements, which are not directly confirmable or falsifiable, and which must be shown to be indirectly confirmable or falsifiable through their logical relations with observational statements" (Hesse, 1969, p. 88)

This clear separation of objective reality and subjective reflection raised some questions, particularly concerning the development and verification of theory. Strictly speaking, theories cannot be verified because they are not observation statements. Meaning of a theoretical statement can result only from the logical analysis of its connection to observable statements. However, since there always exists the possibility of exception in a theoretical formulation that relates to the physical world, the verification principle was replaced with the falsification principle. But here again a negative outcome does not mean the theory is absolutely false. Total certainty appeared to be unattainable in either case.

The meaning and justification of a theory cannot be accounted for by the criteria of empirical meaning. Neither the criteria of verifiability or falsifiability could "tell us whether any parts of a theory were more highly confirmed by observables than others, what the criteria for a good theory would be, supposing its observed consequences to be true, nor how to choose between theories with the same observed consequences, all of which are true" (Hesse, 1969, p. 92). If theory is not essentially or directly verifiable, then some other method is required to provide empirical meaning to a theory, or a better understanding and justification of theory formation is required that fits the reality of the research process.

The bind the logical positivists found themselves in was that theory could not be directly confirmable from empirical data, and therefore, according to their own assumption, theory must be meaningless. The obvious need to explain the process of developing theory using qualitative means could not be accepted by the logical positivists. Theory is not within direct reach of observation, and therefore, the technique of formulating theories and hypotheses will depend largely "upon the intuition of the man of research" (van Laer, 1963, p. 118). Kuhn (1962) stated that he found it impossible to relinquish the viewpoint that theories are "simply man-made interpretations of given data" (p. 125). This question of humankind's role in a scientific endeavor leads us to phenomenology as a reaction to the physicalism of logical positivism.

Phenomenology

The following account of phenomenology is based on the philosophy of Edmund Husserl, who is considered the inaugurator of the phenomenological movement. Although phenomenology consists of many strains, "there is a unity in both Husserl's thought and in phenomenology in general which gives it a philosophical momentum and preserves it from doctrinal fragmentation" (Natanson, 1973, p. 24). It is for this reason we will examine Husserl's work for an understanding of phenomenology.

Husserl's phenomenology was a reaction to the empiricist tradition of separating the physical or natural world from human consciousness. In addition, contrary to logical positivism, phenomenology advocated the philosophical analysis of assumptions. Phenomenology was an interpretation of human involvement in the physical world. Reality in phenomenology is dependent on the apperception and interpretation of a conscious human being. Further, one of the central themes is a suspension of judgment about the reality of the physical world.

Phenomenological reduction temporarily eliminates the empirical or outer world by "bracketing" any presuppositions or beliefs. This is not a denial of the outer world but a natural a priori acceptance of the world in order to reveal the presuppositions of consciousness. The purpose of this bracketing of the outer world is to allow a purely logical philosophical analysis independent of factual states such that attention can be fixed upon the processes of human consciousness. The starting point of knowledge is found in understanding the processes of human consciousness as it searches for the meaning of phenomena. The individual is the centre of philosophical experience and must be open and aware of his/her own life and take nothing for granted in the pursuit of knowledge and meaning. In general, the phenomenologist attempts "to elucidate and bring to a coherent order that which daily life takes for granted" (Natanson, 1973, p. 22).

Phenomenology emphasizes how human beings consciously confront and are confronted by phenomena. Phenomena are analyzed logically in terms of their essential structures "which can be intuited quite apart from the senses" (van Peursen, 1972, pp. 44–45). This investigation and analysis of the essence of the given reality is another integral theme of phenomenology. The manifest role of intuition should also be noted in the investigation and apprehension of essences. Intuition is the necessary condition for locating the experiential world and the investigation and apprehension of essences.

The role of intuition in the phenomenological philosophy precludes the empirical verification of its results. As Natanson (1973) stated:

> . . . the pehnomenologist is deeply interested in the logic of predictive experience, in passive syntheses of meaning, in the covert no less than the overt aspect of action, and in the many facets of intentionality which are involved in tracing out the sedimentation of meaning. Empiricism begins where phenomenology leaves off—that is why it is pointless to ask the phenomenologist for some sort of equivalent for empirical verification. (p. 33).

A Convergence

The philosophical polarity that logical positivism and phenomenology exhibited in the early 1930s revealed dramatic differences. Movements in both philosophical camps have since modified their positions to a point where a confusing variety of perspectives exist. However, the value of describing these early positions not only gives a historical perspective that provides some clarity, but will allow us to show that the practice of research does not adhere strictly to one or another of these positions. Current methodologies are far more eclectic in their practices. This is not only due to pragmatic concerns but is also a result of contemporary philosophical positions of science that have recognized the worth of both phenomenological and empirical forms of information.

One of the goals here is the explanation and justification of theory development in both the physical and social sciences. Logical positivism was essentially concerned only with the hypothetico-deductive aspects of empirical science. The difficulty of this position was accounting for the process of theory formation and its verification—a difficulty which, at one time, seemed more apparent in the social sciences but which is also inherent in research in the physical sciences. It is clear today that empirical methodologies have largely abandoned the "false assumption that observational categories are independent of theoretical ones" (Hughes, 1980, p. 129) and the search for absolute knowledge. The inability of positivism to account for intuition and insight in the creative process of theory and hypothesis formulation and the rejection of the notion of absolute knowledge called into question positivism's ability to account for the practice of scientific inquiry. From a positivist perspective, it could not be claimed that one would know how a hypothesis was arrived at; it would seem, however, that "ultimately the hypothesis arises through intuition" (Strasser, 1963, p. 172). The activities of researchers seldom meet the formalized criteria of the hypothetico-deductive (positivistic) method; "even those who actually work in the 'hardest' sciences now are often satisfied with claiming no more than 'good reasons' and probable knowledge" (Holton, 1978, p. xiv).

Phenomenologists accepted the intuitive and reflective abilities of conscious man to understand and explain phenomena. In this assumption they attempted to explain theory formation but in the process reduced meaning and reality to the psychological or consciousness of man. There existed no comparison to the physical or social world to validate theory, but instead phenomenologists relied on the apperception and reflection of the individual to provide order and structure. However, research methodologies, although aligned with one or the other of these two philosophical perspectives, are not mutually exclusive in terms of their basic assumptions.

The Politics of Educational Research

Throughout this chapter, we argue the proposition that ". . . paradigm differences do not require paradigm conflict" (Gage, 1989; pg. 7). We have assumed that differences among proponents of what have largely been seen to be competing paradigmatic positions could be resolved through rational analysis. However, as Gage observed, ". . . it turned out that Thomas Kuhn had been right (Barnes, 1985). These were rational issues, but not purely rational issues" (p. 7). So, while many writers have advanced in some detail the rational analysis reflected here, it would be a mistake to believe that we have resolved a merely intellectual disagreement by merely intellectual means. As Gage (1989) pointed out in one of the lines of thought he develops in his article, there are other grounds to account for this disagreement, and at the very least, this needs to be recognized so they may be addressed in whatever ways are appropriate.

In the earlier years of the epistemological debate, answers to the questions "What is knowledge?" and "Whose knowledge is legitimate?" were based on the presumption that truth was to be had only through a particular paradigmatic view of science and research. Although there is now wide recognition of ". . . the patently false conclusion that knowledge derived from one source is inherently superior" (Dunn, 1982, p. 295 as cited in Eisenhart and Howe, 1992, p. 655), nonetheless "epistemic privilege" (Walker & Evers, 1986) and "methodological imperialism" (Eisenhart and Howe, 1992, p. 656) persist, for as Gage (1989) posited, "the paradigm wars in educational and social research were, in part, wars between the disciplines" (p. 8). "What had seemed to be merely intellectual disagreement also turned out, as experience accumulated, to be turf wars in the attempt to gain for one's own discipline a greater share of the research funds, the academic positions, and the other kinds of wherewithal needed for a discipline to flourish" (p. 8).

In a less speculative vein, House (1991) made the same point by quoting Campbell and Stanley (1963): "This chapter is committed to the experiment: as the only means for settling disputes regarding educational practice, as the only way of verifying educational improvements, and as the only way of establishing a cumulative tradition in which improvements can be introduced without the danger of a faddish discard of old wisdom in favour of inferior novelties" (p. 171). House (1991) then goes on to observe that, "Whatever the intentions of these theorists, this position hardened into an orthodoxy often supported by federal policies" (p. 7). The emergence of this orthodoxy, reinforced by the development of statistical methods to support the experimentalist paradigm, has lead to a "professional domination of knowledge" and the establishment of a guild of "epistemically privileged researchers" (Walker and Evers, 1986, p. 373). As a result, "Research tends to be an activity conducted by an elite class of professionals" (Sanders, 1981, p. 10) who have been trained and socialized in the paradigms of behavioral science disciplines, "especially in psychology, where positivism was embraced as an accurate portrayal of the scientific method, and then was cashed out in the form of methodological behaviorism" (Howe and Eisenhart, 1990, p. 3).

Walker and Evers (1986) believe a resolution to this undesirable state of affairs is to seek "to replace the traditional view of experiment by relocating the kinds of experiment it endorses (tightly controlled laboratory experiment) within a wider context of theorizing and naturalistic inquiry" (p. 375)—a goal that is compatible with our own point of view. However, this again approaches the dilemma on the high ground of "intellectual disagreement." The political aspects of the debate must be addressed by a relocation that would "involve not only a broader view of educational research, but a rejection of professionalization and epistemic privilege" (Walker and Evers, 1986, p. 375).

To some extent, the movement toward qualitative research can be viewed as a rejection of the traditional experimentalist view of research. However, the question needs to be asked whether the flight is from the deficiencies and strictures inherent in the traditionalist view (and in the results of this research tradition) or whether refuge is being sought from the intellectual demands required to master the methods and to address the matter of standards. It is not sufficient to justify qualitatively oriented research through an enumeration of the shortcomings of quantitatively oriented research. In the extreme case, many who would reject the traditional view of research have sought justification in contrasting the qualitative alternative as tender-minded versus tough-minded, humanistic versus scientific, idiographic versus nomothetic, clinical versus statistical, and hermeneutic versus positivist (Gage, 1989). The rejection of traditional research standards sometimes seems to have been interpreted to mean that qualitative research should be free from the constraints of standards altogether. Such a view can only bankrupt qualitative research conducted in this context inasmuch as "it becomes vulnerable to the familiar charges that it is hopelessly subjective, unscientific, relativistic" (Howe and Eisenhart, 1990, p. 3). The challenge within qualitative research, as it is within quantitative research, is to establish a working framework of standards that would "require that research studies be cogently developed, competently produced, coherent with respect to previous work, important, ethical, and comprehensive" (Eisenhart and Howe, 1992, p. 656).

COMPLEMENTARY METHODS

Floden (1990) offered a general characterization of "methodology" that we find useful for our purposes here. He stated, "Methodology, broadly conceived, goes beyond design and analysis to encompass fundamental questions about how the structure and processes of research justify claims to knowledge" (p. 25).

Research methods used in adult education have often been characterized as either quantitative or qualitative. Although these classifications have commonly been seen as corresponding to epistemological paradigms such as logical positivism and phenomenology, researchers are realizing that in practice the methodologies can be viewed as complementary. Salomon (1991) suggested that on the practical level, the war of the epistemological paradigms should be put to rest. He goes on to say that "No single paradigm provides a fully satisfactory understanding all on its own . . . Complementarity, then, serves better, fuller, and more satisfying understanding" (p. 16). Howe (1985) stated categorically that "researchers who advocate combining quantitative and qualitative methods are thus on solid epistemological ground" (p. 16). With regard to quantitative and qualitative distinctions he argued that "the rigid epistemological distinctions between quantitative and qualitative methods and between factual and value judgements exemplified in present thinking about educational research methodology are unsupported dogmas held over from logical positivism" (Howe, 1985, p. 10).

The reality is that currently most research paradigms and methodologies are concerned with issues of belief, values, and observation of phenomena (Salomon, 1991). Similarly, Howe (1985) believed that "quantification does not eliminate qualitative judgments and therefore is not an alternative to them" (p. 15). Also, Howe and Eisenhart (1990) suggested that "insofar as no standards completely divorced from human judgments, purposes, and values can exist and insofar as there can, accordingly, be no monolithic unity of scientific method—those were the pipe dreams of positivism—standards must be anchored wholly within the process of inquiry" (p. 3).

Judgments are a part of social/educational research and standards guiding these judgments may be found within the methodologies themselves. From a broader perspective, judgments must be made regarding methodologies in terms of the research question being asked. As Shulman (1988) stated:

> Selecting the method most appropriate for a particular disciplined inquiry is one of the most important and difficult responsibilities of a researcher. The choice requires an act of judgement, grounded in both knowledge of methodology and the substantive area of the investigation.

Therefore, selection of methodology is a pragmatic concern in that the appropriateness is dependent upon its functionality in addressing the problem at hand. However, we must also realize that in practice methodology can influence the refinement of the research question. The process of selecting a methodology and refining a research question is an iterative procedure.

The value of research methodology is its distinction from casual observation, speculation, or opinion. Shulman (1988) suggested that all research methodology shares the characteristics of disciplined inquiry. Further, he stated that "What is important about disciplined inquiry is that its data, arguments, and reasoning be capable of withstanding careful scrutiny by another member of the scientific community" (p. 5). To claim, as some qualitative researchers do, that such a methodological approach (i.e., qualitative) "is idiosyncratic, incommunicable, and artistic—and that only those who have been fully socialized and apprenticed in its practice can claim to comment upon it . . . is mostly mystification" (Miles & Huberman, 1985, p. 20).

The examination process by others makes apparent the unavoidable subjectivity of the researcher. Patton (1990) suggested that subjectivity is inevitable but the "point is to be aware of how one's perspective affects fieldwork, to carefully document all procedures so that others can review methods for bias, and to be open in describing the limitations of the perspective presented" (p. 482). The danger is in viewing such issues as competing, mutually exclusive alternatives. Even if knowledge is constructed by humans with particular perspectives, this does not mean we should be free to ". . . cut loose from rational modes of public appraisal." (Soltis, 1984, p. 8) However, there must also be "some notion of reality which gets away from the subject-object split" (Reason & Rowan, 1981, p. 241).

We must bring these views of subjective reflection and objective reality together if our pursuit of understanding and "truth" is to advance in any significant way. Phillips (1990) argues that objectivity is the procedure of reaching for truth. This position is only defensible if objectivity is considered to be an appeal to evidence and to an open and critical analysis of personal perspectives. Objectivity of judgment would have to show that "personal biases and valuations had been exposed to critical examination, and the role that these predilections played in their investigations would need to have been rigorously examined" (Phillips, 1990, p. 37). In turn, objectivity is further assured through the critical judgment (not just consensus) of the larger scholarly community. Objectivity is a property of justification (not discovery) and is in a sense a social matter. Phillips (1990) concluded that "what is crucial for the objectivity of any inquiry—whether it is qualitative or quantitative—is the critical spirit in which it has been carried out" (p. 35). Subjectivity, on the other hand, suggests that researchers "have not been sufficiently opened to the light of reason and criticism" (Phillips, 1990, p. 35).

While there may be little disagreement at this level of what constitutes disciplined inquiry, the problem is that each discipline has developed and adapted particular principles of procedure as well as canons of evidence and verification (Shulman, 1988). When a researcher works within a particular discipline, the principles of disciplined inquiry are less contentious. The challenge for the field of education is that researchers borrow from and operate within a variety of disciplines and, therefore, many research perspectives and procedures may be brought to bear in their "disciplined" inquiry. However, adult education researchers are obligated to adhere to the standards associated with these methodologies. Notwithstanding methodological differences, however, there are issues and standards common to all research methods.

COMMON RESEARCH STANDARDS

Qualitative and quantitative inquiry alike cannot escape the requirement for rigor in developing knowledge if such knowledge is to be of interest for more than its literary merit. Knowledge is the construction of information such that it reduces the complexity of particularization and has meaning for others in similar situations. The nature of knowledge is essentially abstraction and generalization and, therefore, it is "ultimately self-contradictory to hope to develop an idiographic social science" (Goldenberg, 1992, p. 354). At the same time, abstraction in social science must recognize contextual complexities and avoid reductionism.

Regardless of the apparent and real differences among research paradigms, when it comes to interpreting data all methods are subject to similar standards. This important point was made by LeCompte and Goetz (1982):

The value of scientific research is partially dependent on the ability of individual researchers to demonstrate the credibility of their findings. Regardless of the discipline or the methods used for data collection and analysis, all scientific ways of knowing strive for authentic results. In all fields that engage in scientific enquiry, reliability and validity of findings are important. (p. 31).

Guba and Lincoln (1981) also stated that "for naturalistic inquiry, as for scientific, meeting tests of rigor is a requisite for establishing trust in the outcomes of the inquiry (p. 103). Similarly, Kirk and Miller (1986) argued that the concepts of reliability and validity apply equally well to qualitative observation and are "the essential basis of all good research"

(p. 20). And finally, Reason and Rowan (1981) stated that "the issue of validity is of critical importance for inquiry within any research paradigm" (p. 239).

Kirk and Miller (1986) went on to state that "whatever their detailed goals, the natural and social sciences share an aspiration to cumulative collective knowledge that is of interest on its own merits to those other than the friends and admirers of its creators" (p. 13). Research must be systematic in that it builds upon previous research and it is reasonable and open to critical challenge. In short, it must have the characteristics of disciplined inquiry if it is to be cumulative and meaningful.

Validity Considerations

As Salomon (1991) stated, the question of validity, common to quantitative and qualitative research methodologies, asks, "Why should one accept your findings, observations, conclusions, and interpretations?" (p. 10). Validity is closely associated with striving for truth while recognizing that it is not a means to certainty. Phillips (1987) suggested that truth is a regulative ideal, and although it may be an "impossible dream," it is much better to strive for truth than to settle for something less worthy. Issues of validity are concerned with objective procedures in examining biases; providing warrants in terms of the correspondence of facts and reasoning; and conducting tests, particularly in refuting evidence. Such issues cannot be trivialized or dismissed, for they go to the heart of the research process and what is to count as knowledge.

While validity is a common goal to all research, it is essentially an ideal standard. Every attempt is made to maximize validity through critical examination, but the method and standard of addressing this issue are relative to the purpose and context of the research. Traditional methods and views of addressing validity can be found in virtually any standard research methods text. Validation procedures for a variety of qualitative approaches to research are also available (Eisenhart & Howe, 1992; Heron, 1988; Miles & Huberman, 1985; Reason & Rowan, 1981; Smith & Glass, 1987; Wolcott, 1990).

There is a cautionary note to be sounded regarding traditional views of validity, however. The obvious one is that there are a number of validity considerations to be aware of. Validity, while it may be understood as a unitary concept, is not a monolithic matter to be determined through a single course of action. For example, although Eisenhart and Howe (1992) make the case that "it is more fruitful to think in terms of one kind of validity with different design-specific instances" (p. 656), the five validity standards they propose "are not independent of each other; they cannot be applied separately. They are interrelated and must be considered together" (p. 663). General assessments of the validity of any given research activity, then, is an act of judgment dependent on an interplay among the validity standards applied in the assessment (which implies that considerations of who does the judging and refinements or reworking of the standards must also be treated as a part of the dynamic).

We also need to be aware, in a broader sense, of the consequences of the particular view brought to bear in producing and interpreting the standards used. For example, standards that have evolved from the ethos of the traditional, experimentalist-oriented approach will not fit well when applied to so-called qualitative methods. Or, to state it in a converse form, qualitative research will not come off well when measured by standards derived particularly for quantitative methods. An alternative view, as outlined by Eisenhart and Howe (1992), is "deep skepticism or outright rejection of the notion that the conventional conception of validity may be fruitfully applied to alternative methods" (p. 649). An extreme consequence of this line of thought is the position taken by Lincoln and Guba (1985) that an entirely different set of standards should be developed for naturalistic research. However, as Salomon (1991) pointed out, "This line of reasoning could easily lead to the Kuhnian question of incommensurability of paradigms: Empirical research in one paradigm, being based on its own set of assumptions and "pretheoretical" models, cannot be compared with that of other paradigms" (p. 15). So, we again would have two competing and exclusionary views of the world and no definitive reply to the questions of what is knowledge and whose knowledge counts.

A third, more satisfactory approach is to adopt the comprehensive view of validity developed by Eisenhart and Howe (1992), and the associated standards they proposed. Eisenhart and Howe (1992) argued that ". . . some general standards for the conduct of educational research that cut across all forms of educational research can and should be articulated" (p. 656). At the same time, they warn that standards of validity should not be regarded as "static nor mechanically applicable." While they advance the case for broad general standards for the conduct of all research (and specifically qualitative as well as quantitative research), they also recognize that "designs—specific standards—which are subsumed by the general standards and which articulate the particular evidence, knowledge, principles, and technical skills that differentiate alternative designs—are required" (p. 656). These are the discipline-grounded requirements we have referred to earlier.

Eisenhart's and Howe (1992) have proposed five general standards for research. The first of these they label "the fit between research questions, data collection procedures and analysis techniques" (p. 657). The point to this standard is that data collection techniques must be appropriate for answering the research question under consideration. The nature of the research question should determine the data collection and analysis techniques and not the other way around.

The second standard they describe as "the effective-application of specific data collection and analysis techniques." This standard is a requirement that researchers demonstrate they have applied the selected data collection techniques competently and that they have located "their work in the historical, disciplinary, or traditional contexts in which the methods used have been developed" (Eisenhart and Howe, 1992, p. 659).

Standard number three is "alertness to and coherence of prior knowledge." In other words for the results of a study to be credible, they "must be judged against a background of existing theoretical, substantive, or explicit practical knowledge" (p. 659). In this way, the results of new studies may also be appropriately integrated into the field of study to which they pertain and our knowledge in the field is advanced accordingly.

The fourth standard is "value constraints" about which Eisenhart and Howe (1992) observed, "Valid research studies qua arguments must include discussions of values, that is, of the worth in importance or usefulness of the study and its risks" (p. 660). They differentiate between external value constraints which pertain to the worthwhileness of the research (the research must be "valuable for informing and improving educational research" (p. 660) and internal value constraints which pertain to research ethics in regard to the "way research is conducted vis a vis research subjects" (p. 660).

Standard five is "comprehensiveness" and is what Eisenhart and Howe (1992) initially referred to as the "overall warrant" of the research study. That is, "When researchers demonstrate that, or explain the reasons why, other relevant approaches should be rejected or disconfirming data should be questioned, their studies are more comprehensive than when they do not" (p. 662). This standard implies a holistic assessment of the research that embodies the first four standards but goes beyond them as a total exceeding the sum of the parts.

We have explained earlier that the standards were expressly formulated to accommodate design-specific considerations that arise from the disciplinary context in which studies arise. We have also stated that the conceptualization of validity advanced by Eisenhart and Howe (1992) is a unitary construct. Therefore, although the standards are presented as separate considerations, they are interrelated and must be applied as a collectivity.

One aspect of validity in qualitative research that needs to be clarified concerns the question of guiding theoretical frameworks. A source of confusion is the naive notion that because qualitative inquiry is largely inductive or exploratory, the researcher should remain ignorant of relevant literature and knowledge in the area so as not to contaminate the researcher's perspective of the phenomena under study. The literature review adds another perspective to the phenomena for validity purposes. In this regard, Howe and Eisenhart (1990), in proposing their second standard, stated that background assumptions both with respect to the literature as well as the researcher's own "subjectivities must be made explicit if they are to clarify, rather than obscure, research design and findings" (p. 7). The literature review not only provides a means to build upon previous conceptions (a characteristic of systematic inquiry), but it implicitly reveals the perspective of the researcher through the theories that frame the study. Goldenberg (1992) believed that it is impossible to rid oneself of biases and, therefore, "it seems wiser to be familiar with the comparable literature than to enter the field only with preconceptions that have not been tested against the literature" (p. 198). This should not preclude the researcher from being open to new information during the data gathering and analysis phase of the inquiry.

One other issue associated with validity that is worth mentioning explicitly is triangulation. Mathison (1988) suggested that regardless of epistemological or methodological perspectives "Good research practice obligates the researcher to triangulate, that is, to use multiple methods, data sources, and researchers to enhance the validity of research findings" (p. 13). She went on to say that the use of any single method would be biased as would the view of any single individual; therefore, triangulation "is the methodological counterpart to intersubjective agreement" (Mathison, 1988, p. 14). As much as convergence is a possible outcome of triangulation so too is inconsistency and contradiction. The researcher is challenged to make sense of the data regardless of outcome. The value of triangulation "is as a technique which provides more and better evidence from which researchers can construct meaningful propositions about the social world" (Mathison, 1988, p. 15). Triangulation is also identified by Eisenhart and Howe (1992) as an aspect of their Standard 5: Comprehensiveness, and they regard the procedure as "a powerful strategy for establishing the validity of theoretical explanation" (p. 662).

Finally, we note that the traditional view of validity distinguished between external and internal validity. The first four standards proposed by Eisenhart and Howe (1992) may be considered broadly as internal validity considerations. However, the fit between their standards (specifically Standard 5) and external validity (as usually described) is a bit more awkward and it may be worthwhile to describe in more conventional terms what external validity considerations imply. When we study a particular phenomenon in social science research, we are typically interested in the extent to which our findings are applicable to other contexts—that is, whether these findings generalize to other samples and other contexts. The more generalizable are the results of a particular study, the more "comprehensive" we would consider that study to be, and hence, the more fully the study could be considered to have addressed validity considerations.

With Salomon (1991) we believe that generalizability (i.e., "What is this a case of?") is a challenge faced by all paradigms and what "they commonly face is the issue of how useful and applicable (not universal) they can make their research-based assertions" (p. 11). Using the depth and breadth of qualitative and quantitative methodologies, respectively, can provide the basis for speculation "on the likely applicability of findings to other situations under similar, but not identical, conditions" (Patton, 1990, p. 489). If some degree of generalization were not possible, it would put in question the purpose of disciplined inquiry and construction of knowledge. However, as Donmoyer (1990) pointed out, in fields such as education, traditional views of generalizability are problematic. He stated that when concerned with individuals and not groups, research "can only function as a heuristic; it can suggest possibilities but never dictate action" (p. 182). So, while we recognize that absolute truth is an unrealizable ideal, it is possible to abstract principles and provide order that can make sense within a theoretical framework. It must also be kept in mind that any given set of concepts may represent only one of many possible explanations and is not intended to represent an isomorphism from one context to another.

One of the more substantial criticisms leveled at qualitative methods in educational research is the difficulty in making a convincing case that the findings from one study may be generalized to other settings (Patton, 1990). Most researchers would agree with Firestone's (1993) observation that "Generalizability is clearly not the strength of qualitative research" (p. 16). However, as Firestone also pointed out, "past reservations turn out to be overstated" (p. 16). Nor are quantitative methods immune from the conundrum that ". . . generalization requires extrapolation that can never be fully justified logically" (Firestone, 1993, p. 16). The dilemma for qualitative methods has been compounded because there are different senses in which one can claim to generalize findings to other settings. One of these understandings is based on the statistical concept of sampling in which one infers what the characteristics of a population are by extrapolating from sample values. Another aspect of generalizability is what Firestone and others call "analytic generalization" by which "the investigator is striving to generalize a particular set of results to a broader theory" (Yin, 1989, p. 44). Qualitative researchers cannot afford to disregard these considerations as not relevant to the methods they follow. All possible rigor needs to be invoked on all fronts to forestall the dismissal of qualitative methods as "hopelessly subjective" and of limited usefulness. However, as Firestone (1993) pointed out ". . . the long tradition of looking for relationships among variables in a sample of cases has some utility, but does not adequately apply sample-to-population extrapolation to qualitative work" (p. 22). He argued, as do we, that a more rigorous application of analytic generalization holds more promise ". . . partly because there are more ways to make links between cases and theories. One can look for threats to generalizability within cases. Critical and deviant cases can be used to explore or extend existing theories. Multicase studies can use the logic of replication and comparison to strengthen conclusions drawn in single sites and provide evidence for both their broader utility and conditions under which they hold" (Firestone, 1993, p. 22).

Under this view of generalization, it is especially important to recognize the role of qualitative methods in describing and uncovering understandings of phenomena of interest. Qualitative methods are particularly effective in adding context (as opposed to the context-stripping procedures of quantitative methods) through the provision of "thick descriptions" of the situations of interest. While we do need to be concerned that we ought to develop better and more appropriate arguments in support of the generalizability of qualitative research, ". . . qualitative methods should not be avoided because of the fear that their claims for broad relevance are especially weak. That is not the case" (Firestone, 1993, p. 22).

CONCLUSION

Philosophical paradigms do not rigorously determine methodologies. Paradigmatic assumptions do not inherently dictate research methodologies such as quantitative or qualitative approaches. While selection of method often reflects perspectives and values of the researcher, methodologies that reflect qualitative or quantitative approaches are not antithetical and simply present the researcher with different kinds of information (Firestone, 1987). Examples of practice simply contradict the purists who believe that methods are inextricably linked to the paradigmatic assumptions of research philosophies.

Research in adult education, as in other fields of social science, should be concerned with both subjective reflection and objective meaning. Contemporary methodologies, whether they have their roots in positivistic or phenomenological philosophies, have many similarities. Empirical research has accepted the fact that verification cannot be absolute and that subjective interpretation of data within the context of theory is necessary even in the natural sciences. Also, phenomenologically based researchers realize the need to address the validity of their findings. These practices have moved the conduct of research within both paradigms closer to the common goal of constructing valid theory.

In adult education research, consideration must be given to both theory formation and theory validation. These two needs often require different perspectives. Caws (1965) stated that the development of a science results from a continuing dialectic between two absolutely essential processes: rationalism and empiricism. Rationalism proceeds by "developing formal structures in a free and creative fashion," while empiricism investigates the connection of events "without special regard to the significance of those events in any total scheme of things" (Caws, 1965, p. 331).

The two processes about which Caws spoke can be found in the activities of doing research in adult education. One method may begin without formal hypotheses and the researcher may spend considerable amounts of time immersed within the situation to be studied, determining interrelationships and generating general impressions on the basis of data perceived to be relevant to the researcher. On the other hand, a researcher may be seen to be administering predesigned tests that can be quantified and analyzed in a predetermined manner such that a conclusion may be reached as to the probability of accepting a deduced hypothesis. The problem in adult education is that we need to implement the dialectical process to resolve and integrate the rational and empirical phases to complete the research process. Greater efforts need to be made to reconcile seemingly diverse methodologies and findings or, more important, to design research projects that include different methodologies studying the same problem in order that a better understanding may be achieved through a dialectical process.

It would seem that the best chance for adult education to grow as a field of study is to adopt a view of research that allows for a real dialectical process to take place on the basis of diverse findings. Such a perspective must be capable of conceptualizing both subjective and objective realities and promoting a synthesis of seemingly disparate and contradictory findings. The more common view of social science researchers today is that theory and fact are interdependent and result from human activity. As Laszlo (1972) states, "empirical observation is meaningless without the imaginative envisagement of various abstract possibilities" (p. 16). Together, empirical data and theory can provide a holistic view of the reality of man. Solving complex problems requires a synthesis of divergent data, observations, and theory.

With regard to the apparent conflict between phenomenological and positivistic-based methodologies, the two antithetical processes are that data generates theories (induction) and theory exists independent of data (hypothetico-deductive). Cavallo (1979) states that "neither of these two extremes can constitute an acceptable epistemological basis for scientific inquiry, that the potential for knowledge growth resides in the tension between theoretical and empirical concerns" (p. 120). By encompassing a variety of techniques, a creative tension can be realized between theoretical and empirical concerns.

This chapter began by juxtaposing two philosophies of science, logical positivism and phenomenology. Although these philosophies have evolved since their inception in the 1920s, the original positions provide an understanding of the philosophical differences and debate that surround many of the research methodologies currently employed in adult education. By shifting to a pragmatic perspective, we accept the incompleteness of either-or methodological choices and begin to work toward a greater unity and clarity. The methodologies employed in adult education must be seen as being complementary and as contributing to a reality that can encompass and make comprehensible the dualities that we are so prone to create. Only by assuming a broader perspective will new and complex relations reveal themselves, and only in this way can we weave intricate patterns of our objective and subjective worlds.

REFERENCES

Bagnall, R. G. (1991). Relativism, objectivity, liberal adult education and multiculturalism. *Studies in the Education of Adults, 23*(1), 61–84.

Barnes, B. (1985). Thomas Kuhn. In Q. Skinner (Ed.), *The return of grand theory in the human sciences* (pp. 137–169). New York: Cambridge University Press.

Cavallo, R. E. (1979). *The role of systems methodology in social science research.* Boston: Martinus Nijhoff Publishing.

Caws, P. (1965). *The philosophy of science: A systematic account.* Princeton: D. van Nostrand Company Inc.

Donmoyer, R. (1990). Generalizability and the single-case study. In E. W. Eisner & A. Peshkin (Eds.), *Qualitative inquiry in education: The continuing debate* (pp. 175–200). N.Y.: Teachers College Press.

Dunn, W. N. (1982). Reforms as arguments. *Knowledge: Creation, Diffusion, Utilization, 3*(3), 293–326.

Eisenhart, M. A., & Howe, K. R. (1992). Validity in educational research. In M. D. LeCompte, W. L. Millroy, & J. Preissle (Eds.), *The handbook of qualitative research in education* (pp. 643–680). San Diego: Academic Press.

Feigl, H. (1981). The origin and spirit of logical positivism. In R. S. Cohen (Ed.), *Herbert Feigl: Inquires and provocations.* Boston: D. Reidel Publishing Company.

Firestone, W. A. (1993). Alternative arguments for generalizing from data as applied to qualitative research. *Educational Researcher, 22*(4), 16–23.

Firestone, W. A. (1987). Meaning in method: The rhetoric of quantitative and qualitative research. *Educational Researcher, 16*(7), 16–21.

Floden, R. E. (1990). Evolving methods for enhancing validity. *Educational Researcher, 19*(6), 25–27.

Gage, N. L. (1989). The paradigm wars and their aftermath. *Educational Researcher. 18*(7), 4–10.

Goldenberg, S. (1992). *Thinking methodologically.* New York: HarperCollins.

Guba, E. G., & Lincoln, Y. S. (1981). *Effective evaluation.* San Francisco: Jossey-Bass.

Heron, J. (1988). Validity in co-operative inquiry. In P. Reason (ed.), *Human inquiry in new paradigm research* (pp. 40–59). London: Sage.

Hesse, M. (1969). Positivism and the logic of scientific theories. In P. Achinstein and S. F. Barker (Eds.), *The legacy of logical positivism.* Baltimore: The John Hopkins Press.

Holton, G. (1978). *The scientific imagination: Case studies.* Cambridge: University Press.

House, E. R. (1991). Realism in research. *Educational Researcher, 20*(6), 2–9.

Howe, R. K. (1985). Two dogmas of educational research. *Educational Researcher, 14*(8), 10–18.

Howe, K., & Eisenhart, M. (1990). Standards for qualitative (and quantitative) research: A prolegomenon. *Educational Researcher, 19*(4), 2–9.

Hughes, J. (1980). *The philosophy of social research.* New York: Longman.

Kirk, J., & Miller, M. L. (1986). *Reliability and validity in qualitative research.* Newbury Park, CA: Sage.

Kuhn, T. (1962). *The structure of scientific revolutions.* Chicago: The University of Chicago Press.

Laszlo, E. (1972). *Introduction to systems philosophy: Toward a new paradigm of contemporary thought.* New York: Gordon and Breach.

LeCompte, M. D., & Goetz, J. P. (1982). Problems of reliability and validity in ethnographic research. *Review of Educational Research, 52*(1), 31–60.

Lincoln, Y. and Guba, E. (1985). *Naturalistic inquiry.* Beverly Hills, CA: Sage.

Mathison, S. (1988). Why triangulate? *Educational Researcher, 17*(2), 13–17.

Miles, M. B., & Huberman, A. M. (1984). *Qualitative data analysis: A sourcebook of new methods.* Beverly Hills, CA: Sage.

Miller, S. I., & Fredericks, M. (1991). Postpositivistic assumptions and educational research: Another view. *Educational Researcher, 20*(4), 2–8.

Natanson, M. (1973). *Phenomenology and the social sciences.* Evanston, IL: Northwestern University Press.

Patton, M. Q. (1990). *Qualitative evaluation and research methods* (2nd Ed.). London: Sage.

Phillips, D. C. (1987). Validity in qualitative research. *Education and Urban Society, 20*(1), 9–24.

Phillips, D. C. (1990). Subjectivity and objectivity: An objective inquiry. In E. W. Eisner & A. Peshkin (eds.), *Qualitative inquiry in education* (pp. 19–37, 92–95). New York: Teachers College Press.

Reason, P., & Rowan, J. (1981). Issues of validity in new paradigm research. In P. Reason & J. Rowan (eds.), *Human inquiry: A sourcebook of new paradigm research* (pp. 239–250). New York: John Wiley & Sons.

Salomon, G. (1991). Transcending the qualitative-quantitative debate: The analytic and systemic approaches to educational research. *Educational Researcher, 20*(6), 10–18.

Sanders, D. P. (1981). Educational inquiry as developmental research. *Educational Researcher, 10*(3), 8–13.

Schofield, J. W. (1990). Increasing the generalizability of qualitative research. In E. W. Eisner & A. Peshkin (Eds.), *Qualitative inquiry in education* (pp. 201–232). New York: Teachers College Press.

Shulman, L. S. (1988). Disciplines of inquiry in education: An overview. In R. M. Jaeger (Ed.), *Complementary methods for research in education* (pp. 3–17). Washington, DC: American Educational Research Association.

Smith, M. L., & Glass, G. V. (1987). *Research and evaluation in education and the social sciences.* Englewood Cliffs, NJ: Prentice Hall.

Strasser, S. (1963). *Phenomenology and the human sciences: A contribution to a new scientific ideal.* Pittsburgh: Duquesne University Press.

van Laer, P. H. (1963). *Philosophy of science (part one): An introduction to some general aspects of science.* Pittsburgh: Duquesne University Press.

van Peursen, C. A. (1972). *Phenomenology and analytical philosophy.* Pittsburgh: Duquesne University Press.

Walker, J. C. & Evers, C. W. (1986) "Theory, politics, and experiment in educational research methodology." *International Review of Education;* xxxii, 373–387.

Wolcott, H. F. (1990). On seeking—and rejecting—validity in qualitative research. In E. W. Eisner & A. Peshkin (eds.), *Qualitative inquiry in education* (pp. 121–152). New York: Teachers College Press.

Yin, R. K. (1989). Case study research: Design and methods (2nd ed.). Newbury Park, CA: Sage.

CHAPTER 3

ISSUES IN COLLABORATIVE RESEARCH

Allison Tom and Thomas J. Sork

This chapter has two purposes. First, we present the background against which the increasing importance of research collaboration between adult education practitioners and academic researchers can be understood. Second, we discuss theoretical and practical issues to be considered in planning and carrying out collaborative research. We take the position that increased collaboration between practitioners and academic researchers is, in general, to be desired when it is appropriate to the purposes of the study and when it is entered into carefully and thoughtfully. We recognize the importance and potential of research collaboration between other actors in adult education—e.g., between learner and practitioner researchers—but limit the focus of this chapter to the ways practitioner and academic researchers can work together. Collaboration in research helps to increase the practical utility and potential for social change of a piece of research (Gitlin, 1990). Academic researchers' increased awareness of and interest in practitioner involvement in research is an indication of "a growing willingness among researchers to truly ground their critical analyses in the 'trenches' of educational practice" (Anderson, 1989, p. 262).

As we discuss below, practitioners' search for understanding has much in common with academic researchers' search for understanding, and there are justifications for referring to both kinds of activities as research. Members of each group have strengths they bring to the research enterprise and limitations of perspective and skill which must be overcome. In many ways, however, collaborative research differs fundamentally from "traditional" (academic-researcher directed) research, and academic researchers and practitioners who want to engage in collaborative work must be prepared to rethink many of their fundamental assumptions about the conduct and purposes of research. Although the goal of increased understanding is common for all research, there are fundamental issues which must be dealt with if practitioner and academic researchers are to engage in successful collaborations.

NEW AND EMERGING PERSPECTIVES ON RESEARCH

In recent years approaches to research that are noncollaborative, are controlled exclusively by academic researchers, and which produce no direct benefits to the subjects of the research have received considerable criticism. Feminist and postmodern scholars, among others, have raised such problematic issues as scholars' right to enter others' lives and to make and own records about others, power imbalances between researchers and "subjects" and the groups to which they usually belong, the construction of some individuals and groups of people as "other," and the role research plays in supporting or challenging an inequitable social order. "Educational research is still a process that for the most part silences those studies, ignores their personal knowledge, and strengthens the assumption that researchers are the producers of knowledge" (Gitlin, 1990, p. 444, emphasis in the original). Collaborative research—research that involves the "subjects" of research as active agents in shaping and interpreting the research—is often proposed as a partial solution to these challenges.

Generating knowledge is the fundamental purpose of research. By knowledge we mean information that helps us understand, sometimes predict, and occasionally control adult education phenomena. The goal of understanding is the driving force behind all research, but the type of understanding that is sought depends, in part, on the types of questions that we ask and the utility expected of the answers. As educators we are concerned, for example, about matters like how educational policies will affect the provision of educational programs, how educational programs of a certain character will affect the capabilities of those who participate, how the actions of an educational agent will influence the learning process, and how the social or economic circumstances of learners will affect accessibility to and benefits of educational programs. All of these examples illustrate the importance of understanding relationships between various factors, or, more particularly, the effects of an action, event, or circumstance.

Research takes many forms. The most systematic research is conducted by academic researchers who are trained in the principles and practices of "formal" research. But other valuable research is carried out in less systematic and less formal ways by practitioners who simply want to better understand some phenomena related to their work. Indeed, the idea that the production of knowledge is an exclusive and esoteric activity carried on largely by university-based academics is being challenged on a number of fronts (e.g., Belenkey et al., 1986). Participatory and transformational research, in which the primary goal is social action and the researchers are actors in the context being studied, are examples of knowledge production that occurs outside the academy with the aim of moving beyond understanding to action. In describing the defining characteristics of transformational research, Deshler and Selener (1991) make very clear its action orientation:

Transformative research . . . is not a new research methodology, but a particular philosophical stance towards all research without distinction of fields of study: physical, natural, or social science. That stance toward transformative knowledge generation is one that views the focus, the process, and the outcomes of research as the means by which confrontation and action against the causes of injustice, exploitation, violence, and environmental degradation can occur through the research process and the use of research results. (p. 10)

Participatory research was first discussed by adult educators in the 1970s as an alternative to the dominant forms of research. Since that time it has been applied extensively in less developed countries to involve "ordinary people" in knowledge generation. Tandon (1988) explains the basic tenets of the approach:

Participatory research is the methodology of the alternative system of knowledge production. It is not a set of tools, techniques and methods. Embodying the values and philosophy of alternative and popular systems of knowledge production, it is based on the belief that ordinary people are capable of understanding and transforming their reality. Its articles of faith include a commitment to collective participation, and empowerment of the ordinary people in having and knowing their world; in envisioning a new society; and in playing their collective roles in the process of transformation. (p. 13)

Transformational and participatory research respond to what were considered severe limitations of traditional, university-based research. They both call for active participation of people who are not trained researchers and both focus on knowledge generation not as an end in itself, but as a means to empower people to change the circumstances of their existence.

Feminism and ethnography, in different ways, emphasize the notion that the differences between "scientific" knowledge and "everyday" knowledge is not that wide. Feminism emphasizes the need to recognize the knowledge of those whose knowledge is usually neglected or undervalued. Ethnographers also tend to acknowledge that they use rather pedestrian tools in the "production of knowledge"—hanging out, talking to people, looking around. They don't base the validity of their claims to knowledge on the esoteric or arcane nature of the tools they use (or, indeed, of the knowledge they generate) but on the discipline with which they pursue what they want to know (Ayers, 1989; Hammersley & Atkinson, 1983).

If we understand research to be the process of trying to understand phenomena, practitioners in any field are constantly engaged in research. Whenever an educational practitioner tries a new instructional technique or interacts with a learner in a new way, he or she is conducting an experiment. Once the effects of the new approach are observed, the practitioner makes a judgment about whether the approach produced the desired effect. If it does, then a new "principle of practice" has been discovered and the practitioner has another tool to use in his or her work. As practitioners engage in this type of experimentation, they generate practice-based knowledge that has high utility in their work. Yet there is also a need for knowledge that can reasonably be transferred or generalized from the content where it is produced to other contexts with similar characteristics.

So we begin this exploration on collaborative research with the assumption that all practitioners engage in the production of knowledge, that is, research. Further, we assume that understanding is an important— although not exclusive—goal of research and that the knowledge produced through research may be relevant to only a single situation, to several situations that have very particular characteristics in common, or to a broad range of situations that are generally similar in character.

In a university, research is judged by how well it conforms to "accepted" principles of scholarly inquiry, how generalizable or transferable the findings are, and how significant the research problem or question is perceived to be by other academics who serve as gatekeepers—that is, those who control access to publications, research conferences, and grants, and influence decisions about promotion and tenure. Satisfying the gatekeepers is important to the careers of academic researchers, so the focus of their research is often problems or issues viewed as significant or interesting by fellow academics rather than as useful to practitioners. The research done by practitioners is assessed by its practical utility in getting the job done, whether the job is helping people develop basic literacy skills, learn new job-related procedures, become effective activists, or transform society. Practitioners are rewarded for producing knowledge that helps them accomplish their goals; it is not the notion of production of knowledge that counts as much as the improvement in their effectiveness.

The different systems of assessing and rewarding research inside and outside of universities suggest a potential conflict when academics and practitioners engage in research together. At the very least it implies the need for careful articulation of the different interests and different value (and reward) systems within which the two work and negotiation of how the research is to be conducted, shared, used, and publicized.

Some academic researchers have implied that responsibility for making research findings useful rests with practitioners. Because practitioners fail to properly translate findings from scientific research, research findings are so little used in practice. For example, Boyd and Menlo (1984) wrote about a process for translating "scientific information" into a form useful for practice. They argued that university-based research results in what they call "scientific generalizations" that cannot be used directly in practice. In order to use such knowledge, "scientific generalizations" must first be translated into "practice generalizations," then into "design generalizations" that have immediate utility in solving problems of practice in a specific context. Their process is based on the assumption that practitioners should be partaking of the fruits of scientific inquiry, and that in order to do so effectively, they must learn an elaborate process of "translating" information unusable in its original form—that is, as it is published or otherwise disseminated by the academic researcher. This view puts the responsibility for rendering research useful clearly on the shoulders of the practitioner. It is a "top-down" view of research that puts the academic researcher at the "top" and the practitioner facing a problem at the "bottom." Work such as this seems to miss the inherent dialectic between the lives of practitioners and academic researchers. However much academic researchers might like to remove themselves from dependence on practitioners—and indeed on "practice"—the dependence remains, and even the notion that such a separation can work is an exaggeration of opposites.

Both scholars and practitioners know how to "delegitimize" the knowledge of the other; we need to understand this as defensiveness (one against charges of being "useless" or "too theoretical" and the other against charges of being "unsophisticated" or "too parochial") as well as a lack of understanding of the contribution of the "other." Anthropological and postmodern concepts of "the other" help explain this phenomenon. The need/compulsion to separate (and value more highly) what we do in opposition to what some "other" does is a pervading theme that plays into the notion of a dichotomized, either/or world. But efforts to overcome dichotomization usually reveal the greater complexity and richness of the world that has been depicted so simplistically (Tom, in press). Following this notion, we can see that each vision of the "other" is simplistic and that, in a very real sense, the knowledge of practitioners and academics interacts and depends on one another. What could academic researchers study if there was no adult education practice?

CHALLENGES AND ISSUES IN COLLABORATIVE RESEARCH

As practitioner and academic researchers explore the possibilities, challenges, and rewards of working directly together in research enterprises, a number of fundamental issues arise. At first glance, some of these seem to be primarily theoretical or philosophical issues and others seem to be practical issues; closer inspection, however, usually reveals there are practical implications to theoretical questions and theoretical implications to practical questions. We discuss these challenges below in terms of the purposes of research, ideas about academics' and practitioners' roles, bridging the gap between the worlds of academics and practitioners, power issues as they are played out in practical lives, and ethical issues. These categories overlap and interact just as the practical and theoretical aspects of the categories meld with one another.

The Purposes of Research

One way academic researchers have had control over the research process is through their control over the resources necessary to do research. Universities provide their faculty with library support, computer support, and an environment in which research is highly valued. University jobs are structured to encourage and support research involvement; academics have access, through granting agencies, to the funds necessary to support research. For example, the Social Sciences and Humanities Research Council of Canada, although it encourages the involvement of practitioners in research projects, requires that the principal investigator of research projects it funds be employed at a Canadian university. Practitioners and others may have some influence on the structure of research initiatives through pressure on government and granting agencies. Academic researchers help shape research direction by working with granting agencies and are influenced by the policies of granting agencies and their funders. Fraser (1989) has named the process through which women's needs are articulated by women themselves and then adopted and reinterpreted by government agencies a process of "needs interpretation." Adult education practitioners (as well as learners) can be seen to be in a position of articulating their (research) needs to granting agencies but having relatively less control over how those needs are interpreted and met.

These factors have the practical consequence of putting academic researchers, along with granting agencies, in a position to determine what kind of research ought to be done and how it ought to be done. When academic researchers plan research projects, they participate in creating and are subject to a set of norms about what constitutes worthy research questions and acceptable research designs. Practitioner researchers are then put in a position of gaining access to these research resources primarily when they are able to find an academic "advocate" or when they put pressure on granting agencies to respond to their concerns. "One way most traditional research reproduces the hierarchical and alienating relationship between practitioners and researchers is by centering the process of question posing in the hands of the university researcher" (Gitlin, 1990, p. 453). In general, the research that has been done in the academic community is research that the academic community, rather than the community of practitioners, agrees is important and interesting to do.

Because a great deal of educational research does not have immediate or obvious applications or deals with highly abstract or arcane issues, practitioners may consider all research to be irrelevant to their work. If practitioners see research as university-generated "knowledge" that has little concern for the worlds in which they live, they are justified in not seeing research as relevant to their practice. The challenge is for practitioners and academic researchers to move toward a point of mutual respect and collaborative construction of research questions so that the valuable aspects of university-generated research are retained while the relevance of research to practitioners' problems is increased (Rogers et al., 1987). As practitioners and academic researchers begin to work together, they must negotiate practical steps through the research as well as this fundamental notion of what constitutes interesting, important, and respectable research.

Academic researchers have a responsibility to address the issue of accessibility of their research, the topics they choose to address and the places and ways in which they publish the results of their research. As long as academics research is presented in ways and places that delegitimize the expertise of practitioners, the seeming "irrelevance" of their work, and practitioners' indifference to it, will continue (Hooks, 1988; Tobin & Davidson, 1990). Gitlin (1990) believes that practitioners' lack of engagement with the literature is because, ". . . their job is structured to make this difficult; articles also are written in coded ways that limit accessibility" (p. 446).

Ideas About Roles in Research

A traditional model of research separates researcher and subject, researcher and practitioner, and the perspectives of the insider and the outsider. Research that actively involves practitioners challenges these roles if the implications of practitioner involvement are followed to their logical consequences. It is possible, in the abstract, for practitioners to don the "white coat" of the researcher and turn their backs to their ties to the field, but this model of "practitioner involvement" speaks more of recruiting practitioners to the ranks of academic researchers than to research that actively seeks to incorporate the perspective of nonacademics. But collaboration in research also raises the issue of how and when to involve other groups of people who have traditionally been "subjects" of research; in adult education, the involvement of adult learners is immediately raised by attempts to do collaborative research. Practitioners and academic researchers who are not comfortable with less clear lines of division between themselves and "subjects" or themselves and learners may have difficulty with research that involves practitioners in making decisions about and actively contributing to the research process. This discomfort should not be dismissed as individuals' rigid personalities or difficulties in accommodating different roles; it is grounded in experience of the world. "(I)n a social world that is unequal, you don't get a democratic or open conversation simply by saying that everybody's free to talk" (Florio-Ruane, 1990, p. 316). Practitioner and academic researchers must also guard against the temptation to form an alliance that essentially moves the location of powerlessness; that is, they must guard against regarding learners as "subjects" in ways they are struggling to resist for themselves.

Collaborative research challenges more than the relationship between the actors in the research enterprise. It also challenges traditional notions of the relationship between "insiders' " and outsiders' " perspectives. In traditional approaches to research, it was considered important for the researcher to be a more or less objective observer of the phenomenon being studied. The notion of objectivity in research has been challenged in terms of the accuracy of an "objective" or "outside" perspective, in terms of the unattainability of such a perspective, and in terms of the ways in which researchers may evade the responsibility to declare their interests and perspectives by hiding behind the mask of objectivity (Clifford & Marcus, 1986; Harding, 1991; Lather, 1986). In spite of these recent critiques, the idea that practitioners can also be researchers of phenomena with which they are directly involved violates a fundamental principle many scholars and practitioners consider sacred.

Finally, practitioners are rightly concerned primarily with being effective in their day-to-day work. They assume the primary role of teacher, administrator, counselor, planner, and so on, and may not consider assuming the role of researcher at all. Practitioners may also not see themselves as researchers when they subscribe to the university-centered definition of knowledge and its generation. On the other hand, they may choose not to be researchers as an active act of resistance to the scholar-centered production of knowledge.

Bridging the Gap Between the Worlds

As practitioner and academic researchers begin to work together, they face challenges of learning to collaborate while continuing to work and function within their own worlds. Their work environments reward and support them for different kinds of activities and accomplishments. In the academic world where doing research is considered a primary objective, there are often frequent rewards for those who get big grants and publish often in prestigious journals. In the world of practitioners, such activities are less central to the reward system and activities such as making programs work effectively and getting programming funds are rewarded. In addition, neither practitioner nor academic researchers live within job structures that are designed to accommodate work with "the other"; that is, academic researchers' schedules have not been designed with intense work with practitioners in mind and practitioner researchers' schedules have not been designed to accommodate collaboration with academic researchers. Practitioner researchers are likely to be more hard pressed by the difficulties of adding collaboration to their schedules than are academic researchers, but both kinds of researchers will have to put effort into freeing the time necessary to build a close working relationship with someone outside their normal workday world (Florio-Ruane, 1990, p. 327).

Where these issues are neglected, mistrust and misunderstandings can easily arise—as they can from other sources as well. Practitioner and academic researchers need to be clear with each other about the rewards and difficulties that conducting research—and conducting research with someone outside of their accustomed areas of practice—presents for them. This is only one area in which practitioner and academic researchers must consciously work to build trust and avoid miscommunication. Liaisons between practitioner and academic researchers are best begun with deliberate efforts to communicate and require continual attention to building and maintaining trust between the two worlds.

Power Issues in Practical Lives

There is a real concern that when practitioner and academic researchers set out to do research together that the academic researchers' greater experience in playing the game of research—getting grants, writing proposals, and doing the research itself—will, deliberately or not, turn into a situation where this expertise effectively undermines both parties' intentions of working as equal colleagues. The reality that the academic researcher may have these skills should not be ignored any more than the reality of different reward and job structures should be. What should be avoided, however, is the creation of a situation where this greater experience and confidence create an ongoing power imbalance. As Gitlin (1990) puts it, the challenge is to find ways to "enter into a research process that **honors** the questions asked but enables **all** participants to rethink those questions without reproducing the division of labor that privileges academics while silencing practitioners" (p. 457).

Academic researchers are not traditionally trained in many of the skills required to do effective collaborative research. For example, one critical skill is the ability to negotiate the purposes and design of a research project in a way that respects the personal goals of those involved and the autonomy of the researchers as well as the "subjects" of the research. Academic researchers must also learn effective ways of sharing their skills with others whose need for those skills comes from a different source than their own. A practitioner learning to be a researcher may be learning research skills in order to move into an academic environment; on the other hand, many practitioners need to understand research methodology in order to critique the research they read and to participate effectively in the project at hand. Academic researchers often enter an area of practice with theoretical ideas about how the arena of practice works but with very little practical knowledge of how individuals within this field deal with one another, negotiate purposes, and carry out the business of everyday life collectively. Academic researchers must learn the skills that allow them to be effective, nonoffensive participants in the practitioners' worlds.

Both practitioner and academic researchers must be willing to devote the necessary time to teaching and learning the skills required for effective collaborative research. Learning to work together takes time, negotiating the purposes of research takes time, and effective communication takes time (Florio-Ruane, 1990, p. 314). When researchers are working in environments where that time is not easily available, the temptation is to cut corners on the aspects of the research that are least visible: maintaining the human relationships and developing the necessary research skills in all members of the research team. Ensuring that practitioner researchers have an adequate knowledge of the research goals and theoretical issues involved in the research is an ongoing task that is essential to the ethics of the research project and to ensuring that the practitioner researcher has a genuine opportunity to contribute to the formulation, execution, and interpretation of the research. Where academic researchers "save time" by making decisions themselves about issues that seem theoretically complex, they are effectively limiting the real power practitioner researchers have in acting as equal partners.

Ethical Issues

The potential for practitioner researchers to be exploited by collaborative research structures that don't quite work is great. Both parties to the research must be vigilant in ensuring that the research continues to meet the needs of the practitioner researcher. The generally higher status accorded to academic research creates an environment where it may be difficult for some practitioners to be clear about situations where they are being exploited—where they are putting time into a research project that appears to suit their needs but in actuality suits the needs of the academic partner. In collaborative situations, there is also a particularly strong responsibility to ensure that participants are not unfairly encouraged to reveal "more than they ordinarily might do to more obviously authoritarian researchers" (Tobin & Davidson, 1990, p. 279).

Other ethical issues arise as well. In particular, the traditional assumption that research is carried out by someone who has no ties to the research site is often violated by a research alliance between a practitioner researcher and an academic researcher. Solutions to the issues of confidentiality and anonymity must be sought. In some cases, it may become clear that anonymity and confidentiality are not necessary to achieve the goals of the research, but in others these are essential, and a structure that ensures that research "subjects" who wish to have their opinions known in the research but not directly identified as theirs to the practitioner researcher must be devised.

Implementing new research strategies, some of them designed to address ethical concerns with older forms of research, necessarily gives rise to new ethical dilemmas. For example, Tobin and Davidson (1990) designed a "polyvocal" approach to ethnography, intending to "decenter the text from its authors by shifting the power of reflexivity" (p. 272).

Their strategy involved showing videotapes of interactions first to those who had been in the setting, second to others from the same cultural background, and finally to observers from other cultures. The original videotapes and layers of comments from these different analysts produced a "polyvocal" ethnographic account. They found that they unintentionally created situations where new ethical dilemmas arose; actors were embarrassed by the showing of the videotapes within the setting, cultural domination was at least once repeated rather than challenged, and at least one practitioner was left feeling powerless rather than empowered. "To be given the chance to see onself . . . either can be empowering (as we intended) or depersonalizing, an invitation to participate in one's own surveillance, correction, and control" (p. 276). These dilemmas arose not because of bad intentions or poor work of the researchers but because of the tensions inherent in doing research. "The ethical questions raised by our work and by related qualitative investigations are not problems to be solved by right thinking, well meaning researchers. Rather, they are tensions inherent in the research enterprise, in the ongoing negotiation of meaning between scholar and practitioner, and between insider and outsider" (Tobin & Davidson, 1990, p. 272; see also Smyth, 1992).

ENGAGING IN COLLABORATIVE RESEARCH

So far in this chapter we have attempted to discuss new and emerging views on the research enterprise and to identify challenges and issues related to collaborative research. In this final section, we offer some suggestions for those who would like to engage in collaborative research whether or not the intent of that research is to bring about social change. Collaboration has potential benefits regardless of the purpose of the research, but it must be entered into with careful planning, much discussion, and in a climate of mutual exploration and learning if these benefits are to be realized. It is not an easy approach to research and it requires a set of skills that are rarely part of traditional research methods courses taught in universities.

Recognizing and Respecting Different Forms of Knowing

The knowledge that is most highly valued in academic environments is the kind that has been produced using dominant research paradigms, is codifiable, and is generalizable (or transferable). The knowledge that is most highly valued in practice settings is the kind that can be applied to carry out the day-to-day tasks of designing and delivering educational programs regardless of the method of its production, whether it is codifiable, or whether it lends itself to application outside the immediate practice setting. As those from academic and practice settings discuss collaboration, they should acknowledge these differences and discuss the merits and limits of each form of knowledge. Both have strengths and weaknesses that should be understood, and the utility of each depends on the context in which the knowledge is used. Lack of respect for a form of knowing will result in efforts to delegitimize the less respected form, and the words or actions that attempt to delegitimize are certain to strain the collaborative relationship.

Revealing and Discussing Motives and Objectives

Although practitioner and academic researchers share the intention of generating knowledge, they may enter into collaboration with different motives and with different expectations of outcomes. Revealing motives and expectations at the outset and discussing their implications for the collaborative relationship will make the basis of the association transparent and open to discussion and negotiation. A successful collaboration is possible if the objectives of those involved are different as long as they are also seen as complementary. Successful collaborations are not possible if objectives are mutually exclusive or contradictory. It is unwise to assume that initially incompatible objectives will somehow become compatible as the collaboration unfolds. What is more likely to happen is that tensions will develop over whose agenda is being pursued and these tensions will be manifest in frequent disagreements about the focus and conduct of the research. Taking time at the beginning of the collaboration to discuss motives and objectives and their compatibility allows the parties to assess the feasibility of continuing the relationship and drawing it to a successful conclusion.

Understanding Reward Structures

Because practitioners and academics are rewarded for different kinds of performance, some attention should be given to understanding what each party needs from the research to satisfy expectations. Researchers do not operate in isolation of an accountability framework. The sponsors of the research have certain expectations about what it will produce, and the "home" agencies or institutions of those involved in the collaboration will expect that the work being performed will be furthering their respective organizational objectives. Collaborators should work together to make sure that the outcomes of their work will be viewed positively by those to whom they are accountable. This might mean that the outcomes are presented in different ways to satisfy the expectations of the collaborators' "home" organizations. For example, while both may collectively prepare a final technical report to satisfy the sponsor, the academic researcher might focus on articles for publication in scholarly journals while the practitioner researcher might focus on presenting results directly to colleagues either through meetings or practice-oriented publications. Although we might not like these distinctions or that one kind of work may be viewed by some as more valuable or of greater utility than another, it would be naive to ignore the differences. Successful collaborative research acknowledges these differences and provides for them in its design.

Agreeing on Roles and Maintaining Relationships

Collaborative research is, in many respects, more demanding of those involved than research conducted by a single person since collaboration requires shared responsibilities. Where the single researcher is responsible for every aspect of an investigation and does not suffer from confusion over who is responsible for what, successful collaborative research involves reaching agreement on the roles each party will play, the responsibilities each will assume, and the ways in which they will relate to one another. Awareness of one's own strengths and weaknesses, a willingness to compromise, and a readiness to renegotiate responsibilities as the project unfolds all contribute to a healthy collaborative climate.

Maintaining relationships among those on the research team involves frequent meetings, open communication, and a sense of humor. Tensions that develop over any aspect of the work should be discussed early and openly before they become festering annoyances that threaten the success of the project. Other important relationships need attention as well. Examples include the relationships between the researchers and the sponsors of the research, between the researchers and the site where the research is being conducted or the group being researched, and between the researchers and policy makers or others who expect to use the results of the research. In short, diplomacy is required in collaborative research, and neglecting this work can result in serious conflicts that may jeopardize the success of the project.

Training

Research in general and collaborative research in particular requires skills that may not be present within the research team or that may not be as fully developed as they should be. A training component involving everyone associated with the project should run throughout the course of the research. Since by its very nature collaborative research is also collaborative learning, providing opportunities to develop the skills necessary to conduct the study and to share what is being learned during the study is essential. Effective training builds the capabilities of the research team, enhances communication, reinforces the purposes of the study, identifies potential sources of conflict and misunderstanding, and produces more trustworthy (valid and reliable) findings. Training in collaborative research should focus as much on understanding the dynamics and complexities of the site or group being studied as on the technical skills required to collect, process, and interpret data.

Monitoring and Adapting Process

Careful monitoring of the research process reduces the likelihood that methodological errors will compromise the study and increases the chances that formative improvements will be made to the design. Research protocols should be adapted in response to new information that comes from monitoring the process. Developing an explicit monitoring plan with clearly assigned responsibilities acknowledges the complexity of research and the likelihood that the research protocol will have to be adjusted as circumstances change, as initial designs are found to be deficient, and as unexpected opportunities and challenges present themselves. Investigators are often required by funding agencies to report periodically on progress. Such reports would not be complete without a description of what changes were made to the original protocol and why, so recording the circumstances that led to the changes, the specifics of the changes, and the reasoning behind them is an important function.

Protecting Confidentiality and Integrity of the Research

Maintaining confidentiality in research is an important ethical obligation, but the different parties in collaborative research may interpret this obligation differently. Most academic researchers are subject to well-defined and rigidly enforced rules designed to protect the rights of research subjects and other individuals and organizations whose interests might be harmed by the research. Confidentiality, conflict of interest, and informed consent are examples of issues for which guidelines have been developed, but guidelines can never cover all cases. Vigilance is required to ensure that none of the collaborators intentionally or inadvertently violates any of the ethical obligations that all researchers are expected to assume. Although it would be easy to conclude that practitioner researchers are more likely to err in these matters because they lack the formal training of academic researchers and may not work in settings where formal procedures are in place to protect the interests of subjects, this conclusion would be in error. Practitioner and academic researchers are equally subject to self-serving, thoughtless, and expedient behaviors that may jeopardize the subjects or site and, consequently, the integrity of the entire project. These obligations, and the frequent temptations to violate them, must be taken seriously in all forms of research, but collaborative research is even more demanding because so many parties may be involved. Discussing these obligations at the outset of a project and creating a forum for reaching agreement about how they will be respected in the research are both necessary. But a more thorough process may be needed, especially if there are signs that these obligations are not understood by all the collaborators or that the temptation to overlook them is too great.

Disseminating and Applying Results

Findings that are the product of true collaborations between practitioner and academic researchers can and should be qualitatively different from findings produced by either party working alone. We make this assertion because we believe that both parties bring unique and valuable perspectives that enrich the products of research. The value of collaborative research will not be recognized by anyone other than those involved until it is disseminated and applied more broadly. Reaching agreements on how this will be done is an important final step in the process.

For academic researchers there is considerable pressure to *publish* findings in respected journals that are read primarily by other academics. For practitioner researchers there is similar pressure to *apply findings* to improve the design and delivery of programs. The vagaries of different reward systems may mean that joint dissemination and application of results—although the preferred way to end such a project—is not feasible. If all of those who collaborated in the project were equally involved in both disseminating and applying results, the literature and practice of adult education would be enriched.

What is learned through collaborative research is not limited only to research findings; much is also learned about the research process itself. Having good descriptions of the steps involved, the high points, the low points, and strategies used to overcome problems in collaborative research would not only reveal the methods by which new understandings were reached, but would put a more human face on what is often portrayed as a faceless technical process.

Our intention in writing this chapter was to encourage more collaborative research in adult education while recognizing that it is not an easy thing to do. We have argued that collaborative research is consistent with many contemporary ideas about the research enterprise and avoids many of the limitations of "traditional" research approaches. We have discussed challenges and issues involved in collaborative research and suggested tasks that should be addressed by those planning to engage in it.

We end this chapter with the hope that our efforts to illuminate the complexities of collaborative research have not overshadowed its potential to produce *useful* knowledge in adult education. Bringing together the interests, skills, and experience of practitioners and academic researchers to focus on developing new understandings of adult education phenomena can lead to both useful knowledge and an awareness of the important contributions that each can make to improved practice.

REFERENCES

Anderson, G. (1989). Critical ethnography in education. Origins, current status and new directions. *Review of Educational Research, 59,* 249–270.

Ayers, W. (1989). *The good preschool teacher: Six teachers reflect on their lives.* New York: Teachers College Press.

Belenky, M. F., Clinchy, B. M., Goldberger, N. R., & Tarule, J. M. (1986). *Women's ways of knowing: The development of self, voice and mind.* New York: Basic Books.

Boyd, R. D., & Menlo, A. (1984). Solving problems of practice in education. *Knowledge: Creation, Diffusion, Utilization, 6* (1), 59–74.

Clifford, J., & Marcus, G. E. (1986). *Writing culture: The poetics and politics of ethnography.* Berkeley: University of California Press.

Deshler, D., & Selener, D. (1991). Transformative research: In search of a definition. *Convergence, 24* (3), 9–22.

Florio-Ruane, S. (1990). The written literacy forum: An analysis of teacher/researcher collaboration. *Journal of Curriculum Studies, 22* (4), 313–328.

Fraser, N. (1989). *Unruly practices: Power, discourse and gender in contemporary social theory.* Minneapolis: University of Minnesota Press.

Gitlin, A. D. (1990). Educative research, voice, and school change. *Harvard Educational Review, 60* (4), 443–466.

Hammersley, M., and Atkinson, P. (1983). *Ethnography: Principles in practice.* London: Routledge.

Harding, S. (1991). *Whose science? Whose knowledge? Thinking from women's lives.* Ithaca, New York: Cornell University Press.

Hooks, B. (1988). *Talking back: Thinking feminist, thinking black.* Toronto: Between the Lines.

Lather, P. (1986). Issues of validity in openly ideological research. *Interchange, 17* (4): 63–84.

Smyth, J. (1992). Teachers' work and the politics of reflection. *American Educational Research Journal, 29,* 267–300.

Tandon, R. (1988). Social transformation and participatory research. *Convergence, 21* (2/3), 5–18.

Tobin, J., & Davidson, D. (1990). The ethics of polyvocal ethnography: Empowering vs textualizing children and teachers. *International Journal of Qualitative Studies in Education, 3* (3): 271–283.

Tom, A. (in press). Women's lives complete: Methodological concerns in the study of women's lives. In B. Long and S. Kahn (Eds.), *Women's Work, Stress and Coping.* Montreal: McGill-Queens' University Press.

CHAPTER 4

COLLABORATION, NETWORKING, AND THE RESEARCH COMMUNITY

Roger Hiemstra
Ralph G. Brockett

A differentiating characteristic of adult education is that as a relatively new field of study and practice, there are limited numbers of individuals actively engaged in research and scholarship. This has resulted in various unique features of the adult education research community. For example, because of limitations on funding for adult education research, various creative networking efforts have taken place over the years.

An early example is the establishment of the Center for the Study of Liberal Education for Adults (CSLEA). This organization brought together individuals interested in adult education through conferences and the development of publications (Whipple, 1967). An ongoing example since 1966 has been the Educational Resources Information Center (ERIC) database, funded by the U.S. Department of Education. The ERIC Clearinghouse on Adult, Career, and Vocational Education, which is located at Ohio State University, is responsible for collecting and disseminating materials specifically related to adult education. Over the years, the ERIC Clearinghouse has served as a vehicle through which materials not previously widely disseminated have been made available (Imel, 1989). Other recent efforts have included Kellogg Foundation-supported conferences and individual scholar awards on adult education history and other topics at Syracuse University (e.g., Rohfeld, 1990) and conferences and fellowships, also sponsored by Kellogg, in adult learning research at Montana State University (e.g., Fellenz, 1988; Fellenz & Conti, 1990).

Another illustration is the Commission of Professors of Adult Education, a North American organization that has networking among members as one of its major benefits. Since its founding in 1955, it has sponsored or coordinated various collaborative scholarship efforts. The first major product to result from such collaboration was what has become known as the "black book" (because of its cover color) that featured chapters by 18 scholars (Jensen, Liveright, & Hallenbeck, 1964). These authors summarized much of the research and scholarship relative to adult education through the early 1960s and stressed the need for adult education to draw from other disciplines in order to develop its knowledge base. More recently, the Commission (through its umbrella organization, the American Association for Adult and Continuing Education) sponsored the publication of a book designed to "update" the black book in a volume titled (*Adult education: Evolution and achievements in a developing field of study* (Peters & Jarvis, 1991). Two other books on adult education research stress the importance of networking and collaborative efforts (Long & Hiemstra, 1980; Merriam & Simpson, 1984).

Because of the field's unique nature, networking has been especially important to the development and dissemination of adult education knowledge. Indeed, some of the most exciting developments in the field's knowledge base have resulted from efforts to create research networks. For example, the concept of participatory research, discussed later in this chapter, is grounded in the notion of viewing researchers and participants as "co-researchers" in the inquiry process (Gaventa, 1988; Merriam & Simpson, 1984). With its emphasis on equity between researchers and participants, participatory research can be argued to be the "truest" form of collaboration.

A different type of illustration can be found in the area of self-directed learning, where annual symposia on this specialized topic have been held since 1986. Numerous research paper presentations and an annual book of proceedings have contributed to a substantial and progressive development of related knowledge. Long (1992) is a representative example of the several publications emanating from these symposia.

In this chapter, we look at both the potentials and limits of collaboration and networking. Further, we share several strategies that can be used to promote greater collaborative efforts among researchers in the field. Finally, we look briefly at some of the ethical considerations central to networking and collaboration. We believe networking is vital to the future development of knowledge in adult education.

COLLABORATION IN THE RESEARCH PROCESS

Why collaborate? Numerous potential drawbacks and barriers impede collaborative research. Many of these are common sense in nature, yet we believe the potential advantages of collaboration far outweigh these limitations. Several disadvantages and advantages of collaboration and networking are addressed in this section.

Disadvantages of Collaboration

At least five major disadvantages hinder collaborative research. These include barriers due to physical distance among researchers, scheduling and time barriers, irreconcilable differences among researchers, perceptions about the diminished value of collaborative research in some circumstances, and logistical problems in collaboration.

Distance

One of the most easily identified potential barriers to collaboration is the physical distance that exists between some researchers. It is not unusual for one person to live in another region of the country or even in a different country from one or more colleagues with whom networking is desired. This typically creates additional expense in terms of communication and exchanging data or written drafts of collaborative efforts. Distance also reduces the synergistic effects of face-to-face interaction. Yet, with many current developments in technology, such as electronic mail and fax machines, these barriers can be greatly reduced. Some of these are discussed later in this chapter.

Time

Time can become a barrier when there are delays in responding to or critiquing manuscript drafts. The person who is reacting or even the initial author can experience an evolution of personal views that negates or changes original views if too much time lapses between communications. Such a situation can occur, for example, when manuscripts are being transmitted over distance in some manner. The problem can exist even when collaborating with someone in the same location because busy schedules may prevent expeditious responses. The freshness possible from a rapid exchange of perspectives can thus be lost through time delays.

Another time-related concern has to do with the potential false assumption that shared research will require less time than individual research efforts. In fact, there are times when shared efforts will require *additional* time because of the need for engaging with one or more colleagues, dealing with differences in scheduling and working styles, and even scheduling around different time zones.

Irreconcilable Differences

As with the development of any other kind of relationship, those who engage in collaborative research need to recognize and address differences in styles, views, experiences, and beliefs. There will be occasions when co-researchers or co-authors face differences that appear to be irreconcilable, such as views about research methodologies, data analysis approaches, interpretation of results, and strategies for dissemination of findings. In some instances, it is possible to reconcile such differences by negotiating or by simply "agreeing to disagree." However, there will be times when these differences are great enough that they prevent forward movement on a collaborative effort. As will be described in a later section, whenever possible, shared responsibility for decision making and views regarding research should be thoroughly discussed prior to initiating collaborative efforts. Essentially, a spirit of trust is needed that makes possible the kind of "give and take" essential to successful collaborative partnerships.

Perceptions About Diminished Value of Collaborative Scholarship

An unfortunate problem when working collaboratively, but a very real one in some circumstances, is the sometimes held belief that collaborative research simply is not as valued as solo work. In the real life world of academia today, for example, there are some who believe the only true measure of one's ability to produce as a scholar is what one produces on one's own. Further, this often is perceived to mean only the production or dissemination of research results in peer-reviewed periodicals.

When such negative views about collaboration are tied to decisions about promotion, tenure, or merit, the potential for collaborative scholarship is severely delimited. Even the perception that such negative views exist may inhibit or retard collaborative efforts.

Logistical Problems in Collaboration

Collaborative scholarship is a partnership. As with any partnership, specific arrangements in terms of the logistical nature of the working relationship need to be worked out. For instance, misunderstandings can occur if the research and scholarship responsibilities are not divided in a manner clearly understood by all partners from the outset. This includes even such microdecisions as working out the mechanics of who will create the final draft of a product and communicate with editors of periodicals or it may include working collaboratively to create long-term writing and research plans. As with issues related to differences, it is important to establish a sense of trust in one's partners.

Advantages of Collaboration

While the above disadvantages may seem prohibitive to the establishment of collaborative relationships, a number of advantages far outweigh them in scope and value. Some of these advantages include: the value of synergistic relationships; the opportunity to draw upon complimentary skills and abilities; an ability to divide tasks in a way that enhances the level of productivity among partners; the mentoring potential of collaboration; opportunities for inclusiveness; and the chance to truly democratize the research process.

Synergistic Relationships

Synergy as a concept is based on the notion that the whole is greater than the sum of any parts. This works very well in a collaborative research or scholarship relationship in that there is frequently tremendous value in two or more colleagues thinking collectively, discussing all possible issues related to a problem, and determining various research approaches. Quite simply, the flow of energy between two or more people working toward the same end can lead to many insights otherwise not attainable through individual effort.

For example, this chapter was written in a collaborative manner with our brainstorming, gathering background information, writing, and editing carried out in both face-to-face and distance interactions. Our ideas fed off each other. One of us would have an idea about a chapter section and the other would then see possible additions or improvements. One of us would begin writing a section and the other would dictate some ideas as the writing process proceeded. And when we were not working side by side, we were in regular contact via electronic mail and occasionally by telephone. The result, we believe, was a greatly enhanced effort because we were able to work through, clarify, or elaborate on various ideas as they were developing. Although in this instance much of the chapter was created when we were working face-to-face, as we describe later there are ways such synergistic relationships can be enhanced through technological innovations.

Drawing Upon Complementary Skills and Abilities

Another advantage of collaboration is that it allows partners to emphasize or use their greatest skills. Recognizing that each researcher brings to the collaborative effort certain strengths, collaborative relationships allow partners to complement each other's strengths. One partner may have skills in identifying and clarifying conceptual elements of a study, while the other partner might be more adept with certain data analysis techniques. Finding and using each other's strengths also will facilitate the division of tasks in such a manner as to maximize efficiency and productivity. In essence, collaboration facilitates partners obtaining the best they can from each other.

The Mentoring Potential of Collaboration

Brockett (1991) has stated that a purpose of the adult education knowledge base is to socialize people new to the field. This means helping them to develop a sense of identity. Daloz (1986) suggests that mentors "have something to do with . . . the development of identity" (p. 19). A mentoring relationship, which is a form of collaboration, can thus be an effective approach for developing scholarship in the field. For instance, a senior university professor can work collaboratively with a junior professor on the development of research that furthers the knowledge base, provides increased understanding of scholarship, and contributes to products required for subsequent promotion or tenure decisions. The same type of relationship can be developed between faculty and graduate students.

Mentoring by experienced researchers also has an added potential value of enhancing critical thinking, reflection, and writing skills. Having one or more partners that will provide feedback on one's development can be very satisfying and supporting. In addition, a mentoring relationship may lead to long-term collaborations and further networking connections that span several years of a professional career.

Opportunities for Inclusiveness

Collaborative networks provide much potential for increasing the participation of women, minorities, and other groups that have historically been excluded from research participation. Collaboration can do much to increase opportunities for inclusiveness. At recent Adult Education Research Conferences, for example, feminist and African American caucuses have been formed to address issues of inclusiveness, and some initial discussion relative to gay/lesbian issues in adult education research has taken place. Such networks are an important initial step in truly expanding opportunities and emphases in adult education scholarship.

Democratizing the Research Process

The traditional view of research, where the researcher serves as the expert and the participant is the object of study, is often criticized because it creates an artificial environment for studying phenomena. Qualitative research approaches such as participant observation (Bogdan and Biklen, 1982) and case studies (Yin, 1989) allow researchers to investigate phenomena in their natural environments. Other methodologies go a step farther by treating the researcher and participants as "co-investigators" into a problem area. Participatory research (Gaventa, 1988) is an approach that (1) stresses the reappropriation of knowledge from those who have generally controlled such knowledge; (2) values "popular knowledge" that lies outside the "formal scientific structure" (p. 23); and (3) emphasizes democratic participation "in defining the problems to be studied, in setting the research priorities, and in determining the ends to which results are to be used" (p. 25). When participatory research approaches are used, all parties engage in a partnership that results in a network of its own. As such, participatory research holds much potential for creating collaborative partnerships that are virtually unheard of in traditional research paradigms.

COLLABORATION AND NETWORKING ELECTRONICALLY

Various forms of advanced communications and computer technologies provide researchers and practitioners literally throughout the world with many opportunities to collaborate or network. Combining personal computers, main frame computer technologies, and telecommunication services to facilitate such broad interaction is relatively new. In essence, the availability of electronic mail, listserv-supported interchange networks, and various information bases searchable at a distance is creating large numbers of people who engage in collaborative discourse and information retrieval electronically.

Five major collaboration or networking components are discussed in this chapter. Each is described in a separate section. In addition, we present some thoughts about the use of technology for scholarly exchanges, co-authoring, data sharing, and maximizing collaborative efforts.

Computer Networks

Internet and Bitnet are examples of the types of networks that exist to facilitate people communicating with each other via the exchange of electronically transmitted information. The number of gateway connections (communication entry points) that exist among networks is enabling more and more people to connect with each other. LaQuey & Ryer (1993) provide a beginning-level guide to electronic networking via Internet.

AEDNET (the Adult Education Network), a computer-mediated electronic network running on Internet, is an example of such a network aimed primarily at those involved with and/or interested in adult education. The Internet connection enables an interface with a multitude of networks throughout the world. AEDNET was established by the Kellogg Project at Syracuse University in New York and currently is administered by Nova University in Fort Lauderdale, Florida. Today, several hundred members participate regularly over the network and the membership numbers are constantly growing. For information on how to subscribe to AEDNET, please refer to endnote 1 at the end of this chapter.

These networks typically make available to participating members or users such services as electronic messaging, electronic conferencing, electronic forums, and data base searching capabilities. The Distance Education Online Symposium (DEOS) operating out of Pennsylvania State University is another illustration. DEOS consists of both DEOSNEWS (abstracts of research monographs and other information) and DEOS-L (a discussion forum).

A growing phenomenon is the emergence of electronic journals and magazines (Ehringhaus, 1990). For adult educators, *New Horizons in Adult Education* is published by Nova University as a component of AEDNET. Nova faculty and adult education graduate students from throughout North America collaborate in soliciting, reviewing, and publishing research by people interested in the field. Another example of such periodicals is *IPCT—Interpersonal Computing and Teaching: An Electronic Journal for the 21st Century.* This journal is designed to address many issues of potential interest to adult educators interested in distance education. A third example is the *Journal of Extension,* a peer-reviewed publication of the Cooperative Extension Service, which has long been published in hard copy format and has recently expanded to include electronic availability. Subscribers can request articles in various formats, search previously published articles, and obtain a current announcement message. Endnote 2 provides information on how to subscribe to this publication. Various collaboration opportunities exist with such outlets in that all information pertaining to an effort can be moved electronically, thereby overcoming some of the disadvantages described earlier in this chapter.

Electronic Data Bases

The growing accumulation of information data bases worldwide that are accessible electronically is rapidly changing the way researchers find and use information. For example, many such data bases exist within local organizational or institutional levels. These include computerized card catalogues, special interest files, and electronic ties to information stored on CD-ROMs. At a broader level, information accessible through networks like Internet exist on what are called listservs. These are computerized list or informational servers residing on some mainframe computer that provide an electronic groping of knowledge around a common interest area. Currently hundreds exist under a wide variety of topics and many are searchable via an index of past conversations or informational submissions. Darby (1992) presents some useful information for accessing data bases via the Internet.

Computer-Mediated Conferencing (CMC)

CMC is a technique that uses a mainframe computer, personal computers and modems or computer terminals, and sophisticated electronic communication software to facilitate instruction, conversation, and the exchange of information on a given subject. With CMC, people can participate in small or large group discussions, interact with other people asynchronously (at their own convenience to retrieve stored messages and send new ones), and exchange feedback or information via electronic communication. The system facilitates participation around a person's individual schedule and also provides access to various resources as needed through computers anywhere that can be contacted electronically.

The CMC systems (software that regulates the type of communication) are more advanced than normal electronic mail exchange systems in that conversations, messages, or information exchanges can be stored and searched later as needed. Participants also can be enrolled in particular groups, thereby facilitating both large and small group discussion. Although used primarily for instructional purposes to date, a growing awareness is taking place of CMC's value in other ways such as promoting networking or collaboration efforts.

Scholarly Exchange

Tremendous potential exists for people to be able to access so much information electronically (Eastmond, 1992; Heerman, 1988; U.S. Congress, 1989). As Brockett and Hiemstra (1991) note in relation to using such potential for adult learning, "Having access to such a system can add immensely to the power an educator has in meeting the needs of adult learners. Self-directed learners may, in fact, benefit the most from access to increased information and improved retrieval systems, assuming that they have access to the systems and know how to use them" (p. 165).

However, researchers also can benefit in many ways through electronic connections. Data, drafts of manuscripts, and critiques of written material can be exchanged with research partners. In fact, the asynchronous nature of electronic exchanges may even speed up the process of collaboration because partners can provide feedback or new information at their convenience rather than having to negotiate times in already busy schedules for face-to-face or phone conversations. Alternatively, if material is usually sent by mail for critique and feedback, a considerable number of days could be saved if the switch to electronic exchanges was made. In some instances, especially for researchers used to electronic exchange, the synergistic value of rapid transfer or the ability to access a multitude of information sources will even enhance the resulting scholarship.

PROFESSIONAL ASSOCIATIONS AND CONFERENCES

As with most professional fields, adult education has a wide range of professional associations that help to promote professional development across the field. In many cases, these groups play a major role in the dissemination of scholarship and, as such, serve as a vital link in the network of adult education scholars. While it is beyond the scope of this chapter to review the full range of conferences and professional associations in the field, it seems worthwhile to identify certain types of such efforts and to provide illustrations of each type of activity.

The range of professional associations serving educators of adults is vast. These include local, state or provincial, national, and international associations. Similarly, while some associations attempt to unify the field through an "umbrella" approach, others seek to serve needs of specialized segments of the field (Brockett, 1989). The key for those who wish to use associations for networking is to determine which associations will best serve their needs.

To give an example, the American Association for Adult and Continuing Education (AAACE) strives to be an umbrella organization, serving the diverse needs of adult educators throughout the entire field. Many of the networking opportunities, thus, would fall outside of the needs of those seeking specifically to form research/scholarship networks. However, AAACE does sponsor a unit devoted to adult education research and is the "parent" organization of the Commission of Professors of Adult Education, which was mentioned earlier. By identifying such groups as these, a person specifically interested in research networks can focus on such concerns within the larger association.

In addition to umbrella associations, the adult education field has several groups that focus specifically on adult education research and scholarship. Indeed, the adult education field has had a tradition of supporting small, informal gatherings of scholars.

The longest standing of these research groups is the Adult Education Research Conference (AERC), which has been held annually since 1959. This group is not a formal organization per se. Rather, it operates under an informal structure with a rotating four-member steering committee, whose members are responsible for review and selection of presentations and development of conference policy. The AERC draws its participants primarily from the United States and Canada and has a rich tradition of active involvement among graduate students, who typically present a fairly high percentage of the papers.

More recently, the Canadian Association for the Study of Adult Education (CASAE) has been established to serve as a vehicle for networking and research dissemination across Canada. Like the AERC, CASAE publishes its papers in annual proceedings.

Both the AERC and CASAE are targeted toward national and international audiences. An alternative approach, which has had some success but limited implementation, has been the establishment of regional conferences. In the late 1970s through the mid-1980s, the Lifelong Learning Research Conference (LLRC) was held at the University of Maryland. This was an inexpensive, efficiently run conference held during midwinter that initially attracted scholars from the eastern United States, but eventually drew from a broader population base. During the 1980s, the Midwest Research-to-Practice Conference began to operate as a vehicle for sharing research and networking among adult education researchers primarily in the midwestern United States. Unlike the LLRC, the Midwest Research-to-Practice Conference continues to be held annually at various campuses throughout the Midwest. We believe the notion of such regional conferences hold much potential for creating efficient yet inexpensive networking opportunities for adult education researchers.

Professional associations and conferences provide a good point for making contacts that can be helpful in forging networks and collaborative efforts. Very often, the most valuable benefits of attending conferences are found not in the formal sessions one may attend, but in the informal conversations and exchanges that go on "in the halls." As a final example, the two of us recently attended a symposium on self-directed learning. As we talked with other participants, both informally and in presentation sessions, we recognized what we believe to be a gap in the knowledge of self-directed learning. Realizing that several other colleagues attending the conference shared our concerns, the two of us sat down during a break in the conference and drafted a proposal for an edited book of original contributions. We then approached several of the colleagues attending the conference and invited them to write chapters for the book. Once the conference ended, we put the final touches on the proposal, invited a few additional individuals to write chapters, and moved ahead with the development of the manuscript, which is in progress as we write this chapter (Hiemstra & Brockett, in press). This is but one example how a conference can serve as a vehicle for facilitating the formation of a collaborative network.

ETHICAL ISSUES IN COLLABORATION AND NETWORKING

Ethics is clearly an important part of the research or scholarship process. Publications abound on the ethics of research, and there has been some discussion relative to research ethics in the adult education field (Merriam, 1988). However, collaboration adds a different element to the discussion. We believe the most important way to minimize ethical problems is to address such concerns openly as they arise and to avoid, where possible, a confrontational approach. To close this chapter, we briefly identify some major ethical issues to consider relative to scholarly collaboration. Specifically, these deal with authorship, student research, intellectual property/ownership, and failure to fulfill responsibilities.

Who should receive credit for authorship of a collaborative piece of scholarship? Merriam (1988), citing Diener and Crandall (1978), points out that the two major criteria for determining one's level of contribution to a work are the extent to which one has contributed to (1) the conceptualization and design of a study and (2) writing the final publication. Accordingly, the possibilities of acknowledgment "range from being sole author, to being first author among others, to being acknowledged in a footnote" (Merriam, 1988, p. 159).

When dealing with faculty-student collaboration on scholarship, another set of potential ethical conflicts arises. Here, the factor that gives rise to possible problems is the nature of the "power" differential between students and faculty. When a faculty member, for instance, is in a position to "sign off" on a student's dissertation or thesis research, it is important to recognize that the potential for abuse (whether intentional or not) does indeed exist. Where a collaborative student-faculty research project emanates from the faculty member and the student is "brought into" the project at some later point, it seems within the purview of the faculty member to claim first and possibly (depending on the level of student involvement) sole authorship. However, when the research project is student initiated, such as a dissertation or thesis, we support the recommendation of the American Psychological Association (cited in Merriam, 1988) that faculty not claim senior authorship for such work.

A third set of ethical concerns related to authorship centers on the notion of "intellectual property." Ownership of ideas or findings emanating from a research investigation is further confused when more than one partner has been involved in the investigation. Where this has the potential to become a problem is in the event that collaborations decide to "part company" for intellectual or other reasons. What happens, for instance, if two researchers take a very different approach to interpreting data from a qualitative case study investigation? Again, we suggest that issues of ownership be addressed at the outset, prior to the decision to move forward with a study.

Another set of ethical concerns might be described as "failure to fulfill responsibilities." Some would argue that it is unethical for a researcher to gather large quantities of data and then to not proceed with analysis and reporting of such data. Here, it is believed there are obligations to the individuals who were studied as well as to the academic community to follow through on the commitment to complete the research process. When an investigation involves a collaborative relationship, the research partner becomes another source of obligation, for in a partnership, if one partner does not follow through, the negative consequences are also felt by the other partner(s), who may have already fulfilled their obligations.

The intent of this section was to illustrate that, as with any research or scholarship effort, ethical considerations need to be addressed in an open, direct manner. The collaborative relationship poses additional potential ethical dilemmas; however, it also has the benefit of multiple insights that, if addressed openly, can reduce ethical problems in the research process.

CONCLUSION

The various chapters in this volume highlight the potential for enhancing the development of research in the adult education field. In this chapter, we have tried to show that, while it may require more time and energy than solo work, collaborative scholarship allows for innovative efforts not necessarily possible in solo work. While some collaborations form naturally through personal friendships, faculty-student working relationships, or joint projects with colleagues from the same institution, a willingness to engage in networks of like-minded scholars can open doors that one may not have believed to be possible. Networks are a vital element of one's professional development as a scholar and can clearly have an effect on the impact of one's scholarly work.

ENDNOTES

1. To subscribe electronically via Bitnet or Internet, send the following one liner to LISTSERV@ALPHA.ACAST.NOVA.EDU: Subscribe AEDNET Your Full Name.

2. To subscribe electronically to the *Journal of Extension,* post the following command to ALMANAC@JOE.UNEX.EDU: Subscribe JOE Your Full Name.

3. Many listservs have an index of past conversations. If one knows of an electronic address where there are listservs and has the name of a particular listserv, one can determine if they have such as index. For example, TESLIT-L is the name of a listserv at CUNYVM. Use the following one liner email sent to LISTSERV@CUNYVM INDEX TESLIT-L. To search globally for all possible listservs at a site, and continuing to use the same example, one would send an email to LISTSERV@CUNYVM and say "List Global/edu." To search globally

across listservs by topic, send an email to LISTSERV@BITNIC and say "Sendme LISTSERV GROUPS" (that will obtain a partial list of available discussion groups and many electronic journals with a paragraph description for each). It may be necessary to substitute the word "Get" for "Sendme." To obtain a more extensive list but without the descriptive text, just say "LIST." To join that list, the usual one liner email sent to LISTSERV@CUNYVM would be Join TESLIT-L Your Full Name. To signoff that list, send an email to LISTSERV@CUNYVM and say Signoff TESLIT-L.

REFERENCES

Bogdan, R. C., & Biklen, S. K. (1982). *Qualitative research for education.* Boston: Allyn and Bacon.

Brockett, R. G. (1989). Professional associations for adult and continuing education. In S. B. Merriam & P. M. Cunningham (Eds.), *Handbook of adult and continuing education* (pp. 112–123). San Francisco: Jossey-Bass.

Brockett, R. G. (1991). Disseminating and using adult education knowledge. In J. M. Peters & P. Jarvis, (Eds.), *Adult education: Evolution and achievements in a developing field of study.* San Francisco: Jossey-Bass.

Brockett, R. G., & Hiemstra, R. (1991). *Self-direction in adult learning: Perspectives on theory, research, and practice.* New York, NY: Routledge.

Daloz, L. A. (1986). *Effective teaching and mentoring.* San Francisco: Jossey-Bass.

Darby, C. (1992). *Traveling on the Internet.* (ERIC Document Reproduction Services No. ED 350 007).

Diener, E., & Crandall, R. (1978). *Ethics in social and behavioral research.* Chicago: University of Chicago Press.

Eastmond, D. V. (1992). Effective facilitation of computer conferencing. *Continuing Higher Education Review, 56,* 155–167.

Ehringhaus, M. (1990). *The electronic journal: Promises and predicaments* (Technical Report No. 3). Syracuse, NY: Adult Education Program, Syracuse University.

Fellenz, R. A. (Ed.). (1988 August). *Cognition and the adult learner.* Papers from an institute sponsored by The Center for Adult Learning Research, Montana State University, Bozeman, MT.

Fellenz, R. A., & Conti, G. J. (1990 August). *Intelligence and adult learning.* Papers from an institute sponsored by The Center for Adult Learning Research, Montana State University, Bozeman, MT.

Gaventa, J. (1988). Participatory research in North America. *Convergence, 21* (2/3), 19–28.

Heerman, B. (1988). *Teaching and learning with computers.* San Francisco: Jossey-Bass.

Hiemstra, R., & Brockett, R. G. (Eds.). (in press) *Overcoming resistance to self-direction in adult learning.* New directions for adult and continuing education. San Francisco: Jossey-Bass.

Imel, S. (1989). The field's literature and information sources. In S. B. Merriam
& P. M. Cunningham (Eds.), *Handbook of adult and continuing education.*
San Francisco: Jossey-Bass.

Jensen, G., Liveright, A. A., & Hallenbeck, W. (Eds.). (1964). *Adult education:
Outlines of an emerging field of university study.* Washington, DC: Adult
Education Association of the USA.

LaQuey, T., & Ryer, J. C. (1993). *The Internet companion.* Reading, MA:
Addison-Wesley.

Long, H. B. (Ed.), (1992). *Self-directed learning: Application and research.*
Norman, OK: Oklahoma Research Center for Continuing Higher and Professional Education, University of Oklahoma.

Long, H. B. & Hiemstra, R. (Eds.), (1980). *Changing approaches to studying
adult education.* San Francisco: Jossey-Bass.

Merriam, S. B. (1988). Ethics in adult education research. In R. G. Brockett
(Ed.), *Ethical issues in adult education.* New York: Teachers College Press.

Merriam, S. B., & Simpson, E. L. (1984). *A guide to research for educators and
trainers of adults.* Malabar, FL: Krieger.

Peters, J. M. & Jarvis, P. (Eds.), (1991). *Adult education: Evolution and achievements in a developing field of study.* San Francisco: Jossey-Bass.

Rohfeld, R. W. (Ed.). (1990). *Breaking new ground: Worker's education and
adult education between the wars in North America.* Proceedings of the Visiting Scholar Conference on the History of Adult Education. Syracuse University, Syracuse, NY. (ERIC Document Reproduction Services No. ED 328
720).

U. S. Congress, Office of Technology Assessment. (1989). Linking for learning:
A new course for education (OTA-SET-430). Washington, DC: U.S. Government Printing Office.

Whipple, J. B. (1967). *A critical balance: History of CSLEA.* Notes and Essays
on Education for Adults No. 55. Boston: Center for the Study of Liberal
Education for Adults at Boston University.

Yin, R. K. (1989). *Case study research: Design and methods* (Revised edition).
Newbury Park, CA: Sage.

CHAPTER 5

INITIATING RESEARCH

Roger Boshier

The purpose of this chapter is to convince the reader that an idea (or research problem) and a theoretical framework are needed to initiate research. Later, the new researcher will need a design, methodology, some form of data analysis, and a way of deriving conclusions, but these processes are outside the scope of this chapter.

Reviewing books on research does not necessarily produce a project because the origin of ideas and needed "first steps" are treated as a constant. "Finding the idea" and "getting started" are given barely a nod in most standard research methodology books. Authors seem to assume that potential researchers have a surfeit of ideas and thus most attention is given to research design and analysis. The emphasis is on techno-rational questions. For example, in an otherwise exemplary exposition on *The Research Craft,* Williamson, Karp, Dalphin, and Gray (1982) dispose of the origin of "research ideas" in less than three pages. For them, research ideas stem from "curiosity" (researchers are supposed to have plenty), previous pure and applied research, already existing theory, and the "training and experience" of the new researcher.

This chapter is only about initiating research—identifying a problem and choosing a conceptual approach. Why do people choose "their" topics and conceptual approaches? What can the new researcher learn from understanding the circumstances that led Malcolm Knowles to study andragogy or Allen Tough to investigate learning projects? Do the decisions that lead to a commitment to the study of a certain topic and thus use of a particular conceptual framework or antiepistemology stem from some easily understood process? Or does part of the choice reside in serendipity, chance encounters, illogical processes, being a the right place at the right time, or the counsel of a trusted friend or adviser?

All these potential explanations have merit and much can be learned from them. But because of the lack of research on this topic in adult education, and because so few researchers have written their autobiographies, we end up depending on knowledge of what inspires our colleagues and the research choices made by students along with the study of factors that shape the research of people in allied fields.

For example, Sarason's (1988) autobiography *The Making of a Psychologist* is revealing and suggests that initiating research—getting an idea and choosing a framework—has a lot to do with the researcher's life history and sociocultural circumstances. Research is initiated at a point where sociohistorical circumstances and biography intersect. Another outstanding example is Boring's (1957) classic history of experimental psychology that traced the way great events spawned modern psychology. What these works seem to suggest is that nascent researchers should be thoroughly engaged with their society but also open to chance encounters that throw up ideas for research.

This chapter is organized around the notion that research problems are found in what is often erroneously called the "real world." Whether or not the new researcher sees all the research problems scattered around the landscape will have a lot to do with their biography, which will likely influence the extent to which they recognize problems when they see them.

BIOGRAPHY

The *International Biography of Adult Education* (Thomas & Elsey, 1985) shows how life experience begets research and projects intersect with great events. In these 700 pages the reader learns about people as diverse as Condliffe and Te Hau of New Zealand; Coady, Corbett, and Tompkins of Canada; the irascible Colin Badger of Australia; the illustrious Mansbridge and Tawney of the U.K.; Grundtvig of Denmark; Nyrere of Tanzania; Freire of Brazil; and Gramsci of Italy, to name a few.

Individual biographies vary in length and quality, but books like Corbett's (1957) engaging account of life hauling adult education to Canadians in sparsely populated and often frigid places or Kennedy's (1992) analysis of John Friesen provide credible accounts of why these people did their kind of research. Mansbridge's (1940) autobiography *The Trodden Road* was only one of many books written by the distinguished founder of the British Workers' Educational Association. Unfortunately, there have been few attempts to retrace and study the significance of his travels through the British Empire[1] but *The Trodden Road* explains the development of his research interests. Another excellent contribution was Terrill's (1973) elegant biography of R. H. Tawney, the great Fabian economist and brains behind the British Workers' Educational Association, the 1919 Report, and other outstanding examples of English adult education practice and research. The intersection between great events and individual biography will now be explored with reference to three very different people.

Three Researchers

Michel Foucault

Foucault was the famous French philosopher whose benchmark analyses of prisons, mental illness, sexuality, and discourse have significantly influenced an entire generation of scholars. He died of AIDS on June 25, 1984 (see Eribon, 1991; Miller, 1993) but had revolutionized understanding of relationships between power and knowledge. At first he had difficulty finding an authentic voice but, after *Madness and Civilization,* his tone and intellect were unmistakable. His ideas and research flowed from an intellectual "ancestry (that) was a contradictory amalgam of the academic and the insurrectionary" (Said, 1989, p. 2). He was influenced by Marx and Freud, by university courses, and by legendary teachers (Said, 1989, p. 2), but, most importantly, by the political actualities of French life where the great milestones were World War II, the response to European communism, and the wars in Vietnam and Algeria. Foucault's research ideas were rooted in concrete and historical realities. Foucault went beyond recognizable genres of fiction, history, sociology, political science, and philosophy. His work was extraterritorial and involved mixed genres. He worked with constellations of ideas rather than single or inert objects.

Like many adult educators Foucault saw life as a struggle among the marginal, the transgressive, the different and the acceptable, the normal, the same (Carriere, 1993a). At the heart of his work was the notion of *otherness.* He was fascinated with deviation and excess of all kinds and, in the end, this may have killed him (Miller, 1993). But, in this context, deviation and excess alert us to the need to widen the space in which adult educators can assert their biography and search for questions and initiate research. As a busy intellectual and transgressive activist, Foucault's problem was to withstand pressures for academic orthodoxy and conformity (Eribon, 1991; Miller, 1993). In later life, he battled the exhaustion of AIDS at a time when vast and unfinished projects demanded attention. This is usually the way it is with imaginative researchers: they have many ideas and the problem is to find the time to work.

Malcolm Knowles

Malcolm Knowles was the son of a veterinarian who, in the spirit of 1920s entrepreneurship, captured and sold alligators from the Florida Everglades. In 1928 he won a Boy Scout prize and a trip to a jamboree in England. His technique for acquiring 50 scout badges resulted in an early publication (Knowles, 1929) and was a remarkable echo of ideas on program planning that showed up 50 years later (Knowles, 1980). They also provided Carlson (1989) with a focus for an interesting analysis of Knowles's biography. We learn about Knowles's sojourn at Harvard, the way scouting sparked his interest in social service, the impact of the Depression on the Knowles family and young Malcolm, and his move to the YMCA in 1940. We also learn about Knowles's growing consternation concerning the widespread but inappropriate use of the lecture technique and about his treks to the roof of the YMCA building to view the stars. There are the years in Chicago and publication of *Informal Adult Education,* his master's thesis (Knowles, 1950). His wife Hulda, Carl Rogers (1969), and other influences caused Knowles to begin to define and advocate what he would later call andragogy. From there the outlines of the Knowles story are reasonably clear (see Boshier, 1976, 1977; Pratt, 1993).

The research framework for andragogy arose from an interaction of the researcher's biography and crucial sociohistorical events (e.g., the Depression) as well as encounters with educators, psychologists, philosophers and others. The fact that Knowles's work did not contain the critical edge some think to be so essential today was not the point. When viewed against the backdrop of American history from the 1920s to the 1980s, his elaboration of andragogy makes immense sense.

Lorraine Cavaliere

As a child Lorraine Cavaliere sat in the cockpit of breezy pre-World War II aircraft while her father flew to air shows in the northeastern United States. Much later, as a doctoral student at Rutgers University she was invited to a "fly-in" in Maryland. Surrounded by aviation aficionados and old aeroplanes, she began to wonder how Orville and Wilbur Wright, Ohio bicycle manufacturers, had learned about the airfoil effect that propelled them and Kitty Hawk into the annals of aviation history. At the time there was considerable interest in self-directed learning. An offhand remark to Hal Beder a professor at Rutgers University, drew an enthusiastic response—"That's your doctoral dissertation."

Cavaliere went to the Smithsonian Institution to look at the Wright diaries, but the project stalled because she didn't have enough technical knowledge about flight to understand what the Wrights were discussing in their diaries. She learned to fly and, at age 36, got a pilot's license at Mercer County airport. She made two trips to the Royal Aeronautics Museum in London, England; got the knowledge needed to understand Orville, Wilbur, and the airfoil effect; and completed the dissertation (Cavaliere, 1988, 1990, 1992). These days she is a director of continuing education and member of the "Ninety Nines," the Women's Pilots Association founded by Amelia Earhart to celebrate the original 99 women pilots.[2] The essence of this was the paradigm shift that gave the Wrights their breakthrough and, for Cavaliere, it was her biography and the presence of an enthusiastic and noncoercive advisor.

Graduate Students

Adult education graduate students cannot all be compared to Foucault, Mansbridge, Tawney, Cavaliere, Nyrere, or Knowles. But it is nevertheless hard to understand why a presumably well-educated person who has made it to graduate school has difficulty identifying a suitable topic. Why do some people experience their environment as a rich source of research ideas and others don't? What do we make of practitioners who, although they work with exceedingly interesting people and problems, are nonplussed when asked to develop a proposal for research? Some don't see the connections between work, leisure, art, travel, politics, and culture that spawn research questions that lead to viable projects. These variables shape the researcher's biography and their impact can be seen in the work of well-known and less conspicuous adult education researchers.

Students arrive at graduate school with a biography. Most are mature adults who, like organic intellectuals everywhere, too often devalue their common sense understandings of adult education and other processes. Another danger resides in the comfort of course taking. The arrival of yet another "noted" lecturer provides a splendid excuse to avoid political, cultural, and artistic activities wherein research problems are found. Foucault was impressed by his teachers and good research ideas can emerge from courses. But the preoccupation with course taking in North American universities distracts students from the chance to get engaged with doing research. Courses about research are often inept and, like skiing, the best way to learn is to do it.

People who teach courses have plenty to say about research design and methodology, but their vantage point doesn't give them much of a perspective concerning the origins of research problems or ideas. When it is time to get started, look to the professor for support but not for the idea. Most professors don't do research and much of what they do is inconsequential or methodologically flawed.[3] Moreover, as demonstrated in the last part of this chapter, professorial discourse concerning the origins of research ideas and conduct of research can be unduly nested within an ideology of superiority where father knows best and the errant children (thesis or dissertation students) are recipients of discipline. Some professors do research designed to serve the interests of corporate or military elites. it is at the intersections of knowledge and power that professorial discourse concerning what constitutes acceptable and unacceptable ideas (for research) are constructed.

FINDING AN IDEA

Nascent researchers should look for research problems in their own world. While their advisor or professor can help shape the problem into a manageable project, point to relevant theory, and even influence the research design, nascent researchers should choose their "own" topics. This argument will be buttressed by reviewing what research methodology books say about this matter and by examining literature on adult education research that pertains to the question. Nascent researchers excavating the subtext in the discourse on adult education research should realize that when some ideas are reinforced and others extinguished, various interests are served.

Social Research

Table 5.1 lists variables that different authors claim effect the process of getting started. In this table the present author has tried to mirror the extent to which Borg and Gall (1983) as compared to say, Travers (1978), emphasized the importance of a reading program, computer searches, and so on. Most students in adult education graduate programs will recognize these as familiar sources for ideas concerning ways to get started but should critically reflect on implications that flow from getting ideas in these ways.

Reading Program

It is no surprise that almost all authors of textbooks on research urge the new researcher to undertake a reading program. Provided the new

Table 5.1
Origin of Research Ideas

Origin of Ideas	Borg & Gall (1983)	Travers (1978)	Sellitz et al. (1976)	Best (1977)
Reading Program	yes	yes	yes	yes
Computer searches		yes		yes
Extant Theory	yes	yes	yes	
Replication	yes		yes	
Replication/Generalization	yes		yes	
Personal "values"			yes	
Feasibility			yes	
Everyday problems				yes
Graduate "experience"				yes

researcher understands that "the literature" will not necessarily produce a problem or durable conceptual approach, it will show how problems have previously been framed. The problem for adult educators is that a reading program needs to include literature from education, social theory, and a plethora of other fields.

Those on a reading program should note that publishers cannot be blamed for having both eyes on the cash register. Those who think good ideas for new research are found in "the literature" should reflect critically on what gets published. Like it or not, adult education has increasingly become a commodity to be sold (Briton and Plumb, 1993) to those who can afford it, and perspectives not nested in the "applied discipline" discourse are cast in the role of "other." As discussed in Ohliger's (1989) chapter on "alternative" approaches in the *Handbook of Adult Education,* there is a "center" and an "alternative" (or other).

After controversies (see Carlson, 1992; Law, 1992) around the so-called "black and blue book" (Peters & Jarvis, 1991), there might be space created for perspectives from the developing world or constituencies not normally heard (e.g., AIDS activists; First Nations people) in "mainstream" adult education. New researchers embarked on a reading program should realize that the calm and objective realities of North American adult education research are being increasingly challenged by researchers from Britain (e.g., Griffin, Westwood), New Zealand (e.g., Law), Latin America (e.g., Freire), and other places where the conceptions of research and researcher do not conform to the professionalized and credentialed milieu of an applied discipline. If new researchers have time to read, they should secure a plethora of material.

Computer Searches

Travers (1978), Best (1977), and other textbook authors recommend that the new researcher conduct ERIC and other kinds of computer bibliographic searches in order to get started. Unfortunately, the abstract delivered by these services may be written by the author of the study and few have been known to report that "absolutely nothing of any consequence was found." Moreover, the utility of computer data boxes partly depends upon how complete and up-to-date they are. Sometimes helpful things are found in computer searches, but the volume and varied quality are both a strength and a drawback. People walking around with a huge pile of output from an ERIC search are tempted to nest their study within extant traditions, and these are not likely to yield the kind of paradigm shift that got the Wrights off the ground. Many textbook authors are only moderately enthralled by these technologies. This author believes there are better and more dynamic ideas for research nested within discussions on computer bulletin boards associated with INTERNET and other academic networks (see Boshier, 1990b).

Extant Theory

A traditional way to get an idea is to consult an extant theory and apply it or a part to some adult education problem. This is what Boshier (1973) was doing when he used Rogers's (1959) notion of congruence to analyze adult education participation and dropout. Theory developed for one setting (e.g., therapy, organizational change, community development) can be imported and applied to adult education problems. A good example was Miller's (1967) use of Lewin's field theory in a study of adult education participation. There is no doubt that extant theory is a potent source of ideas for new research, and for a positivist, the power of a good theory resides in its generalizability. Theoretical fashions change, and in adult education, after a decade of sometimes very silly "psychology-bashing," psychoanalysis has emerged as a vibrant element in feminist postmodernism (Balbus, 1988) and there is a literature on critical psychology and pedagogy (e.g., Sullivan, 1990).

Replication

For positivists seeking external validity, it is necessary to replicate studies with different populations and settings to see if demonstrated relationships (such as between teacher behavior and dropout) will remain consistent. Most universities will not accept a "replication" for a doctoral degree, but it is acceptable at the masters level. However, the nascent researcher should not uncritically replicate errors that were built into the earlier research. Just because, for example, the users of the Tough (1971) interview schedule made little effort to establish the reliability and validity of the observations (Boshier, 1983b) this will not excuse those attempting a replication. Before replicating a study, the new researcher should also be sure it concerns something of significance for theory or practice. There is an extended discussion of issues pertaining to replication in Sellitz, Wrightsman, and Cook (1976) and Borg and Gall (1983).

Personal Values

It is a serious error to think research is somehow "value-free." However, the extent to which the researcher's values influence the first steps are often shaped by the social conditions pertaining at the time the work is performed. At the end of the 1960s, the architects of lifelong education and advocates of self-directed learning rode the "anti-institution" ethos that was so prominent. These days issues of race, gender, and class are in the foreground and researchers interested in such matters will find an interested audience for their work. The extent to which personal values interact with the outcomes of the research has become exceedingly problematic for new and old researchers of both a positivist and postpositivist persuasion (Boshier, 1989a; Lather, 1986).

Feasibility

Much of what the general research literature says about assessing the feasibility of a project constitutes common sense. But seeing projects fail causes the more experienced researcher to proceed with caution. For example, most new researchers, particularly in adult education, want to change the world and, in the earlier stages, tend to include too much. The first project does not have to be the last work on the topic and there is no shame in paring it down. Now there is such a preoccupation with

"context" and apprehension about "reductionism" that some researchers wallow more so than in the past. Also, the project will likely take
longer than expected, and there are ethical review and other time-
consuming procedures.

In North American academic research circles, there is a distracting
and unhealthy obsession with money. The best ideas cost nothing. However, if equipment is needed and subjects have to be paid and there are
vast expenses for royalties on educational or other tests, the new researcher had better know where these funds are coming from. In addition, the extent to which people in agencies, adult learners and others
who might be involved in the study, will be inclined to cooperate with a
project that probably has little or no "payoff" for them needs to be
considered. For an elaboration on this and other considerations pertaining to feasibility, see Sellitz, Wrightsman, and Cook (1976).

Everyday Problems

Best (1977) reminds researchers of the "acres of diamonds" that "in-
quisitive" and "imaginative" researchers can find in their own back-
yards, just as popular writers (e.g., Shekerjian, 1990) have tried to
detect how great ideas are born. The everyday is not just a commodity
or "alternative" source of research ideas but a "site of contestation"
(Aronowitz & Giroux, 1991, p. 67. de Certeau, 1984) that highlights
perspectives, memories, stories, and approaches that oppose orthodox
or conventional wisdom. A strong endorsement of this approach is at the
center of this chapter.

Graduate Experience

Enrolling in a graduate program at a university is supposed to stimulate
the kind of "questioning attitude" (Best, 1977, p. 22) that yields an idea
and conceptual perspective. Unfortunately, many adult education graduate students study part-time and it is difficult to take full advantage of all
the stimulation that can be secured by attending seminars, engaging in
debates, and participating in coffee room discussions at the university.

With the advent of home computers and e-mail, the need to go to the
university has been lessened, and unfortunately, graduate programs that
were once a hotbed of discussion (involving the core students) have gone
silent. Nevertheless, the adult education graduate student can secure
good research ideas by attending some of the more stimulating research

conferences (such as the annual Adult Education Research Conference), by organizing or participating in nonformal (out-of-school) intellectual activities, and by engaging with other students who seem to have their projects well underway.

There have been attempts to trace the influence of mentors but few studies on the intersection of biography and graduate study in adult education (for a top-down view, see chapter 7). Unfortunately, just at a time when adult education has been recognized as an essential element of social, economic and political development, resources have been lost and departments closed.[4]

ADULT EDUCATION RESEARCH

Ideas transformed into adult education research problems can be secured from the same sources as those identified by Borg and Gall (1983) and the authors of other standard research texts. There is nothing particularly unfamiliar or surprising about what they have to say. But at the center of this analysis is the fact that their very familiarity attests to their commitment to the past, to previous research, extant traditions, and familiar conceptualizations.

Simply put, our advice is to keep a close eye on whose interests are being served and go forth and find your own problem. In a postmodern world, adult educators ought to contemplate the extent to which they should continue fishing for ideas in traditional and, to a certain extent, stagnant reservoirs. Researchers should also worry about the quality of advice received from professors and mentors who insist on framing adult education as an applied discipline, who seek to solve practical problems in the field, who eschew theory in favor of running errands designed to meet the needs of funding agents, and who happily collaborate with corporations or the military. It is also perilous for the new researcher to hang around with "those who have spent their professional lives prowling the corridors of community colleges, those who have said all there is to say—and precious little there is to say—about program planning or curriculum development, and those who have fallen sideways into the field for the want of anything better to do" (Courtney, 1986, p. 164). The immediate and practical concerns of these professors obscures the importance of more theoretical, aesthetic, or personal kinds of research. Adult education research should not be hamstrung by the need to produce results, solve problems, or lead to any immediate or noticeable improvement in the quality of people's lives. Indeed, an insistence on these kinds of principles will, in Courtney's view, "destroy the refreshing if bewildering pluralism that now flourishes" (p. 164).

The Landscape

Some of the best work (e.g., Grattan, 1955; Brunner et al., 1959) is done by people not primarily identified as adult educators. When we survey the adult education landscape looking for advice about how to choose a research problem or get a theoretical framework, not much will be found. Deshler and Hagan (1989) highlighted the contributions of Brunner (1959); Krietlow (1965, 1972); Jensen, Liveright, and Hallenbeck (1964); and more recently, Long & Hiemstra (1980); Long (1983); and Darkenwald and Merriam (1982). Krietlow (1965, 1972) deserves mention for the effort he put into making lists of "needed research." Deshler and Hagan (1989) also speculated about seven "promising directions." However, there is little evidence that these lists generate much new research.

Long and Hiemstra (1980) devoted two pages to choosing a topic and described some students as "highly promiscuous, entranced by a different topic daily. Other novices choose a topic so broad that the narrowing process is both painful and difficult. Sometimes the researcher is spared this dissonance: the major advisor or employer assigns the topic" (p. 27). These writers advise new researchers to pick a topic that is "of interest" to them, preferably one related to their "future goals." But new researchers were also warned that their selection of a topic will attest to their "maturity and . . . competence" (p. 29). Long and Hiemstra claimed that researchers have to be familiar with the subject matter before they can derive a researchable problem. There are several problems with this analysis; for example, "dissonance" is not necessarily disabling and can often be desirable. We revisit this later.

Preeminent Authors

Another perspective on getting started was provided by Garrison and Baskett (1987; 1989) as well as Baskett and Garrison (1989) who interviewed 17 "preeminent" North American adult education researchers. These stellar performers had each published an *average* of 38 articles, nine book chapters, four books, and six monographs. They were asked how they "generated ideas" and the most frequently cited source was "the literature," "colleagues" was next, then "teaching," "practitioners," "students," "reflection," and "conferences." Only 3 of the 17 reported having just one line of research and one interviewee claimed that "adult education, by definition, is a . . . generalist activity" (Garrison & Baskett, 1987, p. 92). Virtually all interviewees thought that having some experience as a practitioner or "direct contact" with the field helps generate research ideas.

LOOKING IN AND OUT

In the past there have been Herculean attempts to build a discipline of adult education and concepts indigenous to adult education. Boyd and Apps (1980) said the "first principle that distinguishes our theory from others is that we believe it is an error to seek assistance from recognized disciplines until we have clearly understood the structure, function, problems and purposes of adult education" (p. 2). Their project was an extension of the historic attempt to "demarcate" adult from other branches of education so as to establish it as an "emerging" field of university study (see Jensen, Liveright, & Hallenbeck, 1964).

This project failed. Boyd and App's (1980) call to cease the unbridled borrowing from other disciplines was 30 years late and fell on exceedingly deaf ears. The 1980s were probably the most exciting era in the history of adult education research because of the embrace of outside knowledge, the collapse of universal explanations (e.g., the idea that adults are goal-, learning-, or activity-oriented) and the widespread and swift slaughter of sacred cows that previously stood unsullied in the fields of the academy (e.g., the notion that *all* adults are self-directed or engage in learning projects).

Boshier and Pickard (1979) showed that by 1977, 60% of citations in articles published in *Adult Education* were to "primary adult education literature." Our sense is that this situation changed dramatically in the 1980s and the most energetic researchers, the sort of people who make the Adult Education Research Conference such a lively event, largely eschewed exhortations to look inward at the field. These days adult education researchers embrace a plethora of disciplines, epistemologies, anti-epistemologies, and problems of unparalleled scope and significance.

Throughout the 1980s and into the 1990s the walls came tumbling down. Boyd and Apps (1980) lay silent in the rubble, rarely mentioned, only occasionally cited in major journals. Their attempt to discipline the transgressors, those who engaged with other disciplines, was reduced to a murmur. The same epistemological break and rejection of totalizing explanations for phenomena that had signaled the arrival of a postmodern architecture, art, or popular culture had reached adult education research. Courtney (1986) called it a "bewildering pluralism."

This did not mean everything was well in the academy because it was not. In times of slow change or social inertia, it was probably acceptable to assume that future research would be more or less an extension of the past. We certainly cannot berate those who read "the literature" and most hard-pressed researchers wish they had more time for it. But, before new researchers rush to the library in the hope of picking up a good idea, they must realize that the literature represents only a tiny slice of what is possible. Moreover, exhortations to look in the literature for research ideas are often nested within a functionalist or institutional paradigm, content area, or methodology. Those who yield to these exhortations can produce durable and useful research. But our sense is that now is time to look outward—at the everyday experience of people, the insights of the organic intellectual, the lived experience of ordinary people, commonsense knowledge (Luttrell, 1989).

In some graduate programs students get the impression that everyday or commonsense constructions of problems will not suffice when held up against the apparatus of formal theory or the proclamations of preeminent or even less distinguished researchers and professors. Common sense has been characterized as a cultural form of knowledge (Luttrell, 1989, p. 37). It tends to be class-based and acquired from friends or others who "know the ropes." It depends not on professional experts but on the advice of others who share the same problems. Unfortunately, in graduate programs there is a tendency to set aside commonsense knowledge in favor of "real intelligence" acquired through reading books, engaging with a mentor, or submitting to the demands of the graduate experience. Ironically, it appears that early in their careers many young researchers work on problems that are not authentically theirs, but as they mature, they start doing what they really want to do. Hence, in the twilight of his career, B. F. Skinner wrote novels, and in adult education, Allen Tough turned from learning projects to UFOs, extraterrestrials, and futures.

The best research problems are found in the "real" world. The way to encounter them is to become an active participant in the community and to pay attention to the arts, popular culture, and politics. Ours is a commitment to ordinary people living their lives, and we are suggesting that, in the first stages of a research project, people not take too much notice of their teachers. Regard this as permission to be naughty in school.

At the University of British Columbia, we try to value commonsense understandings of phenomena and encourage students to get their "own" projects. This doesn't suit everyone and when so many; do "one-shot" research, there is an absence of cumulative inquiry. But it leads to a commendable pluralism of epistemology and exceedingly interesting work on, for example, the conceptions of learning held by schizophrenics in Vancouver (Price, 1993), the way African urban agriculturalists respond to information about environmental degradation (Mlozi, 1993), lifelong education in Hong Kong (Shak, 1989), andragogy and art galleries (Clark, 1990), education in the B.C. Christian Task Force on Central America (Dykstra, 1990), the literacy play *Marks on Paper* (Andruske, 1993), and why men choose nontraditional health care careers (McAulay, 1991). Sometimes a faculty member has an interest in a project and encourages a student to move accordingly, but ensures that ownership lies with the student. A recent history of Canada's John Friesen is an excellent example (Kennedy, 1992).

CHOOSING A THEORETICAL PERSPECTIVE

The nascent researcher doing a modernist project needs to know how various conceptual approaches can be used to shape initial ideas into researchable problems. Although it is not necessary to have a theory in mind when developing an idea, it will soon be necessary to develop a theoretical perspective on the chosen problem. For example, let's say a new researcher has recently witnessed the death of a friend from AIDS and now wants to do research on the implications of AIDs for education. This person would not get far before encountering the social dimensions of the epidemic (see Shilts, 1987; Watney, 1987) and discovering that AIDS education has been differentially constructed to serve some interests better than others. The researcher would also soon have to make a decision about the extent to which the project will be anchored in an objectivist or subjectivist ontology. The same decisions will be required if the researcher decides to work on program planning, distance education, literacy, communications technology, agricultural extension, community development, or the hundreds of other areas that fascinate adult education researchers.

At an early stage of the project, the researcher will also have to decide if theory is the *goal* of the researcher or a *tool* used to foster understanding of the problem. In other words is the frame of reference, model, or theory (see Boshier, 1979) going to be used as lens through which to view the data or phenomenon of interest or will the purpose of the study be to create theory? At about the same time the researcher will have to decide whether to proceed *inductively* (and let the theory arise from the data) or *deductively* (in which case the theory will be identified before data is collected). At this stage the professor might have a helpful perspective.

Figure 5.1 shows an elaboration of a model adapted from Burrell and Morgan (1979), and in this context it will be used as a heuristic device to

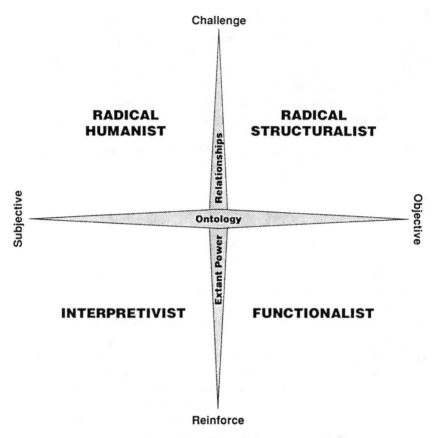

Figure 5.1: Four paradigms that are informed by or inform adult educational research.

help new researchers move their ideas into researchable problems. It is not our intention to suggest the future will be an extension of the present, but the research discussed here shows that ideas can be derived and reformulated from both "commensense" and "academic" perspectives. After this model is presented, the author will present a contrary, antifoundational, antiparadigmatic, postmodern perspective. However, for present purposes, assume the four paradigms shown here are those that inform and are informed by adult education research nested within a modernist ideology.

The two axes in Figure 5.1 lie in an orthogonal relationship to each other. Treat them like latitude and longitude on a nautical chart. They identify epistemological positions in adult education research. Adult educators who have been looking for a "map of the territory" (e.g., Rubenson, 1982) should be able to locate themselves and others within it. Although used here to bound a discussion about research, it can and has been used to analyze a broad array of adult education phenomena, including education about AIDS (Boshier, 1989b; 1990a; 1992b) and boating safety (Boshier, 1992c). Part of its power resides in the fact it is pluralistic, it embraces a broad spectrum of thinking about research, and it could lead to a lessening of the artillery duels that go on between so-called positivists and so-called post-positivists (see Boshier, 1989a).

This model was stimulated by Paulston (1977), who did a large-scale review of literature to help the World Bank understand why their massive "investments" in "development" had not yielded expected "dividends." At the end of this review, Paulston concluded that much functionalist-oriented education failed because it had inadequate regard for patterns of power and privilege. It is necessary to realize that education can be cast within a **conflict** as well as an **equilibrium** paradigm. In the equilibrium paradigm, Paulston identified evolutionary, neoevolutionary, systems, and structural-functionalist approaches to education and development. In the conflict paradigm he identified Marxian and neo-Marxian approaches, anarchist-utopianism, and education for cultural revitalization. He gave equal weight to the conflict paradigm so as to present an alternative to functionalist, or equilibrium approaches (Paulson, 1989). (Interested readers should note that Paulston (1992) and Paulston and Liebman (1993) have now insinuated a postmodern perspective into the problem of mapping social theory).

The orthogonal axes in Figure 5.1 embrace four distinct epistemologies. The unique contribution of this part of this chapter is to locate recent adult education research within each quadrant and hopefully stimulate readers to consider possibilities for elaboration, refutation, or "spin-off" ideas that have little to do with the past or present. With this in mind, consider Figure 5.1 to be a map of the territory that offers choices for theoretically anchoring research.

ASSUMPTIONS

All educators base their research on assumptions about the nature of the world and their role within it. Sometimes these assumptions are implicit and so deeply embedded in consciousness they are never brought forth for explicit examination. For example, the widespread adoption of new-rightist political ideology has created a situation where much adult education research (particularly in A.B.E.) is widely thought to be for remedial purposes, for "skills training" and "reskilling" for economic "development" and the relentless pursuit of an improved "bottom line."

Ontology

The first set of assumptions that buttress Figure 5.1 concerns ontology—the essence of the phenomena. Researchers vary with respect to the extent to which they think there is an **objective** "reality"—out there—external to the individual. For some there is an objective world inhabited by lawfully interrelated variables. For others, reality is essentially a **subjective** phenomenon that exists within consciousness. It exists "in the mind." Associated with ontology are other assumptions related to preferences concerning epistemology (anti- or post-positivist; positivist), one's beliefs about the nature of human nature (free will; determined), or preferences concerning research methodology (qualitative; quantitative).

Extant Power Relationships

A central assumption of this analysis is the notion that somebody's interests are always being served when educational programs are mounted and research conducted. Sometimes these interests are clouded by rhetoric about the public good. For example, initially AIDS was dismissed as a gay plague and many politically active homosexuals claimed that education, research, and prevention measures were not energetically pursued until the transmission pattern threatened heterosexuals.

Functionalist-oriented education systems and research are concerned with consolidating the status quo. Research based on conflict theories of the type identified by Paulston is committed to explaining deep-seated structural change of a type that invariably threatens the interests of certain individuals and groups. Functionalists also seek change, but it is ephemeral and superficial compared to that sought by theorists informed by a conflict perspective.

Burrell and Morgan (1979) spoke of a sociology of "regulation" and a sociology of "radical change." This was to distinguish between theorists who "explain" society in terms that emphasize an underlying unity and cohesiveness and those whose explanation for change resides in deep-seated structural conflict, modes of domination, and structural contradiction. Those preoccupied with regulation focus on how societies maintain themselves as an entity, how they hold together rather than fall apart.

Those concerned with radical change focus on material and psychic deprivation, are often visionary and utopian, and are concerned with possibilities rather than acceptance of "what is."

One problem with contrasting research designed to maintain equilibrium with that designed to foster conflict is that conflict can be functional. It is not necessary to restage the old "conflict/order debate" here, so in Figure 5.1 we refer to the extent to which research reinforces or challenges extant power relationships. For example, most research on continuing professional education, training, and program planning has been anchored in a functionalist perspective that does not anticipate upsetting power relationships.

FOUR PARADIGMS

Functionalism

Returning to Figure 5.1, functionalism provides an essentially "rational" explanation for social affairs. It is the dominant ideology of our time and is characterized by a concern for social order, consensus, and social integration. Its epistemology tends to be positivist, determinist, and nomothetic. A new researcher anchored in a functionalist perspective will need to consult Parsons (1967) and recent reifications of his theory (e.g., Munch, 1987). Functionalists want practical solutions to practical problems and are usually committed to social engineering as a basis for change with an emphasis on gradualism, order, and the maintenance of equilibrium. Functionalists attempt to apply models derived from natural sciences to human behavior. They assume there is an "objective" world "out there" that consists of observable, lawfully related empirical entities. Mechanistic and biological analogies appeal to functionalists and, in radical functionalist states, such as Singapore, it is engineers who control adult education and shape research (Boshier, 1993).

Research

Functionalism is an epistemology and ideology. Adult education research informed by it includes projects associated with government training; manpower or reskilling programs; so-called upgrading programs; most research on continuing professional education (e.g., Houle, 1980); and nearly all research on technical or vocational training and adult basic education run by schools, colleges, and other school-like institutions.

At the 1992 Adult Education Research Conference (Saskatoon), the editors of the then recently published *Adult Education: Evolution and Achievements in a Developing Field of Study* (Peters & Jarvis, 1991) were assailed for purporting to represent the "state of the art" in adult education. There were thoughtful chapters by Griffin (1991), Deshler (1991), and several others. But other authors were very selective in what they chose to include and exclude. Some observers saw this book as located in the functionalist orthodoxy of professionalization which has increasingly become an "academic cul-de-sac" (Law, 1992, p. 258). Although the book was organized by the Commission of Professors of Adult Education and publication was sponsored by the American Association of Adult and Continuing Education, the professors apparently had second thoughts. Their *Newsletter* (Commission of Professors, 1992) reported that there was "considerable discussion as to whether the book was representative of the field. In particular the inclusion of two women and no person of colour among seventeen authors was questioned" (p. 8). Another issue was concerned with whether "only one particular interpretation of the field" (i.e., functionalism) was presented. The attack on this book was late coming because for decades the discursive parameters of North American adult education research have been excessively shaped by the functionalist notion that adult education is an "applied" discipline, and as result, adult education departments lay at the marginalized fringes of university operations. Later, we recall these events in the context of postmodern critique.

A corollary of this is that the value of research depends upon its "relevance" to practice and practitioners (see chapter 7). Kaestle's (1993) allegations concerning the "awful reputation" of educational research were similarly based on its alleged lack of utility.

Interpretivism

Researchers and theorists located within an interpretive paradigm are "subjectivists" in that "reality" is what it is construed to be. Great effort is devoted to adopting the frame of reference of the participant. Social "reality" is a network of assumptions and "shared meanings." The subjectivist ontological assumptions shared by interpretivists stem from the notion that human affairs are ordered, cohesive, and integrated. Interpretivists are more concerned with understanding subjectively construed meanings of the world "as it is" than with any utopian view of how it might be. While they are at the subjectivist end of the ontological dimension, they do not anticipate any threat to extant power relationships.

Research

Adult education movements, perspectives, and researchers located in this corner include Mezirow and associates (1990), with their concern for perspective transformation; the Swedish phenomenographers (Marton, 1981, 1986) and their disciples (e.g., Pratt, 1992a, 1992b); studies of African-American women (e.g., Peterson, 1991); and to a certain extent, the notion of andragogy (Knowles, 1980; Pratt, 1993), which has some regard to the way adults construe their experience within an "independent" self-concept.

Mezirow (1990, 1993) is interesting because like Tough, 20 years earlier, the impact of his work was greatly enhanced by the context in which it landed. Whereas Tough's (1971) work on learning projects was exceedingly congruent with the anarchist utopianism of the late 1960s and early 1970s, Mezirow's radical subjectivism appealed to a broad range of scholars and practitioners who had grown disenchanted with "objective" science in the 1980s. However, Mezirow (1993) is a modernist and firmly committed to reason and the existence of an "objective" world. He claims that "rational thought" is impeded by sociolinguistic, epistemic, and psychic distortions.

Radical Humanism

The radical humanist paradigm encompasses researchers and theorists who want to upset extant power relationships but are anchored within a subjectivist ontology. Those in this paradigm are usually anti (or "post") positivist, nominalist, and voluntarist. But, unlike the interpretivists, the radical humanists want to overthrow or transcend existing social arrangements. Many radical humanists employ concepts developed by the young Marx to describe how people carry ideological superstructures that limit cognition and create a "false consciousness" which inhibits self-actualization or fulfillment. Radical humanists want to release people from constraints, which largely reside in their own cognitions. Radical humanism thus seeks transformation, emancipation, and a critical analysis of modes of domination. It wants people to reconstruct their "view" of "reality" and take appropriate action. Thus praxis becomes reflection (or reconstruing) followed by action.

Research

Freire's notions of conscientization and popular education are the clearest exemplars of this paradigm. Participatory research, popularized by the International Council of Adult Education (see Park et al., 1993), springs from similar ontological and ideological roots. Giroux's (1983, 1988) analyses of American education and resistance theory are other examples. Most research on movements that employ education for cultural revitalization, whether among Maori people in New Zealand (Harker & McConnochie, 1985; Smith, 1993; Walker, 1980, 1990), Indians in Latin America, or the Lap people in the Nordic countries, are informed by radical humanism. A good example of participatory research in North America was Wright's (1988) study of housing tenants.

A persuasive argument for critical theory can be found in Kincheloe and McLaren (1994). They define a criticalist as a researcher who uses his or her work as a form of social or cultural criticism and accepts the following assumptions. First, "all thought is fundamentally mediated by power relations that are social and historically constituted; that facts can never be isolated from the domain of values or removed from some form of ideological inscription" (p. 139). Second, relationships are never stable or fixed and mediated by the social relations of capitalist production and consumption. Language is central to the formation of subjectivity.

A criticalist would also start from the position that certain groups in any society are privileged for reasons that vary, that oppression is reproduced when subordinates accept their social status as "natural, necessary, or inevitable; that oppression has many faces and that focussing on only one at the expense of others . . . often elides the interconnections among them (p. 140). A criticalist would also believe that "mainstream research practices" are often unwittingly implicated in the reproduction of oppressive systems . . .

Critical researchers begin their projects with their assumptions on the table. The task is to expose contradictions accepted by the dominant culture as inviolable and natural. "Natural" or taken-for-granted situations often conceal unequal and unjust social relationships. Moreover, as Kincheloe and McLaren (1994) point out, ideologies are not simply deceptive or imaginary states that exist in the heads of individuals or the collective understanding of groups, but are also "inscribed in the materiality of social and institutional practices" (p. 140). Thus hegemony is only possible when oppressive states are accepted as consensus.

When Little (1992) tried to secure literature to test three questions to "assess" adult education research informed by a critical perspective, he claimed there was a paucity of reports in mainstream journals. However, since Little performed his analysis, there has been a discernible quickening of interest in critical perspectives. Most readers in North America have ready access to Hart (1990), McTaggart, (1991), Collins and Plumb (1989), Finger (1989), Collard and Law (1991), Dykstra and Law (1994), Quigley (1990), and the special "critical" issue of the *Canadian Journal for the Study of Adult Education* (Vol. 5, 1991) which, among others, contains an article by Welton (1991), whose more recent analysis of new social movements as sites of "revolutionary" learning is also noteworthy (Welton, 1993). A succinct and clear mapping of critical theory in adult education is in Collard and Law (1991).

Feminism constitutes a special problem, although out of its most energetic branch resides within this paradigm. So does most of what goes on in the Frankfurt school and critical theory (Benhabib, 1989; Horkheimer, 1989; Kellner, 1989). Existentialism belongs here as well as anarchist-utopians like Illich (1979) and Rahnema (1988, 1990, 1991) or those in UNESCO preoccupied with human consciousness and the need to deschool society in the name of lifelong education (Faure, 1972) "learning to be" or the "learning society" (Boshier, 1980; 1983a). Most adult education researchers whose work is informed by radical humanism are nested within an ideology of modernity.

Radical Structuralism

Radical structuralists share fundamental assumptions that buttress functionalism and are committed to the overthrow of social structures that build "false consciousness." If the radical humanists focus on consciousness and meaning, the radical structuralists focus on structures, modes of domination, deprivation, and contradictions within an objective social world. Within this paradigm are those who focus on deep-seated internal contradictions within society while others focus on power relationships. But common to all theories in this paradigm is the notion that each society is characterized by inherent conflicts, and within these lie the basis of change. The "later" Marx was the chief architect of this position.

A Marxist approach to adult education would focus on the economic and political context in which it was located. An analysis of the "political economy" of adult education shows how its shape and character are determined by the distribution of political and economic power in society. Not all adult education is determined by economic factors, but it is "not an autonomous institution that generates all of its own characteristics" (Youngman, 1986, p. 11). As a cultural and ideological institution (part of the "superstructure") education is always linked to political and economic structures and is never neutral. Education is one of the ways the ruling classes perpetuate their own privileges and controls. People are socialized to "fit in," accept authority, and "buy into" orthodox ways of viewing their "lot" or place in life. Underclasses have been indoctrinated with and largely "bought into" the illusion of healthy competition and the possibility of upward social mobility (Apple, 1990). Marxists are particularly critical of humanistic (largely North American) adult educators who reinforce the illusion that in a capitalist society individual freedom is possible without a fundamental transformation of the system. Moreover, when "radical" techniques become divorced from revolutionary ends, they become reactionary, such as when Freire's notion of dialogue was used to domesticate Third World peasants (Kidd & Kumar, 1981).

Research

The diligent student of Marxist pedagogy would need to read Marx, Lenin, Engels, Gramsci, Althusser, and Lukacs as well as Habermas and other critical theorists that became as disillusioned with bureaucratic state capitalism as they did with western corporate capitalism (see Collins & Plumb, 1989).

It is ironic that the collapse of the Soviet state has been accompanied by a terrific surge of interest in the emancipatory aspects of radical structuralism. Regrettably, these interests are not welcomed in North American universities where there is a strong commitment to liberalism, humanism, and an ideology of individualism. Thus, North American graduate programs house few faculty members or students whose research is significantly informed by radical structuralism. However, some of the most energetic members of the Adult Education Research Conference have been committed to structural perspectives. Examples include Zacharakis-Jutz (1993) who examined the FBI files on the Highlander Folk School (see Gaventa et al., 1994); Fieldhouse (1980) who analyzed adult education and the activities of the British security authorities; Boshier (1969) who scrutinized the stumbling ineptitude of the New Zealand Security Intelligence Service; Hellyer (1986) who studied the repressiveness the U.S. government in 1919–1920; Law (1988) who traced the influence of McCarthyism in adult education; and Quigley and Holsinger (1993) who studied the "happy consciousness" of A.B.E. participants.

Examples of research that concerned structural relationships between education and society, with a focus on class and power, include

Bowles and Gintis's (1976) classic study of the American school system. They propose a "correspondence" theory wherein it is claimed social relations of education directly parallel those of capitalist production. In similar fashion, Carnoy and Levin (1985) claim schooling is class-structured and contributes to "bourgeois hegemony" by being at the center of the ideological apparatus of the state. In adult education these ideas inform Apple's assertions about relationships between "ideology" and "curriculum"; Giroux's preoccupation with "resistance"; Lovett's community focus and the work of the Highlander Folk School in Tennessee (see Heaney, 1992); Law's series of theoretical analyses, mostly presented at the Adult Education Research Conference (e.g., Law, 1992b); and Schied's (1992) analyses of labor education. Altenbaugh's (1990) analyses of the relationships between three labor colleges and Gramsci's notion of hegemony can also be considered as exemplifying a radical structuralist perspective.

Most feminisms are nested within the interpretivist or radical humanist paradigms, and by and large, feminists have manifested considerable disdain for the kind of radical objectivist ontology that informs radical structuralism. Some unwisely claim that feminist research, by definition, must be nested in subjectivist ontology. However, there are now various "structural" feminisms. For example, O'Brien (1989) is clearly a feminist Marxist; Lather's (1991) focus on "research as praxis," a work written in the company of New Zealand Maori activists; and parts of Nicholson's (1990) exceedingly erudite collection of postmodern perspectives on feminism all owe something to radical structuralism. So also does the collection made by Luke and Gore (1992).

There are numerous examples of research on counterhegemonic adult education organized by social movements concerned with peace, ecology, women's rights, or liberation. All these challenge the dominant ideology and involve a wide variety of qualitative and quantitative methodologies. Most adult education research informed by radical structuralism concerns informal and nonformal settings for education.

POSTMODERN TURN

By 1994 the situation in adult education was exceedingly interesting. For almost a decade criticalists have berated mainstream adult education for its functionalist, professionalizing, "applied discipline" emphasis. The sometimes oppressive and exclusionary critical tumult (always nested within a superficial discourse of inclusion) reached a zenith at the 1992 Adult Education Research Conference where a polite symposium on the recently published *Adult Education: Evolution and Achievements in a Developing Field of Study* (Peters & Jarvis, 1991) turned into a full frontal assault on functionalist ideology, gatekeeping, publishing ethics, the Commission of Professors, and what is sometimes characterized as an old boys network. The lively assault on functionalist orthodoxy, largely led by Canadians and New Zealanders, was well worth the price of admission (Carlson, 1992). But now the tables are turning and criticalists, most of whom anchored in objectivist ontology, informed by the "grand narrative" of Marx and committed to the study of material conditions (or the "concrete reality"), are the target of postmodern critique.

Kincheloe and McLaren (1994) are erudite exponents of Marxist critical theory and attempted to coopt postmodernism into critical theory. The problem is that criticalists are largely committed to the "reality" of (usually unequal) material conditions; postmoderns claim that "reality" is socially constructed or semiotically posited. If critical theory can successfully coopt postmodernism, it would make life easier for this writer because postmodernism would be regarded as a moment in modernism and nicely assigned to the radical humanist paradigm. However, critical modernism (e.g., Habermas, 1987) is not the same as postmodernism.

Postmodernism, in its most stark sense, denotes the death of reason and poses a problem for researchers committed to the notion that individuals can think critically and behave rationally to "remake the world in the interest of the Enlightenment dream of reason and freedom" (Aronowitz & Giroux, 1991, p. 57). For many educators and social theorists of the type located in the four quadrants just described, modernism and progress denote a commitment to rationality, science, technology, and the progressive unfolding of history. In this scheme, education legitimates notions of "progress." But now the notion that knowledge is only knowledge if it reflects the world as it "really is" has been replaced by the postmodern idea that "reality" is socially constructed or semiotically posited.

Modernism, a western industrial kind of idea, is often assumed to have begun as a reaction to feudalism, religion, and superstition. There are plenty of arguments about when the modernist era began, but when Narvaez, Galiano, Valdes and the first PhD (Dr. Tadeo Haenke) arrived in the west coast of America in the 1790s, they were on great voyages of discovery and were equipped with astronomical instruments and the other paraphernalia of science. Like latter-day scientists they believed there was an objective world of lawfully interrelated variables and their task was to theorize about and investigate relationships among them. Thus, theory invoked in this brand of scientism became the great meta-epistemology of enlightenment or modernist thinking just as Jose Cardero's drawings of the west coast indigenous people, the headlands, the fauna and flora became invaluable records of "reality" as he saw it. "Truth" lay outside the human organism and the task of enlightenment thinking was to understand, make predictions about, and finally control "nature."

Today, there is growing uncertainty about modernist assumptions and methods deployed to explain and interpret human experience. This uncertainty has been expressed, almost simultaneously, in the rise of feminism and postmodernism. Postmodernist critique radically challenges western enlightenment ideas concerning the self, science, philosophy, and art as ways of establishing truth, justice, or beauty. According to postmoderns, the world is constituted in a "shared language" and can only be known through the particular forms of discourse language creates.

These days the position occupied by the researcher has been problematized and "critique" has become a method of analysis along with the "subject" of the "research." For some postmodern critics, theory is a disciplinary mode of thought by which so-called truth or privileged perspectives are imposed as unproblematized ideology. Where power intersects with theory, the effect is inevitably to silence someone (Carriere, 1994; Foucault, 1979, 1980), to include some things, and to exclude others. Theory is disciplinary because it normalizes acceptable and unacceptable ways of thinking. Hence, for Carriere (1993a) theory "is a privileged epistemological strategy of a modernist ideology of rational humanism." As such, it is systemized speculation concerning a reified but idealized truth. Modernist theory of the type laid out in Figure 5.1 is also almost exclusively based on European models of culture and civilization, what postmodernist Jean-Francois Lyotard (1984) calls the "great story" of the Enlightenment. It is also largely constructed by elite white men who look down on or dismiss the validity and importance of popular culture or everyday experience.

THREE EXPONENTS OF POSTMODERNISM

As with modernism and the kind of epistemologies nested in Figure 5.1, there is considerable diversity within the postmodern map. However, there are communalities and, following Hassard (1993), we briefly examine the ideas of three lading exponents of postmodernism.

Baudrillard and Simulations

Postmodern critique challenges the dominance of western cultural models and focuses attention on electronic mass media, the changing nature of class and social formations in post-industrial societies, and the growing tendency to transgress boundaries that formerly separated image and "reality," high and popular culture, life and art (Baudrillard, 1988). Modernity, industrial capitalism, and production are being replaced by postindustrial postmodernity represented by alternative forms of technology, culture, and society. In the postmodern society, it is simulation that structures social affairs. "Simulacra"—copies or representations of objects or events—constitute the "real." There is a universe of nihilism where concepts float in a void.

Hyperreality is a term used to describe an information society where there is an accelerating emphasis on representation—on film, television, print media, and computers. These have a profound effect on cultural and political narratives. For example, when we saw the smart missiles and televised Gulf War constructed as the "Fourth of July" or a "football game," there was a feeling we'd seen it all before. Macho posturing by Bush and Saddam and the death of thousands were reduced to pastiche. The outcome seemed assured and natural.

Lyotard and *The Postmodern Condition*

For Lyotard, postmodernism is primarily a type of knowledge, not a condition of society. Unpredictable moves are needed for researchers or science to make progress but these are antithetical to the stability needed to control and regulate inputs and outputs. Lyotard is opposed to the "grand narratives" of modernist science which acquires legitimacy through its grand narratives (objectivity, reason, detachment). In Lyotard's epistemology no one discourse is privileged. Instead there is a concern with "localized understandings and acceptance of a plurality of diverse language forms" (Hassard, 1993, p. 9). Hence, grand narratives are fragmented and meta-narratives discredited. In the English edition of *The Postmodern Condition,* Lyotard (1984) says "let us wage a war on totality; let us be witness to the unpresentable; let us activate the differences and save the honour of the name" (p. 82).

Derrida and Deconstruction

Derrida wants us to celebrate "difference." His process of deconstruction shows how "rational" processes obscure phenomenological ambivalence. His concept of "text" refers to an interplay of social, political, and philosophical perspectives. His goal is to expose contradictions that lie within any text. He argues that language is not just a medium for communicating thought. He is concerned about "logocentrism," that is, the notion that thoought is primary and language merely a vehicle for transmittal. To offset the "censoring" that arises from logocentrism, deconstruction involves "overturning" and "metaphorization." We have to overturn the hierarchy nested within polar opposites of language (e.g., kind, cruel), and to avoid the problem of simply replacing the superordinate with the subordinate term, the author reveals or unmasks the double-dynamic or mutual dependence within the polar opposites. This is "metaphorization."

THREE NOTIONS OF POSTMODERNISM

Many ideas reside in the writings of Baudrillard, Lyotard, Derrida, and other postmoderns, but three are crucial.

Representation

Postmoderns do not accept a "picture theory" in which the physical properties ("realities") of the world are regarded as fixed and language is adjusted to describe them (Hassard, 1993). For postmoderns, knowledge of the world is constructed more as a representation than on the basis of facts or "accuracy." This means there is no point in attempting to discover a fixed or objective reality. Postmoderns do not accept the modernist view that language is a "slave to observation and reason" (Hassard, 1993). Findings produced through the "scientific method" reflect existing intellectual categories in which some things are included and others excluded.

Reflexivity

Postmoderns are critical or suspicious of their own and others' intellectual assumptions. Hence knowledge should not be elevated to some "prestigious and objective estate" (Hassard, 1993, p. 13). Forms of language labeled knowledge should be treated with humility and not be the source of ultimate commitment. We should be particularly suspicious of the grand narratives concerning the inexorable nature of "progress" because its unitary nature precludes competing or alternative narratives.

Writing

For postmoderns, writing (and reading) relates as much to representation (and its structures) as it does to conveying messages. As noted earlier, Derrida invests considerable effort in overturning what he calls logocentric writing wherein language is only a sign system for concepts which are thought to have some kind of independent existence in the "real" world. For the postmodern, writing is only a process of inscribing marks on a surface. It merely illustrates how the writer is reflecting on his or her social world.

Theoretical writing reflects the "expert" position of the writers (Carriere, 1994). Readers also employ "ideologies of reading" (Cohen, 1992, p. 70) to engage with theoretical texts, and to a postmodern critic the notion of any "fixed truth" quickly recedes. Hence, postmodern critics are skeptical of radically reductive analyses or theoretical explanations of complex events that have a universalized "story line" (e.g., class, patriarchy, deficit, God) that ignores local and historical particularities. Postmodern critics are particularly focused on the position of the reader and writer and relationships between the subjects and objects of theory (see Boshier, 1992b, 1993b; Miller & Usher, 1993).

POSTMODERNISM AND RESEARCH

Postmodernism raises crucial questions concerning the hegemonic aspects of modernism and, by implication, adult education research. Discourses on postmodernism appear to embrace a plethora of reactionary or progressive possibilities. Postmodernism involves much more than a simple-minded repudiation of the kind of modernism that produced Dachau, Hiroshima, Chernobyl, Bophal, or the Gulf War. As Laclau (1988) noted, it involves a different modulation of the themes and categories of modernism. In a broad sense it refers to an intellectual position and mode of criticism and set of sociocultural and economic conditions associated with global capitalism and the crisis of industrialization.[5] It is both a condition and critique and its celebration of plurality and the preoccupation with the politics of race, gender, and ethnic difference has sparked major debates (see, for example, Bloom, 1987; Fraser, 1989; Habermas, 1987; Hebdige, 1986; Lather, 1991; Nicholson, 1990).[6]

This postmodern turn has infused new energy and perspectives into adult education research. Biography, autobiography, and ethnography all involve exploration of subjective perspectives in local and particularized ways. New ways of establishing reliability and validity have been developed (see Lather, 1986). Genealogical records of historical particularities of institutional, domestic, and popular or everyday practices are being explored afresh (e.g., de Certeau, 1984; Foucault, 1978, 1979) as are relationships between popular culture and education (Giroux & Simon, 1993; Pittman, 1990; Pittman & Ohliger, 1988). An excellent example is Falk's (1994) analysis of "postmodern doors" into the modern community college.

Most importantly for adult education, the boundaries between educational and other disciplines are disintegrating, and to a certain extent, researchers now seek knowledge about adult education through analysis of popular media (Boshier, 1992b, 1993b; Briton & Plumb, 1992a, 1993), everyday discourse (Carriere, 1993a), and narrative (Carriere, 1994). The body has also become politicized as a site of surveillance and discipline (Foucault, 1978; Sawicki, 1988) and the libido, previously suppressed by the Cartesian obsession with distinguishing mind from body, has become a focus for attention.

There are many discourses on postmodernism and, in adult education, great concern about its embrace of radical relativism (Briton & Plumb, 1992b; Collard & Law, 1990; Collins, 1994). But in adult education research, as elsewhere, there is no doubt that the postmodern turn has opened space for "other" voices. Examples include Chovanec's (1993) study of abused women, La Paglia's (1993) analysis of stories told by women in the much maligned 2-year American college, Hall et al.'s (1992) poetry at a meeting of the "learned societies," or bell hooks's (1993) dialogue with herself (Gloria Watkins) about Paulo Freire. There is also an invitation to the reader to participate in the construction and deconstruction of meanings; these days few people automatically accept orthodox wisdom (e.g., all adults are self-directed; participants are goal, learning, or activity oriented). Postmoderns have also debunked the calm rationalities of "scientific" or "academic" writing as yet another meta-narrative. Postmodern "writerliness" admits and celebrates the insertion of apparently incongruent styles and this will almost certainly become an arena of struggle in graduate programs where modernist professors will have a hard time coping with what appear to be the transgressive and disrespectful excesses of student writing nested in postmodernism.

DISCURSIVE FORMATIONS

Postmodern critics are preoccupied with discourse as the locus of effects (as well as causes), subject/object relations, and multiple subjectivities, and with the theorist or researcher as a fully engaged player in "theoretical operations." The postmodern preoccupation with power and privilege, the disdain for universal or foundational explanations for phenomena, and the way theory is deployed by "coercive institutions and practices" (Gruber, 1989, p. 192) have created an immense challenge for researchers comforted by the notion that theory or research is ideologically benign.

An absence of perspective concerning the positioning of the research expert or advisor can lead to situations where authority or the power to discipline is automatically and almost inadvertently assigned to an unnamed and unbodied authority. For example, consider Long and Hiemstra's (1980) claims concerning the "promiscuous" graduate students struggling to give birth to research ideas. The discursive formation in these exhortations is a familiar one and poses no threat to the learned professors in charge. Students who cannot get focused are "promiscuous" and if they give birth to an idea, it will be "painful" and "difficult." If they have been totally inept the "major" (or superior) advisor will "assign" a topic and the recalcitrant candidate will be more decisive and, one may assume, repentant when facing this problem in the future. In this discourse on graduate supervision, the professors are subjects. The students are objects of surveillance and discipline. In the contest for power, the professors have it and the students don't.

Now consider the subtext in the employer discourse used by Griffith in chapter 7 of this volume. Griffith is a past president of the American Association for Adult and Continuing Education. His recommendations concerning ways to increase "research production" specifically and unquestionably privilege the interests of companies and other employers of adult education graduates and dismiss professors and others "obsessed with the idea that adult education must be the world's sole engine of social change." Even the most diligent advocates of social change do not tout adult education as the "sole engine" of change; the notion that it is only an adjunct has been thoroughly canvassed elsewhere (Hall, 1992). But what matters here is that Griffith (at the "center") thinks graduate study and research are threatened by those ("others") who see it as "excessively ideologically laden."

Put simply, ideology refers to the production of sense and meaning. It is a "way of viewing the world, a complex of ideas, various types of social practices rituals and representations that we tend to accept as *natural* or *commonsense*" (McLaren, 1988, p. 176). Ideology tends to structure the nature of perceptions in a particular direction and often conceals or legitimates unequal power relations. Ideology is usually linked to a pattern of domination which privileges some groups over others. Ideology works through four modes:

1. Legitimation—Domination is sustained by being presented as inherently legitimate or worthy of respect.
2. Dissimulation—Relations of domination are concealed.
3. Fragmentation—Groups are fragmented so as to oppose each other.
4. Reification—Transitory states are presented as permanent.

As discussed in chapter 7 of this volume, Griffith's ideology privileges and legitimates employers of graduates and consumers of their research, professional groups such as National University Continuing Education Association, the Association for Continuing Higher Education and the American Society for Training and Development. Concern for future employers, Griffith says, "is not simply a marketing ploy; it is a vehicle for designing research of demonstrable relevance to the most influential practitioners in the field." Relevant to who? And which influential practitioners? If this analysis were pursued and money and numbers were the sole criteria of influence, we would hitch our research wagons to the U.S. military. It is, without doubt, the most influential employer and adult educator in North America and there is no question about whose interests it serves.

THE FUTURE

Future researchers will be less inclined to move through the familiar rhythms of stating a problem, choosing a theory or model, developing a methodology, acquiring results, and deriving conclusions than at present. There will probably be a much greater preoccupation with the experience of ordinary people and an increasing tendency to "smoke out" or illuminate the patterns of power and privilege that surround formal theory. The notion of what constitutes "acceptable knowledge" and "research" will be broadened.

In the past established senior members in the field of adult education did not have to endure awkward questions hurled by those outside the inner circle. But, these days the hallowed concepts and assumptions of the past, concerning the alleged self-directedness of learners, their "voluntary" participation, and other dependable certitudes, have been shaken by the postmodern and other counter-epistemological or counter-hegemonic challenges. The collapse of old ideas has enervated the adult education research academy. This is, without doubt, the most perplexing but exciting period in the history of adult education research.

ENDNOTES

1. The record of Mansbridge's travels to Australia and New Zealand are clear, but his trip to Canada, which included a stop in small Vancouver Island coal field towns, and presumably Vancouver City itself, remains obscure. Here is a thesis-in-waiting.

2. When Cavaliere presented this work at the 1990 Adult Education Research Conference, various pundits, including New Zealanders, claimed that the Wrights were not the first to make a powered flight. However, this does not mask the fact this project nicely incorporated the author's interests in technology transfer, communication networks, and self-directed learning.

3. Throughout the 1970s dozens of graduate students produced theses, dissertations, or papers based on "adult learning projects." Each of these studies seemed to confirm the notion that there was an epidemic of self-directed learning going on. These conclusions were probably an artifact of a flawed methodology that had no regard to the reliability, let alone validity of the observations made or error induced by the pressing and persistent interviewing techniques employed. With many polities moving to adopt a broadened definition of education, it is a shame that, to this day, we do not know much about who is doing "learning projects" and whether or not they learn anything. For a further elaboration of this point, see Boshier (1983b).

4. In North America, the adult education holdings in the Syracuse University library are invaluable, yet senior administrators closed the graduate program in 1992. At the University of British Columbia, the Coolie Verner Memorial Reading Room was threatened by the politics of centralization (Centre = Teacher Education; Other = Nonformal Education) and a top-down planning process done in the name of "restructuring" (see Boshier, 1992a).

5. For an analysis of the "sustainability crisis" in twentieth century capitalism and the transition to a postmodern world see Orr, D. W. (1992). *Ecological Literacy: Education and the Transition to a Postmodern World*. Albany: State University of New York Press.

6. Readers wanting an introduction to these debates could consult the bibliography in Connor (1992) which concerns postmodernity in literary and cultural theory, philosophy, architecture, art, photography, literature, performance, feminism, television and film, and popular culture. it also lists 25 special issues of journals devoted to the subject.

7. An early warning of this was received in a graduate program at a Canadian university where a student committed to postmodern analysis deconstructed and critiqued the assumptions in comprehensive examination questions instead of "answering" them in the usual way. He failed the exam and the matter was appealed to higher authorities.

REFERENCES

Altenbaugh, R. (1990). *Education for struggle*. Philadelphia: Temple University Press.

Andruske, C. (1993). *Marks on paper: Exploring literacy through theatre— Impact of performing on literacy and upgrading students*. Unpublished master's thesis, University of British Columbia, Vancouver.

Apple, M. (1990). *Ideology and curriculum*. London: Routledge.

Aronowitz, S., & Giroux, H. (1991). *Postmodern education: Politics, culture and social criticism*. Minneapolis: University of Minnesota Press.

Balbus, I. E. (1988). Disciplining women: Michel Foucault and the power of feminist discourse. In Arac, J. (Ed.), *After Foucault: Humanistic knowledge, postmodern challenges* (pp. 138–160). New Brunswick: Rutgers University Press.

Baskett, H. K., & Garrison, D. R. (1989). Research writing: Patterns and strategies of some of North America's most prolific adult education researchers. *Proceedings of the 30th Annual Adult Education Research Conference* (pp. 19–24). University of Wisconsin, Madison.

Baudrillard, J. (1988). *Selected writings*. Stanford: Stanford University Press.

Benhabib, S. (1989). *Critique, norm and utopia*. New York: Columbia University Press.

Best, J. W. (1977). *Research in education*. New Jersey: Prentice Hall.

Bloom, A. (1987). *The closing of the American mind*. New York: Simon and Schuster.

Borg, W. R., & Gall, M. D. (1983). *Educational research: An introduction*. New York: Longman.

Boring, E. G. (1957). *A history of experimental psychology*. New York: Appleton-Century-Crofts.

Boshier, R. W. (1969). *Footsteps up your jumper: The activities of the New Zealand Security Service*. Perspectives, No., 6. Wellington: Farm Road Branch of the New Zealand Labour Party, p. 40.

Boshier, R. W. (1973). Educational participation and dropout: A theoretical model, *Adult Education* (USA), 23(*4*), 255–282.

Boshier, R. W. (1976). Andragogy: A conversation with Malcolm Knowles about the meaning and use of the term. *Continuing Education in New Zealand*, 8(*1*), 20–26.

Boshier, R. W. (1977). The design and implementation of adult education experiences: A conversation with Malcolm Knowles. *Australian Journal of Adult Education*, 27, 7–12.

Boshier, R. W. (1979). A perspective on theory and model development. In *Yearbook of Adult and Continuing Education*, 1979–80. (pp. 37–44). Chicago: Marquis Academic Media.

Boshier, R. W. (1980). *Towards a learning society: New Zealand adult education in transition*. Vancouver: Learningpress.

Boshier, R. W. (1983a) *Education inside*. Ottawa: Solicitor General of Canada and University of British Columbia Program in Correctional Education.

Boshier, R. W. (1983b). *The adult's learning projects: An alchemists fantasy?* Invited Address Delivered to Division J, American Educational Research Association, Montreal, Canada.
Boshier, R. W. (1989a). Jumping to conclusions on the post-positivist bandwagon. *Proceedings of the Adult Education Research Conference* (pp. 37–42). University of Wisconsin, Madison.
Boshier, R. W. (1989b). When it comes to sex the process is the product. In International Development Research Centre, *Human Sexuality: Research perspectives in a world facing AIDS* (pp. 1–27). Ottawa: International Development Research Centre.
Boshier, R. W. (1990a, March). *Epistemological foundations of international AIDS education programs.* Paper Presented at the Annual Conference of the Comparative and International Education Society, Anaheim, CA.
Boshier, R. W. (1990b). Socio-psychological factors in electronic networking. *International Journal of Lifelong Education, 9(1)*, 49–64.
Boshier, R. W. (1992a). *History and significance of the Coolie Verner Memorial Reading Room.* Unpublished paper circulated during the reading room closure crisis, University of British Columbia, Vancouver.
Boshier, R. W. (1992b). Popular discourse concerning AIDS: Its implications for adult education. *Adult Education Quarterly, 42(3)*, 125–135.
Boshier, R. W. (1992c). Theoretical and empirical perspectives on marine incidents and their prevention through education. *Canadian Journal for the Study of Adult Education, 6(2)*, 1–16.
Boshier, R. W. (1993a). Education for docility: The problem of Singapore and education for the next lap (pp. 131–150). In Stromquist, N. P. (Ed.), *Education in urban areas* (pp. 000). Westport: Praeger.
Boshier, R. W. (1993b). Constructing HIV and Magic Johnson: Discourse, education and power. *Proceedings of the 34th Annual Adult Education Research Conference* (pp. 19–24). Pennsylvania State University, University Park.
Boshier, R. W., & Pickard, L. (1979). Citation patterns of articles published in *Adult Education, 1968–1977. Adult Education, 30(1)*, 34–51.
Bowles, S., & Gintis, H. (1976). *Schooling in capitalist America.* New York: Basic Books.
Boyd, R., & Apps, J. (Eds.). (1980). *Redefining the discipline of adult education.* San Francisco: Jossey Bass.
Briton, D., & Plumb, D. (1992a). Robo ed: Re-imaging adult education. *Proceedings of the Annual Conference of the Canadian Association for the Study of Adult Education* (pp. 38–43). University of Saskatchewan, Saskatoon.
Briton, D., & Plumb, D. (1992b). Vaclav Havel, postmodernism, and modernity: The implications for adult education in the West. *Proceedings of the 33rd Annual Adult Education Research Conference* (pp. 19–23). University of Saskatchewan, Saskatoon.
Briton, D., & Plumb, D. (1993). The commodification of adult education. *Procedddings of the 34th Annual Adult Education Research Conference* (pp. 31–36). Pennsylvania State University, University Park.

Brunner, E. S., Wilder, D., Kirchner, C., & Newberry, J. S. (1959). *An overview of adult education research.* Chicago: Adult Education Association of the U.S.A.

Burrell, G., & Morgan, G. (1979). *Sociological paradigms and organizational analysis.* Loudon, NH: Heinemann.

Carlson, R. (1989). Malcolm Knowles: Apostle of andragogy. *Vitae Scholasticae, 8(1),* 217–233.

Carlson, R. (1992, Fall). Open season on gatekeepers (at the 1992 Adult Education Research Conference). *Newsletter of the Commission of Professors of Adult Education,* pp. 4–6.

Carnoy, M., & Levin, H. (1985). *Schooling and work in the democratic state.* Stanford, CA: Stanford University Press.

Carriere, E. (1991). Racism in Canada: A conceptual outline. *Proceedings of the 32nd Annual Adult Education Research Conference* (pp. 33–38). University of Oklahoma, Norman.

Carriere, E. (1993a). Writing wrongs: Implications of Foucauldian theory for researching racism discourse. *Proceedings of the Adult Education Research Conference* (pp. 54–59). Pennsylvania State University, University Park.

Carriere, E. (1993b). *De/scribing racism in theory and everyday discourse: Implications for antiracism education.* Unpublished Working Paper on Racism, University of British Columbia, Vancouver.

Carriere, E. (1994). Re-enchanting research: Using narrative in anti-racism education. *Proceedings of the Adult Education Research Conference,* University of Tennessee.

Cavaliere, L. (1988). *The self-directed learning patterns and processes used by the Wright bros. which led to their invention of the airplane.* Unpublished doctoral dissertation, Rutgers, The State University of New Jersey.

Cavaliere, L. (1990). Using naturalistic inquiry and content analysis as a qualitative approach to conduct historical case study research. *Proceedings of the Adult Education Research Conference* (pp. 43–48). University of Georgia, Athens.

Cavaliere, L. (1992). The Wright Brothers odyssey: Their flight of learning. In L. Cavaliere & A. Sgroi (Eds.), *Learning for personal development* (pp. 51–59). San Francisco: Jossey Bass.

Chovanec, D. (1993). The experience of consciousness-raising in abused women. *Proceedings of the Adult Education Research Conference,* (pp. 72–78). Pennsylvania State University, University Park.

Clark, J. R. (1990). *Andragogy and art galleries.* Unpublished major essay, University of British Columbia, Vancouver.

Cohen, P. (1992). 'It's racism what dunnit': Hidden narratives in theories of racism. In J. McDonald & A. Rattanksi (Eds.), *Race, culture and difference* (pp. 62–103). London: Sage Publications.

Collard, S., & Law, M. (1990). Universal abandon: Postmodernity, politics and adult education. *Proceedings of the Adult Education Research Conference* (pp. 54–58). University of Georgia, Athens.

Collard, S., & Law, M. (1991). The impact of critical social theory on adult education: A preliminary evaluation. *Proceedings of the Adult Education Research Conference* (pp. 56–63). University of Oklahoma, Norman.

Collins, M. (1994). From self-directed learning to postmodern thought in adult education. *Proceedings of the Adult Education Research Conference,* University of Tennessee.

Collins, M., & Plumb, D. (1989). Some critical thinking about critical theory and its relevance for adult education practice. In *Proceedings of the Adult Education Research Conference* (pp. 95–100). University of Wisconsin, Madison.

Commission of Professors of Adult Education (1992, Spring). *Commission of Professors of Adult Education Newsletter—AERC.* De Kalb, IL: Commission of Professors of Adult Education.

Connor, S. (1992). *Postmodernist culture.* Oxford: Blackwell.

Corbett, E. A. (1957). *We have with us tonight.* Toronto: Ryerson.

Courtney, S. (1986). On derivation of the research question. *Adult Education Quarterly, 36,* 160–165.

Darkenwald, G., & Merriam, S. B. (1982). *Adult education: Foundations of practice.* New York: Harper and Row.

de Certeau, M. (1984). *The practice of everyday life.* Berkeley: University of California Press.

Deshler, D. (1991). Social, professional and academic issues. In J. M. Peters & P. Jarvis (Eds.). *Adult education: Evolution and achievements in a developing field of study* (pp. 384–420). San Francisco: Jossey Bass.

Deshler, D., & Hagan, N. (1989). Adult education research: Issues and directions. In P. Cunningham & S. B. Merriam (Eds.), *Handbook of adult and continuing education* (pp. 147–167). San Francisco: Jossey Bass.

Dykstra, C. (1990). *Education for social transformation: A quest for the practice of democracy.* Unpublished master's thesis, University of British Columbia, Vancouver.

Dykstra, C., & Law, M. (1994). Popular social movements as social forces: Towards a theoretical framework. *Proceedings of the Adult Education Research Conference,* University of Tennessee.

Eribon, D. S. (1991). *Michel Foucault.* Cambridge, MA: Harvard University Press.

Falk, C. (1994). Postmodern Doors Into a Modern Community College. *Proceedings of the Adult Education Research Conference,* University of Tennessee.

Faure, E. (1972) *Learning to be.* Paris: UNESCO.

Fieldhouse, R. (1980). *Adult education and the Cold War.* Leeds: Leeds University Department of Adult and Continuing Education.

Finger, M. (1989). New social movements and their implications for adult education. *Adult Education Quarterly, 40,* 15–21.

Foucault, M. (1978). *History of sexuality.* New York: Pantheon.

Foucault, M. (1979). *Discipline and punishment.* New York: Vintage Books.

Foucault, M. (1980). *Power/knowledge. Selected interviews and other writings, 1972–1977.* New York: Pantheon Books.

Fraser, N. (1989). *Unruly practices: Power, discourse and gender in contemporary social theory.* Minneapolis: University of Minnesota Press.

Garrison, R., & Baskett, H. K. (1987). Research and publishing in adult education: A study of the approaches and strategies of the field's most successful researchers. *Proceedings of the Adult Education Research Conference* (pp. 90–95). University of Wyoming, Laramie.

Garrison, D. R., & Baskett, H. K. (1989). A survey of adult education research in Canada. *Canadian Journal of Adult Education,* 3(2), 32–46.

Gaventa, J., Heaney, T., Austermiller, J., & Williams, L. (1994). Learning from the Highlander experience. *Proceedings of the Adult Education Research Conference,* University of Tennessee.

Giroux, H. (1983). *Theory and resistance in education.* South Hadley, MA: Bergin and Garvey.

Giroux, H. (1988). *Teachers As intellectuals: Toward a critical pedagogy of learning.* South Hadley, MA: Bergin and Garvey.

Giroux, H., & Simon, R. (1993). *Popular culture: Schooling and everyday life.* New York: Bergin and Garvey.

Grattan, C. H. (1955). *In quest of knowledge.* New York: Association Press.

Griffin, C. (1991). A critical perspective on sociology and adult education. In J. M. Peters & P. Jarvis (Eds.), *Adult education: Evolution and achievements in a developing field of study* (pp. 259–281). San Francisco: Jossey Bass.

Gruber, D. F. (1989). Foucault and theory: Geneaological critiques of the subject. In A. B. Dallery & C. E. Scott (Eds.), *The question of the other: Essays in contemporary continental philosophy* (pp. 189–196). New York: State University of New York Press.

Habermas, J. (1987). *The philosophical discourse of modernity.* Cambridge: Massachusetts Institute of Technology Press.

Hall, B. (1992). Rich and vibrant colours: 25 years of adult education. *Convergence,* 24(4), 4–16.

Hall, B., Kounusu, S., Munro, J., & Welton, M. (1992). Epistemology and voice: Poetry, transformation and adult education. *Proceedings of the Adult Education Research Conference* (pp. 294–315), University of Saskatchewan.

Harker, R. K., & McConnochie, K. R. (1985). *Education as cultural artifact: Studies in Maori and aboriginal education.* Palmerston North: Dunmore Press.

Hart, M. (1990). Critical theory and beyond: Further perspectives on emancipatory education. *Adult Education Quarterly,* 40(3), 125–138.

Hassard, J. (1993). Postmodernism and organizational analysis: An overview. In J. Hassard & M. Parker (1993) (Eds.), *Postmodernism and Organizations* (pp. 1–23). London: Sage.

Heaney, T. (1992). When adult education stood for democracy. *Adult Education Quarterly,* 43(1), 51–59.

Hebdige, D. (1986). Postmodernism and "the other side'. *Journal of Communication Inquiry,* 10(10), pp. 78–99.

Hellyer, M. (1986). Adult education and government repression in the U.S., 1919–1920—revolutionary radicalism. *Proceedings of the Education Research Conference* (pp. 134–139), Syracuse University.

Hooks, b. (1993). Bell hooks speaks about Paulo Freire—the man, his work. In P. McLaren & P. Leonard (Eds.), *Paulo Freire: A critical encounter* (pp. 146–150). London: Routledge.

Horkheimer, M. (1989). *Critical theory: Selected essays.* New York: Continuum.

Houle, C. O. (1980). *Continuing learning in the professions.* San Francisco: Jossey Bass.

Illich, I. (1979). *Deschooling society.* New York: Harper and Row.

Jensen, G., Liveright, A. A., & Hallenbeck, W. C. (Eds.) (1964). *Adult education: Outlines of an emerging field of university study.* Chicago: Adult Education Association of the U.S.A.

Kaestle, C. F. (1993, January). The awful reputation of educational research. *Educational Researcher,* 23–31.

Kellner, D. (1989). *Critical theory, Marxism and modernity.* Baltimore: John Hopkins University Press.

Kennedy, K. (1992). *John K. Friesen: Adult educator, mentor and humanitarian.* Unpublished master's thesis, University of British Columbia.

Kidd, R., & Kumar, K. (1981, January). Co-opting Freire: A critical analysis of pseudo-Freirean adult education. *Economic and Political Weekly,* 16(*1,2*), 3–10, 27–36.

Kincheloe, J. L., & McLaren, P. (1994). Rethinking critical theory and qualitative research. In N. K. Denzil & Y. Lincoln (Eds.), *Handbook of qualitative research* (pp. 138–157). Thousand Oaks: Sage.

Knowles, M. S. (1929, October). How to earn fifty merit badges. *Boys' Life,* 19:32.

Knowles, M. S. (1950). *Informal adult education.* New York: Association Press.

Knowles, M. S. (1980). *The modern practice of adult education.* Chicago: Association Press and Follett.

Krietlow, B. (1965). Needed research. *Review of Educational Research,* 35(2), 240–245.

Krietlow, B. (1972). Research and theory. In R. M. Smith, G. F. Aker, & J. R. Kidd (Eds.), *Handbook of adult education* (pp. 137–149). New York: Macmillan.

La Paglia, N. (1993). Story-tellers: The image of the two-year college in American fiction and in women's journals. *Proceedings of the Adult Education Research Conference,* (pp. 161–165). Pennsylvania State University.

Laclau, E. (1988). Politics and the limits of modernity. In A. Ross (Ed.), *Universal abandon* (pp. 63–82). Minneapolis: University of Minnesota Press.

Lather, P. (1986). Issues of validity in openly ideological research: Between a rock and a soft place. *Interchange,* 17 (*4*), 63–84.

Lather, P. (1991). *Getting smart: Feminist research and pedagogy with/in the postmodern.* New York: Routledge.

Law, M. (1988). Adult education, McCarthyism and the Cold War. *Proceedings of the Adult Education Research Conference* (pp. 181–186), University of Calgary.

Law, M. (1992a). The new black book: What does it tell us about adult education? *Adult Education Quarterly, 42(4)*, 253–259.

Law, M. (1992b). Engels, Marx and radical adult education: A re-reading of a tradition. *Proceedings of the Adult Education Research Conference* (pp. 150–157). University of Saskatchewan.

Little, D. J. (1992). Criteria for assessing critical adult education research. *Adult Education Quarterly, 42(4)*, 237–249.

Long, H. B. (1983). *Adult learning: Research and practice.* New York: Cambridge University Press.

Long, H., & Hiemstra, R. (Eds). (1980). *Changing approaches to studying adult education.* San Francisco: Jossey Bass.

Luke, C., & Gore, J. (1992) (Eds.). Feminisms and critical pedagogy. London: Routledge.

Luttrell, W. (1989). Working-class women's ways of knowing: Effects of gender, race and class. *Sociology of Education, 62(1)*, 33–46.

Lyotard, J. (1984). *The postmodern condition.* Minneapolis: University of Minnesota Press.

Mansbridge, A. (1940). *The trodden road.* London: J. M. Dent and Sons.

Marton, F. (1981). Phenomenography—Describing conceptions of the world around us. *Instructional Science, 10*, 177–200.

Marton, F. (1986). Phenemonography—A research approach to investigating different understandings of reality. *Journal of Thought, 21*, 29–49.

McAulay, J. (1991). Why men chose nontraditional health care careers. *Unpublished master's major essay,* University of British Columbia, Vancouver.

McLaren, P. (1988). *Life in schools.* New York: Longman.

McTaggart, R. (1991). Principles for participatory action research. *Adult Education Quarterly, 41(3)*, 168–187.

Mezirow, J. (Ed.) (1990). *Fostering critical reflection in adulthood.* San Francisco: Jossey Bass.

Mezirow, J. (1993). Conceptions of transformation in adult education: Views of self, society, and social change (Paper presented in a symposia chaired by J. M. Dirkx). *Proceedings of the Adult Education Research Conference* (pp. 354–359). Pennsylvania State University, University Park.

Miller, H. L. (1967). *Participation of adults in education: A force field analysis.* Boston: Center for the Study of Liberal Education for Adults. Occasional Paper No. 14.

Miller, J. (1993). *The passion of Michel Foucault.* New York: Simon and Schuster.

Miller, N., & Usher, R. (1993). Discourse and difference in academic communities: An examination of how adult educators talk to one another. *Paper Issued as a Supplement to the Proceedings of the Adult Education Research Conference,* Pennsylvania State University, University Park.

Mlozi, M. (1993). Inequitable agricultural extension services in the urban context: The case of Tanzania. In N. P. Stromquist (Ed.), *Education in urban areas* (pp. 105–128). Westport: Praeger.

Munch, R. (1987). Parsonian theory today: In search of a new synthesis. In A. Giddens & J. Turner (Eds.), *Social Theory Today* (pp. 116–155). Stanford: Stanford University Press.

Nicholson, L. (Ed.). (1990). *Feminism/postmodernism*. New York: Routledge.

O'Brien, M. (1989). Feminist praxis. In A. Miles & G. Finn (Eds.), *Feminism: From pressure to politics* (pp. 120–128). New York: Black Rose Books.

Ohliger, J. (1989). Alternative images of the future in adult education. In S. B. Merriam & P. Cunningham (Eds.), *Handbook of adult and continuing education* (pp. 628–639). San Francisco: Jossey Bass.

Park, P., Brydon-Miller, M., Hall, B., & Jackson, T. (Eds.). (1993). *Voices of change: Participatory research in the United States and Canada*. Toronto: OISE Press.

Parsons, T. (1967). *Sociological theory and modern society*. New York: Free Press.

Paulston, R. (1977). Social and educational change: Conceptual frameworks. *Comparative Educational Review, 21,* 368–395.

Paulston, R. (1989). Personal Communication. Teleconference with the author's ADED501 "Adult Education and Society" class, University of British Columbia, Vancouver.

Paulston, R. (1992). Ways of seeing education and social change: A phenomenographic perspective. *Latin American Research Review, 27(3),* 177–202.

Paulston, R., & Liebman, M. (1993, March). *Invitation to a postmodern reflection on critical social cartography*. Paper Presented at the Comparative and International Education Society Annual Conference, Kingston, Jamaica.

Peterson, E. A. (1991). A phenomenological investigation of self-will and the relationship to achievement in African-American women. *Proceedings of the Adult Education Research Conference* (pp. 197–202), University of Oklahoma, Norman.

Peters, J. M., & Jarvis, P. (Eds.). (1991). *Adult education: Evolution and achievements in a developing field of study* (pp. 97–120). San Francisco: Jossey Bass.

Pittman, V. (1990). Adult students in film: Andragogy goes to Hollywood. *Proceedings of the Adult Education Research Conference* (pp. 153–158). University of Georgia.

Pittman, V., & Ohliger, J. (1988). Adult education and works of the imagination: A new direction for research. *Proceedings of the Adult Education Research Conference* (pp. 236–241). University of Wisconsin.

Pratt, D. (1992a) Conceptions of teaching. *Adult Education Quarterly, 42(4),* 203–220.

Pratt, D. (1992b). Chinese conceptions of learning and teaching; A Westerner's atttempt at understanding. *International Journal of Lifelong Education, 11(4),* 301–319.

Pratt, D. (1993). Andragogy after twenty-five years. In S. B. Merriam (Ed.), *An update on adult learning theory.* (pp. 15–23). San Francisco: Jossey Bass.

Price, C. (1993). *The learning and empowerment of people with schizophrenia.* Unpublished master's thesis, University of British Columbia, Vancouver.

Quigley, A. (1990). Hidden logic: Reproduction and resistance in adult literacy and adult basic education. *Adult Education Quarterly,* 40(2), 103–115.

Quigley, A., & Holsinger, E. (1993). "Happy consciousness": Hegemony and hidden curricula in literacy readers between 1977 and 1991. *Proceedings of the Adult Education Research Conference* (pp. 221–226). Pennsylvania State University.

Rahnema, M. (1988). Power and regenerative processes in micro-spaces. *International Social Science Journal,* 117(3), 361–375.

Rahnema, M. (1990). Participatory action research: The last temptation of Saint Development. *Alternatives,* 15, 199–226.

Rahnema, M. (1991). Global poverty: A pauperizing myth. *Interculture,* 24(2), 1–51.

Rogers, C. R. (1959). A theory of therapy, personality and inter-personal relationships, as developed in the client-centered framework. In S. Koch (Ed.), *Psychology: The study of a science, Vol. 5* (pp. 184–256). New York: McGraw-Hill.

Rogers, C. R. (1969). *Freedom to learn.* Columbus, OH: Charles E. Merrill.

Rubenson, K. (1982). In search of a map of the territory. *Adult Education Quarterly,* 32(2), 57–74.

Rubenson, K. (1989). Adult education research: General. In C. Titmus (Ed.), *Lifelong education for adults* (pp. 507–511). Oxford: Pergamon.

Said, E. W. (1989). Michel Foucault, 1926–1984. In J. Arac (Ed.), *After Foucault: Humanistic knowledge, postmodern challenges* (pp. 1–11). New Brunswick: Rutgers University Press.

Sarason, S. B. (1988). *The making of an American psychologist.* San Francisco: Jossey Bass.

Sawicki, J. (1988). Feminism and the power of Foucauldian discourse. In J. Arac (Ed.), *After Foucault: Humanistic knowledge, postmodern challenges* (pp. 161–178). New Brunswick: Rutgers University Press.

Schied, F. (1992). Connecting workers' education to the working class: Labour schools and informal education in cultural context. *Proceedings of the Adult Education Research Conference* (pp. 221–226). University of Saskatchewan, Saskatoon.

Sellitz, C., Wrightsman, L. S., & Cook, S. (1976). *Research methods in social relations.* New York: Holt, Rinehart.

Shak, T. (1989). *Lifelong education: Definition, agreement and prediction.* Unpublished doctoral dissertation, University of British Columbia, Vancouver.

Shekerjian, D. (1990). *Uncommon genius: How great ideas are born.* New York: Penguin Books.

Shilts, R. (1987). *And the band played on: People, politics and the AIDS epidemic.* New York: St Martins Press.

Smith, G. (1993, May–June). *Kaupapa Maori: Resistance and intervention in Aoteoroa (New Zealand)*. Paper presented at the International Conference on Higher Education and Indigenous People, University of British Columbia, Vancouver.

Sullivan, E. (1990). *Critical psychology and pedagogy: Interpretation of the personal world*. New York: Bergin and Garvey.

Terrill, R. (1973). *R.H. Tawney and his times: Socialism as friendship*. Cambridge, MA: Harvard University Press.

Thomas, J. E., & Elsey, B. (Eds.). (1985). *International biography of adult education*. Nottingham: University of Nottingham.

Tough, A. (1971). *The adults learning projects*. Toronto: Ontario Institute for Studies in Education.

Travers, R. M. (1978). *An introduction to educational research*. New York: Macmillan.

Walker, R. J. (1980) Maori adult education. In R. W. Boshier (Ed.), *Towards a learning society* (pp. 101–120). Vancouver: Learningpress.

Walker, R. J. (1990). *Ka Whawhai Tonu Maori: Struggle without end*. Wellington: Penguin Books.

Watney, S. (1987). *Policing desire*. Minneapolis: University of Minnesota Press.

Welton, M. (1991). Shaking the foundation: The critical turn in adult education theory. *The Canadian Journal for the Study of Adult Education, 5*, 21–42.

Welton, M. (1993). Social revolutionary learning: The new social movements as learning sites. *Adult Education Quarterly, 43*(*3*), 152–164.

Williamson, J. B., Karp, D. A., Dalphin, J. R., & Gray, P. S. (1982). *The research craft*. Boston/Toronto: Little Brown and Company.

Wright, L. (1988). Tenant management: A study of empowerment through a participatory research project. *Proceedings of the Adult Education Research Conference* (pp. 306–311), University of Calgary.

Youngman, F. (1986). *Adult education and socialist pedagogy*. London: Croom Helm.

Zacharakis-Jutz, J. (1993). Highlander Folk School and the industrial labor movement: Using the FBI files to develop a third perspective. *Proceedings of the Adult Education Research Conference* (pp. 341–346), Pennsylvania State University, University Park.

CHAPTER 6

WRITING AND SUBMITTING A MANUSCRIPT FOR PUBLICATION

Sharan Merriam

It is 2:00 on a Sunday afternoon as I begin writing this chapter. It occurs to me that in sitting down to write, I am mirroring many of the things I plan to say about the writing process. First of all, it is about 75° F outside and a gorgeous spring day. Glancing out the window, I long to do what my neighbors are all doing—mowing lawns, planting gardens, relaxing. But this is the first of three consecutive days during which I have committed myself to large chunks of time to write this chapter. Over the years I've discovered several things about writing. First, it takes discipline to sit down and write; there's *always* something else you could be doing that would be more fun. Specific times have to be designated for writing and rigorously adhered to, regardless of there being more interesting things to do. Second, everyone has a preferred working style. I need long blocks of time as close together as possible. I would rather write for 6 to 8 hours three days in a row, than 2 to 3 hours each day for a week.

Looking around in my immediate surroundings, I see other trappings characteristic of my working style. I have a spelling dictionary and thesaurus close by. I also have a soft drink and will soon be taking a break to get the candy I use to reward myself along the way, and/or to fill in periods of no writing. To my left is a rather detailed outline for this chapter (I'm on the introduction now, to which I've allocated about two pages—but more about this later); 10 pages of notes from books and articles that I have read in preparation for this chapter; and on the floor next to me, the books and articles that I might quote from. All this is to say that writing, like exercising, is an activity that takes preparation, time, and commitment. Further, writing is an idiosyncratic process; getting published is a mechanical process. Neither writing nor getting published should be seen as mysterious processes, fathomable only to a select few. The purpose of this chapter is to offer suggestions for facilitating the writing process and for getting published.

117

But first it is important to underscore the commitment you have to have to write and to publish. This commitment is to contribute to the knowledge base of your field. In adult education, the theory and knowledge base is young; there is much still to be understood about our practice. From the university professor to the trainer in business, to the health professional working with adults, to the classroom literacy instructor, there is room (and publishing outlets) for all to contribute. Contributions can take the form of conference and workshop presentations, in-house or staff publications, public media, and so on, in addition to the usual journal and book outlets. This commitment is a crucial prerequisite to doing any writing.

Once you commit to contributing to the field through writing for publication, the task can become less formidable and more manageable by knowing how to go about doing it. The first section of this chapter deals with the writing process itself, including reviewing the components of a standard research report. The second half of the chapter focuses on the publication process—how the process differs for articles, chapters, or books, and things you can do to increase your chances of getting published.

THE WRITING PROCESS

While many **intend** to write for publication, and many have something to say that surely would be of interest to others, few actually take the steps necessary to bring it about. This is particularly lamentable if you've gone to all the trouble of actually having done some research, as is always the case with graduate students. Some of the finest research in the field is being conducted by graduate students who have the benefit of a committee making sure the research is done well, while potential pitfalls are avoided. Graduate students have even written up the research and defended it before the committee. Yet most of this research never reaches others, never contributes to the knowledge base of the field, and never comes to the attention of practitioners who might benefit from knowing about this research. The same is true for those working in adult education who often investigate something about their daily practice that puzzles them or challenges them to find better ways to do something. Most of these applied research projects are never written up for others to read and benefit from. Unless you can write up the research you "may as well have never started [the] task, for as far as the rest of the world is concerned, [the] work on that problem doesn't yet exist" (Bertrand, 1987, p. 15).

Why More People Don't Write

Why is it so difficult to write something that others in the field might benefit from reading? Graduate students talk about being "burned out" or too sick of their research to want to revisit it to write something from it. This typical postprogram reaction is more of an indictment of our graduate programs than of those who go through them. If research could be demystified and made exciting and fun, and requirements made less archaic and formal, maybe students would retain some enthusiasm for disseminating the results of their investigations. More often, postprogram inertia recedes as busy professional lives take over. The same is true for those doing research to solve some immediate work-related problem. Once the problem is solved, once one has graduated, there is little time or inclination to pursue publication of the results.

For those who are committed to sharing their work with others through publication, there are other barriers. Becker, in a marvelous book titled *Writing for Social Scientists* (1986), identifies two powerful obstacles. One is thinking that there is One Right Way; if we don't know the right way to write up research, we can't do it. Applied to graduate students and professionals, the myth works like this: "Since what you are writing is something new, the One Right Way does not exist, but its Platonic ideal exists somewhere and it is up to you to discover it and put it down on paper" (p. 47). Becker goes on to note that

some very common, quite specific writing difficulties have their origins in this attitude: the problem of getting started and the problem of "which way to organize it." Neither one has a unique solution to be discovered. Whatever you do will be compromise between conflicting possibilities. That doesn't mean that you can't arrive at workable solutions, only that you can't count on finding the one perfect one that was there all along waiting to be found. (pp. 48–49).

A second obstacle to writing, and perhaps the most powerful deterrent of all, is the *risk* one takes by writing up something for others to see. Fear of rejection, fear of criticism, fear of being thought of as unscholarly, fear of being found out, paralyze many beginning writers. Richards, in Becker's book, writes:

For me, sitting down to write is risky because it means that I have to open myself to scrutiny. To do that requires that I trust myself, and it also means that I have to trust my colleagues. By far the more critical of these is the latter, because it is colleagues' responses that make it possible for me to trust myself. (p. 113)

Dealing With Barriers to Writing

Assuming you at least cognitively agree there is no One Right Way, and you are willing to risk, there are some things you can do to get on with it, so to speak, and to overcome instances of what is known as "writer's block." As I pointed out by the way in which I began this chapter, you need to determine what your modus operandi is. Where are you most comfortable writing? At home? In the office? The library? What do you need to do before you sit down to write? Everyone has little rituals that lead up to the moment. Do you need to water the plants? Check your email messages? Unplug the phone? What particular accouterments do you need? Snacks? Pens? Reading glasses? What is your rhythm when writing? That is, do you need to get up and wander around regularly, thinking as you go, or do you stay glued to the chair until you get a certain amount written? Do you need large blocks of time close together as I do, or do you do better spreading the task out over a longer period of time? I suggest identifying and indulging in these idiosyncracies; by doing so you set optimum conditions for actually producing something.

Once underway, everyone hits periods of not being able to write a word, or being utterly dissatisfied with what was written. It has been my experience that a writing block is really more a thinking block—you just can't *think* what to say next. This is usually a signal to me that I need to back up and do some more reading, thinking, or talking about the project. Talking about what you are trying to write is one of the best ways to bring some clarity to the task. Talk to anyone—spouse, kids, the dog, your mother; sometimes those least knowledgeable about the topic force you to be most clear. Colleagues who will push you to articulate your thoughts are also worth approaching.

Another startegy is to force yourself to write anything—however remotely related to the topic—just as long as you get something down. You can also skip over where you are stuck, and go to another section where you know what you want to say. This is in fact a general writing strategy for many people—working first on those parts that come readily. My preferred strategy is to follow an outline. One technique I use is to estimate the number of pages I plan to write for each portion of the outline, and then write until I fill up that many pages. For this section on writer's block, for example, I allocated about one page. I have a good sense of where I'm going and how much I need to write to get there. As I meet these little, within-project goals, I reward myself with the candy I have situated prominently next to the computer.

Wolcott, in *Writing Up Qualitative Research* (1990), speaks to what he calls "The Plan." This plan consists of a clearly written statement of purpose of what you are trying to write about and a *"detailed written outline or sequence"* (p. 16). He has his doctoral students write a table of contents for their dissertation proposal, estimating "the number of pages they plan to devote to each chapter" (p. 17). This activity, which he calls "tight outlining" (p. 23), "helps to give a sense of the piece as a whole" and "may prevent overwriting in introductory sections" (p. 17). You will have to experiment to determine whether the outlining approach or the more shotgun approach discussed earlier (or some other) works best for you. For some forms of writing, such as writing up a report of research, there are conventions and guidelines, outlines if you will, already in place that you can follow.

The Structure of a Research Report

Since the focus of this chapter is on writing up research for publication, it would probably be helpful to review what the typical research report consists of and what variations there might be depending upon the type of research conducted.

All research, whether it be experimental, survey, or some form of qualitative, historical or philosophical, is generated by a research problem. That is, there is something that puzzles you, something you wonder about, something that just doesn't play out the way you would expect it to, given what is understood about the phenomenon. This problem is introduced and identified early in the report. Often interwoven with the problem itself is a presentation of what else is known about this problem, what others have said about it, as well as what investigations have been conducted in the same area. This is the literature review and it is this component that sometimes brings an end to writing up research before one has barely started. Writers worry that they haven't uncovered important previous work that everyone but they know about, therefore risking exposure for being not very scholarly or thorough. "No one wants to discover that their carefully nurtured idea was in print before they thought of it (maybe before they were born) and in a place they should have looked," writes Becker (1986, p. 136) in a chapter aptly titled, "Terrorized by the Literature." But no one person will be familiar with everything available on a particular topic. The best thing to do is to give it your best shot and expect that someone will suggest a reference you don't have, but that you can then look up and incorporate into a revision.

A third component of all reports of research that comes after the research problem and review of relevant literature is a methodology section. Basically, this section tells the reader how the research was conducted. What was the design of the study? Was this a survey? An experiment? A case study? How were the data collected and from whom? How were they analyzed? What precautions did you take to ensure that your interpretation of the data was trustworthy (valid and reliable)?

Once you've told readers how you conducted the study, you tell them what you found. This is the results or findings section. Typically, results are presented without comment; rather, discussion and interpretation of the results follow the findings. It is in this section that you tell the reader why you think you got the results you got, and how you make sense of (interpret) those results. Often, literature reviewed earlier is referred to at this point to help interpret the results and/or to show where this particular study fits into, extends, or refines what is already known about the phenomenon. Finally, most reports of research in applied fields such as adult education end with implications and/or recommendations for applying the results to practice.

In spite of several years experience as co-editor of *Adult Education Quarterly* (AEQ) and as author of numerous publications in other journals, the above format still looks easier to follow than it actually is in practice. Decisions have to be made at every step in the process regarding what and how much to include. This is particularly problematic with regard to writing up qualitative, participatory, and critical forms of research because universally accepted formats and styles for reporting research do not exist. How detailed should the methodology section be for a study employing one of these less familiar methodologies? How much "raw" supporting data should be included versus analysis and interpretation? What "voice" is most appropriate? Van Maanen (1988), for example, in his book, *Tales of the field,* describes three very different ways to write up an ethnographic study. Realist tales are direct, matter-of-fact portraits of a studied culture; confessional tales are highly personalized and focus more on the researcher's point of view than the culture; impressionist tales are "personalized accounts of fleeting moments of fieldwork cast in dramatic form" (p. 7). There are also critical, formal, literary, and jointly told tales. All these formats are acceptable and publishable by some outlets but not others. The trick is to find the best match between how you want to write up your research study and a publishing outlet that will accept that format (this point will be discussed later).

Another common problem I have encountered as a journal editor is the difficulty researchers have in reducing a thesis, dissertation, or other large-scale study into a journal article. You would think that since these are already written, most likely in the format outlined above, it would be easy to put a reduced version together for a journal or book chapter. However, these manuscripts rarely make it through the review process, not because the research is flawed, but because reviewers can't make sense out of the presentation of the study. Most likely the author has tried to include in 20 pages all the important and exciting things found in the 150-page larger study. It simply can't be done. What can be done is to think of the larger study as holding the potential for several articles, each focusing on a slightly different aspect, dimension, or finding of the study. Wolcott (1990, p. 62) compares this problem to the traveler who has too much for the suitcase:

> Faced with the dilemma of having more to pack than a suitcase can possibly hold, the novice traveler has three possibilities: rearrange so as to get more in, remove nonessentials, or find a larger suitcase. . . . If clever repacking is not remedy enough, some items will have to be left out. As to the third possibility, seasoned travelers and researchers alike are aware that large containers are unwieldy, often require special handling that entails additional costs, and may be prohibited by regulation.

Wolcott reiterates that the solution to this problem lies in focusing the report. "*Do less, more thoroughly*" (p. 62), he recommends. This problem is so prevalent that at AEQ we have developed guidelines for converting theses and dissertations into journal articles. These are sent out regularly with reviewer comments to authors who have tried (usually unsuccessfully) to tell all in a few short pages.

THE PUBLISHING PROCESS

Most people experience a great sense of accomplishment once they have written something; having it published is even more exciting. It is also very affirming, since some editor somewhere (and probably several reviewers) has deemed your ideas or research significant enough to be of interest to others in the field. However, you won't ever know if your writing is publishable unless you send it somewhere for review. A surprising number of people have drafted manuscripts that end up in their file cabinet, or at the most, are shared with a few trusted colleagues. For various reasons, they are never actually sent for review. For some authors, the risk factors alluded to earlier are too daunting; for others, the mauscript is never perfected enough to send out. Becker (1986), in a chapter titled "Getting It Out the Door," speaks to the tension all writers feel between "making it better and getting it done" (p. 122). He describes intellectual life as "a dialogue among people interested in the same topic. You can eavesdrop in the conversation and learn from it, but eventually you ought to add something yourself" (p. 124). A manuscript can be indefinitely revised, updated, and perfected. Rather than becoming paralyzed by the thought that it is not as good as it *could* be (but it never will be), you need to take control and at some point decide that enough is enough. When is that point? My suggestion would be to have a couple of colleagues critique a draft, take their comments into consideration in crafting a final revision, and then send it off. I plan to do just that with this chapter. In fact, I already have a couple of people in mind who will give me a good "read" on the first draft. *Where* to send it is an important consideration in getting published.

Where to Send it

Where you send your manuscript depends upon whether you see it as an article, a chapter, or a book. If you are writing a book chapter, as I am doing now, you will most likely have been invited to write the chapter based upon your expertise in the field. The editor of the book will have already conceptualized the project, delineating how each chapter contributes to the whole. The focus of your chapter will have been fairly well defined before you agree to writing it. Specifics of the chapter may have been negotiated through an outline submitted by you early in the process. The book editor, and sometimes reviewers commissioned by the publisher, will review your draft chapter and make suggestions for a revision. Typically, the editor retains the option of ultimately not including your chapter if it fails to meet the agreed-upon specifications. A very accessible outlet for writing of this kind in our field is the *New Directions for Adult and Continuing Education* series published by Jossey-Bass. These are monograph-length quarterly publications on various topics in adult education. Many new writers contribute to these sourcebooks. You can also propose a topic for which you would be the editor. Book chapters are an excellent route to publishing in the field. Your task is to make your area of expertise known so that you will be considered for these opportunities.

Short of publishing (which gets us into a chicken-and-egg situation), you can make your area of expertise known through approaching someone whom you've heard is developing a book, through networking, and through conference attendance and presentations.

Hundreds of journals publish reports of research. Deciding which journal is most appropriate for your report takes a bit of detective work. First, go to the library and browse through journals that represent the content area of your study. For example, if your research deals with undergraduates, then look at the journals in higher education; if it deals with counseling undergraduates you might also check journals with a counseling focus, and so on. Another thing to look for is the type of articles a journal publishes. Are various research methodologies acceptable? How detailed are the write-ups? Who is the intended audience for this journal? Other researchers? Practitioners? The general public? What is the tone of the articles? Chatty? Scholarly? Personal? Basically, try to find the best match between your manuscript and a prospective journal. In actuality, I often recommend to those who are new to publishing to identify the journal *first,* then slant the write-up of the article to match the journal.

All journals provide guidelines for the submission of manuscripts. These guidelines can usually be found on the inside front or back cover; sometimes you are told to send for more complete instructions. Rigorously adhering to these guidleines regarding format, referencing style, number of copies, and so on can save you time in the long run. Some editors will return your manuscript unreviewed if guidelines are not adhered to. The "ethics" of journal publishing require that you send your manuscript to only one journal at a time. If a particular journal seems to be taking an inordinate amount of time to render a decision, you can request that it be withdrawn from consideration and then send it on to another journal. Most journals take about 3 months to review a manuscript.

Where to send a manuscript or a proposal for consideration as a book is somewhat more complicated. Let's assume that your research or your idea is more comprehensive or complex than can be reasonably covered in an article-length manuscript. You have enough to say that a book-length manuscript is a more appropriate vehicle. How do you find a publisher for this manuscript? We have to also assume that this book will be of interest to professionals in a particular field such as adult education. Popular book publishing where your book would be of interest to potentially anyone who walks into a bookstore is another game entirely. For this type of book you are best advised to hire an agent who will negotiate with publishers for you. But back to a book for a professional or academic audience.

The strategy is similar to journal searching in that you find out who is publishing books in your field. Armed with the names of several publishers, the next step is to get the name of an editor at a publisher who handles books in your field. You can do this by calling the publisher "cold" or by contacting the author of a recent book and asking who the editor was. The next thing I would do is to call the editor and briefly present your idea; the editor will be able to tell you whether the idea is within the scope of the publisher, and if it is, how to go about submitting a proposal.

My experience with book publishers is that they each have their own guidelines for the submission of book proposals and the process varies somewhat depending on the publisher. Typically, a proposal consists of a rationale for the book, that is, why it is needed; a statement explaining how it differs from other books already published on the topic; a description of the potential market for the book (who's going to buy the book); and a chapter-by-chapter overview. Most publishers will want a couple of completed chapters, and may even want a draft of the entire book, especially if you are an unknown to them. Usually these materials are sent out to reviewers; comments from these reviewers in conjunction with the "gut" sense of the editor leads to a recommendation for or against publication. If the manuscript is recommended for publication, you will be sent a contract spelling out the conditions that have to be met for it to be published. Unlike journal articles, book proposals can be sent to several publishers simultaneously. Of course, once you and a publisher negotiate a contract, proposals at other publishers must be withdrawn from consideration.

The Review Process

All manuscripts submitted for publication are reviewed by someone at some point in the process. This process ranges from very formal and rigorous to rather informal and casual. Book chapters are usually reviewed by the book editor, although sometimes even book chapters undergo what is called a blind review; you will not know who reviewed your chapter. Often book manuscripts that are under contract, and most journal articles, especially research or theory articles, are subjected to what is known as a double-blind review. In this process, the author does not know who is reviewing the article, and the reviewers do not know who wrote the manuscript. Supposedly this frees reviewers to say what they really think of the article. Of course, reviewers often have a good idea who has written a piece, just as authors sometimes can tell who has reviewed their work by the nature of comments returned. Sometimes reviewers and authors wish to contact each other, a process that is mediated by the editor. Reviewers' comments are adjudicated by the editor who ultimately makes the final decision as to whether the manuscript should be published. Sometimes extensive revisions are asked for before the manuscript is finally accepted.

Nothing is more disheartening to a novice writer than to have a manuscript rejected, especially if such rejection is accompanied by scathing reviews. Although some rejections aren't explained, in most of my experience, the editor either summarizes the problems with the manuscript and/or sends along copies of the reviews. It is at this point that a little perseverance goes a long way. First, realize these reviews are not *personal*—after all, the reviewers didn't know who you were. Second, all reviewers have their own agendas, perspectives, and world views that influence and may distort the reading of your manuscript. I was once told by a reviewer of one of my book manuscripts that it was well written, had lots of helpful material, etc., etc., but that it had one "fatal flaw"—basically, ny orientation to the material was diametrically opposite the reviewer's. At my editor's suggestion, I finessed this "fatal flaw" by recognizing the range of views on this topic and by delineating where I positioned myself vis-a-vis those views.

What do you do with reviewers' comments? It depends whether the manuscript has been flatly rejected or whether it may be accepted pending revisions based on the comments. Unless a reviewer has pointed out an error, problem, or omission in the manuscript, you can ignore the comments accompanying a rejection and send it to another journal or publisher. My personal rule of thumb is that a manuscript has to be rejected three times before I'll consider revising it. I have had a number of articles accepted on second and third tries without changing a word. After all, rejections can be explained by factors other than the quality of the manuscript. Perhaps the content or the style of presentation was not a good match with the journal; perhaps the reviewers weren't appropriate for this manuscript. AT AEQ, for example, we have some 50 reviewers on our board, three of whom are assigned to each manuscript. Taking into consideration the content area and methodology of the manuscript, we try to assign the three most knowledgeable reviewers that we can to each manuscript. On occasion we get back three different recommendations on the same manuscript that we as editors must then mediate.

Rather than ignoring the comments, you may feel that your manuscript will be improved by incorporating reviewers' suggestions into a revision. After all, reviewers are like a trial audience; others who read your manuscript might have the same questions, might suggest the same additional references, or might not understand what you are trying to say. Some authors use the review process for just this purpose—to get a "read" on their article, to get some suggestions as to how to handle troublesome sections, etc. From an editor's perspective, I don't recommend this use of reviewers' time unless you have exhausted other avenues of help.

Increasing Your Chances of Getting Published

Several things can be done to increase your chances of getting published. First, ask colleagues to critique a draft of your article. Graduate students should not hesitate to ask professors, other graduate students, and even professors in your interest area at other institutions to read and critique a draft of your article. Most people in an academic setting, whether they be students, faculty, or administrators, enjoy the intellectual challenge of being asked to respond to a colleague's ideas or research. Some will be more helpful to you than others, but that will also be true of "official" reviewers of your manuscript when you send it out. Those not in an academic setting can ask friends, colleagues at work, fellow professional association members, or other experts in the field to review their manuscript. The point is to get another set of eyes, another perspective that will bring potential problems to your attention. Even the most experienced writers suffer from not being able to "see" gaps in logic. What happens is that "the writer's own knowledge . . . may automatically supply the missing steps in the arguments and clarify the ambiguities in the wording. This hypothesis . . . explain[s] why it is often much easier to identify faults in other writers' texts than in one's own" (Thomas, 1987, pp. 104–105).

If you cannot find someone to critique your manuscript, a backup strategy would be to put it away for a period of time. Getting some distance from what you've written will often allow you to read it from a fresh perspective when you go back to it. You may have forgotten what you were thinking when you wrote a particular passage (which now seems unclear), and you don't feel a pressing need to defend what you've written since you're no longer quite as invested in it. This strategy is actually a good one to use in conjunction with the above.

A few technical issues come to mind that will help your manuscript along in the process. In addition to strictly adhering to a journal or publisher's guidelines about style and length, pay particular attention to the title and abstract. These need to be clear and concise, conveying what the manuscript is about. While clever or catchy titles will no doubt favorably predispose a reviewer towards your manuscript, going over-board here will have a negative effect. Also, avoid being apologetic about what you have *not* done. This merely alerts reviewers to possible shortcomings in your treatment of the topic, some of which may reflect their own biases and agendas.

Another suggestion, covered above but worth underscoring again here, is the importance of matching your writing with a potential publishing outlet. Whether you write first and then find an outlet, or find an outlet first and then write to it, doesn't matter. What matters is that the format, style, focus, and audience to whom you are writing are aligned as closely as possible to the journal or publisher where you intend to send your manuscript for review.

My final suggestion for increasing your chances of getting published is to begin modestly. Review a book, for example, or write a response to an article that might go in a "forum"-type column. For those in education, the Educational Resources Information Centers (ERIC) system publishes hundreds of manuscripts through *Resources in Education,* which are accessible on disk and microfiche. New journals have no backlog of manuscripts and are often looking for submissions. Major professional journals that have been around for years typically get many more manuscripts than they could possibly publish. They can thus afford to be highly selective in what they do accept. Reserve your very best efforts—those that you think are particularly strong and for which you've gotten good informal feedback—for the more prestigious journals.

SOME RELATED ISSUES

Several issues related to writing and publishing research need to be considered up front. First is the issue of co-authoring. Theoretically, co-authoring can cut your time and effort in half, but it also means you share the credit. If that's not a deterrent, the trick is to find someone who will truly be a co-author, someone who can contribute conceptually in the framing of the manuscript as well as technically in the writing of it. Can you agree on a time line and will it be adhered to? Can your working styles and your writing styles be made compatible if they aren't already? Unfortunately, some of these things are difficult to determine ahead of time. Openly explore the *possibility* of co-authoring with a discussion of these issues, leaving the option open to retreat if you have any doubts.

A second related issue has to do with multiple authorship. How are responsibilities to be divided? In what order will authors' names be listed? Typically, names are listed alphabetically or randomly (according to some random selection strategy) if everyone has contributed equally. Otherwise, names are listed in order of who has contributed the most (Winston, 1985). This issue becomes a particular problem with articles or books based on graduate student research. Should your advisor and/ or your committee members be listed as co-authors? There are few guidelines to go by on this question. Much depends on how much your advisor has contributed to the conceptualization of the research, the interpretation of data, and the structuring and writing of the article (or other manuscript). Much also depends on the personal ethics of the advisor; some are scrupulous about not taking advantage of the power differential inherent in the student/advisor relationship; unfortunately, others are more self-serving. If in doubt about a situation, check with your major professional association. The American Psychological Association (APA), for example, has published guidelines dealing with authorship questions and graduate research. According to their guidelines, only second authorship is acceptable for the dissertation director. Furthermore, depending on the amount of involvement, second authorship may be obligatory, a courtesy, or not acceptable at all (Fields, 1983).

A third issue pertains to publishing research in particular. Some authors wonder how many articles can be derived from the same study. Since more than one question is often asked in a research study, it is quite common practice to write a number of articles based on the same data set, as long as each article focuses on a different aspect of the study. Even though the sample and perhaps some of the literature and procedures will be the same across several write-ups, each question can form the focus of a separate article. As was discussed earlier, many studies are simply too complex and too long to be reduced to a 20-page article. The writing of several articles (or a book) is the only solution.

SUMMARY

Writing and submitting manuscripts for publication, particularly research manuscripts, is a process perceived as being frought with so many dangers and having such a low return on investments that even the Indiana Joneses among us are reluctant to enter the foray. In this chapter I have attempted to demystify the process by breaking it up into smaller, less formidable tasks in the hopes that you will feel it is at least a possibility. The development of our field depends upon people taking the risk involved in disseminating knowledge gained from research and practice. Without written input from fellow scholars, practioners, and students, the field stagnates and fails to germinate new ideas and solutions to old problems.

There is no "secret" formula for writing and publishing. Commitment, perseverence, and strategizing are the keys to doing both. With regard to writing, take stock of the conditions under which you are most likely to be productive; indulge in those things that will maximize your efforts. Employ whatever tricks you can to get around writer's block. Become familiar with the typical or standard format for writing up a research study. While there are many decisions to be made along the way, and many variations on this structure, the standard format does offer a place to begin—and beginning is one of the hardest things about writing.

The second half of this chapter was devoted to strategies and tips I have found useful in negotiating the publishing maze. The major topics discussed here were where to send your manuscript and how the review process works, including what to do with reviews once you get them. Finally, related issues of co-authoring, multiple authors, multiple articles from the same data set, and graduate student research were discussed.

REFERENCES

Bertrand, P. (1987). Writing for academic publications. In P. Hills (Ed.), *Publish or perish* (pp. 7–24). Guildford, Great Britain: Peter Francis Publishers.

Becker, H. S. (1986). *Writing for social scientists*. Chicago: The University of Chicago Press.

Fields, C. M. (1983, September 14). Professors' demands for credit as 'co-authors' of students' research projects may be rising. *Chronicle of Higher Education, 27*(3) pp. 7, 10.

Richards, P. (1986). Risk. In H. S. Becker, *Writing for social scientists* (pp. 108–120). Chicago: The University of Chicago Press.

Thomas, G. (1987). The process of writing a scientific paper. In P. Hills (Ed.), *Publish or perish* (pp. 93–118). Guildford, Great Britain: Peter Francis Publishers.

Van Maanen, J. (1988). *Tales of the field: On writing ethnography*. Chicago: University of Chicago Press.

Winston, R. B. (1985). A suggested procedure for determining order of authorship in research publications. *Journal of Counseling and Development, 63,* 515–518.

Wolcott, H. F. (1990). *Writing up qualitative research*. Qualitative Research Methods, Volume 20. Newbury Park: Sage Publications.

CHAPTER 7

GRADUATE TRAINING AND RESEARCH

William S. Griffith

The place of research training in graduate adult education programs continues to be a matter of dispute among those who write about this field. Although the research produced by more than 4,000 individuals who have earned doctorates in this field constitutes a significant proportion of the total amount of research reported and published in adult education, serious differences exist in the perspectives of professors, practicing adult educators, and contributors to the literature about the role of research training in doctoral degree programs. In this chapter an overview of the historical as well as the current situation are presented, followed by a discussion of possible approaches to improving the situation. Finally, a brief examination of the mentoring process and its relationship to apprenticeships are presented as a possible means for making improvements in the present system of research production and dissemination in adult education.

A TRADITION OF ACTION ORIENTATION

Since the establishment of the first doctoral degree program at Teachers College, Columbia University, in 1930, most of the attention of the faculty members in such programs has been directed to the training of adult education adminstrators and teachers. Such research training as is included in graduate programs is often regarded as an unavoidable requirement imposed by universities as a condition for conferring the doctorate. The interest of the faculty in preparing administrators and teachers is understandable in that the largest number of individuals who are recognizable as full-time workers in adult education are employed in these roles. Because of the national interest in Americanization programs early in this century, universities were inclined to offer special courses for the teachers in such programs. The National Education Association established a Division of Adult Education, the focus of which was the provision of practical, applied, how-to-do-it information that was sought by and used by inexperienced individuals who were faced with the responsibility of teaching groups of non-English-speaking adults for the first time. This practical perspective on training was appealing to both teachers in Americanization programs as well as those in adult vocational education.

The university educators who set up programs for these Americanization teachers intended to provide practical training. Research, per se, was evidently not perceived as an important part of graduate study be either the neophyte teachers or by the educators who sought to provide useful educational programs. Accordingly, training in the designing, conducting, and reporting of research was not seen to be an essential in what were perceived as in-service training activities.

However, in the 1920s a small number of individuals in strategically located positions had a sense of the potential importance of research in adult education to the sound development of the field. Frederick Keppel, president of the Carnegie Corporation of New York, had spent some time in England where he had become quite impressed with the visions reflected in The 1919 Report (Wittshire, et al., 1980) and the liberal education that was being provided by a partnership between the universities and the Workers' Education Association. Returning to the United States, Keppel drew upon the resources of the Carnegie Corporation to convene educators and other national leaders for the purpose of persuading them of the value of establishing a national adult education organization, the American Association for Adult Education. The philosophy of the association, which was composed largely of university-affiliated educators, was that the rational and appropriate way to establish adult education as a district field was to demonstrate, through well-designed and widely reported research, that those who were engaged in the work of educating adults, regardless of the level of instruction, the learners' previous level of education, or the specific nature of the content being taught, were engaged in a common pursuit, adult education. Therefore, they should recognize their common concerns and work together to expand and to improve the learning opportunites for adults and to upgrade the quality of instruction provided. The A^3E advised the Carnegie Corporation on the selection of suitable reserach projects that were likely to be persuasive in demonstrating the existence of the field.

Although the demonstration of the existence of the field through publishing research reports was ostensibly academically sound, there is little evidence to suggest that this approach was effective in making practicing adult educators aware that they were in fact engaged in a common cause. The involvement of the Carnegie Corporation, however, may have been responsible for the involvement of major national figures in adult education research, publication, and other association activities. Clearly the subsidization of research and publication was a distinct contribution of the Carnegie Corporation to laying a foundation for the development of further research activities.

Dean James E. Russell and Edward L. Thorndike at Teachers College, Columbia University, maintained a relationship with the Carnegie Corporation and were also involved in the American Association for Adult Education, so it is not surprising that Columbia University established the first full doctoral program in adult education and hired the first full-time professor of adult education. The first full-time professor was not an academic with a history of research involvement in adult education. Instead the individual selected, John D. Willard, was a seasoned adult education administrator, having served as director of extension first at Michigan State University and subsequently at the University of Massachusetts (Houle, 1964, p. 70). At the time Willard was appointed, agricultural extension workers were possibly the largest category of full-time adult educators with career expectations in that field. The field orientation and the focus on administration in doctoral programs were appropriate, given the nature of the potential students and their career aspirations, and probably was an important consideration in the minds of those who hired Willard.

The Carnegie Corporation provided the funds for fellowships in adult education at Columbia and later at the University of Chicago and other less prestigious universities. These fellowships were not intended to produce adult education researchers, but rather to facilitate the further development of practicing adult educators. Other foundations, especially the W. K. Kellogg Foundation and Ford Foundation, also underwrote the costs of graduate fellowships, although the focus was typically on the continuing development of individuals who were perceived to demonstrate leadership qualities and, in some cases, to have been identified by their employing institution as individuals who were marked for promotion. The research training provided for these fellows was not in preparation for their pursuing a career in research in as much as their career line focused on the practice of administration of adult education programs.

The faculty interests and background in adult education administration were completed by the psychological orientation and disciplinary expertise of Thorndike. While it might seem reasonable to assume that the content of adult education graduate study was determined after a rigorous examination of the role expectations of the potential students or the required competencies for various kinds of adult educators, apparently the actual curriculum was shaped more by the personal interests, disciplinary training, and professional expertise of those who were giving direction to the program.

The number of adult education graduate programs and professors in the field grew slowly. When the first meeting of these professors was held in 1955, there were 28 programs and 15 full-time professors. Although Houle (1964) traced the establishment of graduate programs in adult education in North America, neither he nor any other scholar has conducted historical research that would reveal what role the characteristics of the initial professors had on those programs and the nature of doctoral study.

CHANGING DIMENSIONS OF ADULT EDUCATION
GRADUATE STUDY

The graduate study of adult education was properly regarded as an "emerging" field of university study by the small core group of professors when they collaborated on the writing of the "black book" (Jensen, Liveright, & Hallenbeck). The table of contents of the black book reflects the thinking of those leaders regarding the conceptual foundations of the field. The editors claimed that the book introduced new ideas and ways of thinking about the conceptual foundations of adult education as a university discipline. Section II of the black book identified five "other disciplines" from which adult education was seen as borrowing and reformulating knowledge: sociology, social psychology, psychology, history, and organization and administration. These five disciplines were included partly because they were the disciplinary roots of charter members of the Commission of Professors of Adult Education.

Despite the restricted list of disciplines that the black book highlighted, the commission, in its statement "Adult Education: A New Imperative for Our Times," noted that in addition to the five disciplines already mentioned:

Anthropology has contributed experience relating to the introduction and acceptance or rejection of change in ideas and technology. Economics has provided information about the relationship between human competence and societal well-being, as well as principles for the sound use of resources for lifelong learning (Commission of Professors of Adult Education, 1964, p. viii).

So it is clear that the first members of the commission did consider other disciplines, though they chose not to include them in the initial volume. When the successor to the black book was published 27 years later, the only additional disciplines included were philosophy and political science. The fact that these are the only additional disciplines after nearly three decades could reflect a lack of interest in this field by those whose academic preparation was in economics or anthropology, or it could reflect the breadth of perception of the editors (Peters & Jarvis, 1991; Rubenson, 1989).

Peters and Jarvis (1991) noted that all of the related disciplines included in the black book are included in their successor volume with the exception of social psychology. Philosophy and political science have been added, and the selection of disciplines is justified on the grounds that the editors believe these disciplines are the ones that have made the greatest contributions to adult education knowledge (1991, p. 187). Jensen had noted in 1964 that the list of "other disciplines" is highlighted "merely because adult educators have had more experience with them" (Jensen, 1964, p. 111). This explanation by the senior editor of the black book helps to explain the somewhat happenstance collection of root disciplines on which adult education graduate programs have been constructed and may give some hint of the breadth of research perspectives reflected in the editing of books that purport to outline adult education as an evolving field of graduate study.

The Commission of Professors is perceived as demonstrating stability or lack of flexibility in its identification of core areas for graduate study in this field, depending on the orientation of the observer. In the "Standards for Graduate Programs in Adult Education" produced by the Commission of Professors of Adult Education in 1986, the core areas listed for master's degree-level study in adult education are history, philosophy, and sociology. Further, in describing the desired academic backgrounds for full-time faculty members in adult education, the Standards include as examples of relevant fields only philosophy, psychology and sociology (Brookfield, 1988, p. 235–237). The prevailing perception continues to be limited to only a selected group of the social sciences.

The nature of the knowledge produced by adult education graduate students and other academic researchers is a function of the kinds of questions they ask and the methods they use in seeking answers. Both the kinds of questions and the favored methodologies are shaped largely by the previous academic preparation of the investigator or the investigator's research supervisor. Merriam (1991, p. 42–65) has traced the nature of adult education researchers' perspectives through three phases: positivist, interpretive, and critical, noting that all three exist simultaneously, though the most widely accepted world view continues to be that of the positivist. Where professors subscribe to a positivist orientation, it would not be surprising to find that the graduate students whose research they supervise tend to follow a positivist perspective. Similarly, those professors who are inclined to an interpretive or critical world view attract and supervise students who share those perspectives.

Although it is not possible to demonstrate on logical grounds that any one of these approaches is unquestionably superior to the other two, the advocates of each view often appear to be rather intolerant of the other two. At this time the field is probably better served by entertaining all three perspectives on knowledge and research and gleaning whatever insights are produced by proponents of each of the three views.

The approach taken by the Commission of the Professors suggests that the commission regards research training as an essential component of graduate study. In describing appropriate research training of magistral students, the commission listed "an understanding of basic statistics and research," while for doctoral candidates it added "research methodology entails methods of inquiry as preparation for writing the dissertation" (Brookfield, 1988, p. 240). The importance of research is reflected in the commission's view that one of the primary indicators of a "quality graduate program" is publications in refereed journals by faculty members, students, and alumni (Brookfield, 1988, p. 241). So while it is unclear just how important the commission believes the development of expertise in conducting research is in the preparation of practicing adult educators, there is no doubt that disciplined inquiry and scholarly publication are perceived as clear indicators of program quality.

Doctoral students in North American universities have typically been subjected to more statistically oriented research approaches than have their counterparts in the United Kingdom. Brookfield (1988) observed that:

> Despite the acknowledgement of the validity of qualitative approaches on the part of American researchers, American journals and research conferences still favour articles and papers which can be located within either the experimental design paradigm or the survey research paradigm. Research is frequently reported in terms which require a good knowledge of statistical techniques and analysis . . . (pp. 301–303.

Although Brookfield's claim of favoritism being shown may be valid, there is no evidence available to demonstrate that referees receive equal numbers of quantitative and qualitative proposals and manuscripts, or that qualitative proposals and manuscripts are more likely to be rejected than quantitative ones, conditions that would have to exist to provide the empirical data to support this claim of favoritism.

Peters and Kreitlow reported that 35 of the 57 magistral programs they studied were requiring courses in research methods and statistics (1991, p. 152). They expressed some concern over the fact that the literature dealing with graduate programs shows little difference between the coursework that is required for master's and doctor's degrees. They state: "Often doctoral and master's students participate together in the same courses, further indicating that few distinctions are made in the level of content available to students seeking different degrees" (Peters & Krietlow, 1991, p. 172). The fact that graduate programs are often restricted to offering either the doctor of education (Ed.D.) degree or the doctor of philosophy (Ph.D.) degree means that the supposed distinction between the two (the Ed.D. being practice oriented and the Ph.D. being oriented toward theory advancement) does not exist in reality. Graduates of programs with a single degree (either Ed.D. or Ph.D.) may have had either focus in their degree program. Where only one degree is authorized but adult educators with vastly different educational interests are admitted to the programs, it is not surprising that the interpretation of the degree requires a knowledge of the proclivities and preferences of the research supervisor of the direct examination of the dissertation itself.

IMPROVEMENT OF PRACTICE VERSUS ADVANCEMENT OF KNOWLEDGE

Even the importance of research in the graduate education of adult educators remains a matter of debate among academic and professional leaders in the field. Major contributors to the literature such as Knox (1979), in writing about enhancing the proficiencies of continuing educators, directed the first in the series of well-known source books to three categories of personnel: administrators, resource persons, and policy makers. He noted that the major areas of proficiency covered in the book "seem important for all categories of practitioners (except researchers and professors)" (Knox, 1979, p. 8). Clearly, future researchers and professors are but a very small proportion of the total number of graduate students found in adult education doctoral programs and so their special needs are not addressed by most of the authors who attempt to analyze the training of adult educators. Those who direct such programs focus primarily on the acquisition and upgrading of practical administrative and instructional skills rather than on training for conducting research.

The emphasis on the development of practical skills and the downgrading of the importance of research training is not a recent development. In discussing the nature of adult education graduate education in 1964, Jensen stated:

> . . .adult education is a practical discipline . . . its primary objective is coping effectively with some unsatisfactory state of affairs or problem of everyday life. Its system of knowledge is organized in ways requiring taking action on problems faced by adult education practitioners . . . Though the adult educator does indirectly test a theoretical system, his main purpose is to deal with problems that continuously arise, and to gain more effective control of them . . . He thinks first of a system of ideas in terms of its usefulness for dealing with problems of practice and only secondly of its empirical or logical validity (Jensen, 1964, p. 106).

Looking to the future, Rossman and Bunning (1978) conducted a Delphi study in an effort to identify the future knowledge and skill requirements of successful adult educators. After surveying 141 university professors of adult education from the United States and Canada, they found that none of the 67 highest ranked knowledge and skill statements called for an adult educator to have knowledge about conducting research or to have skills in actually conducting research. In fact, only 2.6% of the responses to the fourth round of questionnaires listed "completing a thesis, dissertation, or similar work" as a suitable learning experience to develop the knowledge and skills required by tomorrow's adult educators (Rossman & Bunning, 1978: 152). It should be noted that these researchers did not restrict their study to the skills and knowledge required by tomorrow's adult education professors and researchers, but rather left the definition open, probably resulting in an emphasis on practicing adult education administrators and teachers.

The findings of this study are consistent with those of others who sought to identify competencies of adult educators and that characteristically did not reflect an appreciation for research competence. The perspective of Rossman and Bunning may be inferred from their recommendation that "The Utility of theses, dissertations and similar topics could be questioned in the professional preparation of most adult educators" (Rossman & Bunning, 1978, p. 153–154). No explanation was provided by the authors for their use of the word "most" though one might surmise that they were thinking about adult education professors and career researchers as exceptions. When graduate adult education is discussed in the literature, the author is most likely to be addressing the preparation or upgrading of

administrators and teachers and giving scant attention to the special requirements of future researchers and professors.

An even more distressing note regarding the importance of any kind
of graduate education for adult educators was reported in a 1981 survey.
Ingham and Hanks reported on a survey of 37 graduate departments of
adult education that they had conducted in 1977–78 which included the
respondents' perceptions of graduate education. They found that:

> The respondents recognize that the field has failed to accept the no-
> tion that training is required to become an adequate adult education
> practitioner. After fifty years of graduate studies in adult education, it
> is still possible for persons with no university training in the field to
> assume positions of leadership. The inability of graduate programs in
> the field to clearly established the superiority of the university-trained
> adult educator over the untrained one must be seen as a major failure
> of our graduate departments (Ingham & Hanks, 1981, p. 21).

Graduate adult education departments continue to be under considerable stress, trying both to acquire and maintain full acceptance within
the university context while at the same time striving to achieve validation by those who employ their graduates. The disparate and often
conflicting perspectives of professors, practicing adult educators, and
university graduate faculties present perplexing problems to the manag-
ers of graduate education for adult educators.

Some sense of the evolution of thinking about graduate study in adult
education is shown in a book Brookfield edited in 1988, bringing together a collection of previously published essays on the training of
educators of adults. He included articles that had been published between 1938 and 1986, showing the persistence of certain kinds of characteristics and problems endemic to such programs. Included in Knowles's
(1988) 1962 exposition on the theory of the doctorate in adult education
were four competencies, one of which was: Participation in the advancement of education which included ability to conduct and report original
research, a competency that would be acquired through guided experience in conducting and reporting original research. The fact that
Knowles himself had received a doctorate under the guidance of Cyril
Houle two years before he wrote the article may have had an influence
on his identification of appropriate competencies.

Two years later Liveright, another of Houle's students, identified five
attributes to be developed through graduate study in adult education, the
fourth of which was: "Zest for continued study which will steadily increase knowledge and skill required by practice" (Liveright, 1964, p. 98–

99). The fifth attribute was "Enough competence in conducting or interpreting research to enable the practitioner to add to human knowledge
through either discovery or the application of new truths." He stated that
the medical profession subscribes to the notion that "By the time a student has completed his undergraduate medical program, he should have
developed a genuine spirit of curiosity and be in possession of methods of
study which foster the accumulation of facts that lead to new knowledge
and the wisdom to utilize it" (Liveright, 1964, p. 99). Liveright then
expressed the view that "Because adult education is a new and emerging
profession and needs increasingly thoughtful and sophisticated research
in the areas of adult learning and teaching, it can hardly settle for less than
the research requirements established by the medical profession" (Liveright, 1964, p. 99). So, an appreciation for the acquisition of competence
in disciplined inquiry has been perceived as essential for practicing adult
educators by some authors for at least 28 years.

Chamberlain, yet another of those who studied under Houle, reporting on a survey to determine the perceptions of 90 leaders in the practice
of adult education regarding the importance of various concepts, skills,
and values, found that the ability to plan and to conduct research in
matters relating to adult education was ranked 38 out of a total of 45
items (Chamberlain, 1961, p. 78–83). Accordingly, it seems clear that
those who are providing leadership in the practical administration of
adult education programs neither have a high regard for research competence nor an appreciation of the value of acquiring those skills. Until or
unless such an appreciation is acquired, there will continue to be a
mismatch between the research competencies required in adult education doctoral programs and those regarded as useful and appropriate by
a significant number of those who are the potential employers of the
graduates of such programs.

The fundamental reason why administrators appear to have such a
limited appreciation of research skills has not been established, but
Daniel and Rose (1982), in examining the work of adult education practitioners, commented that:

> By expending all of their energy on practical problems, they are left
> without sufficient time, energy, or resources to attack the basic prob-
> lems. Included in the basic problems are those dealing with the adult
> as a learner, the field of adult education and what it is, the purposes of
> continuing education, the content of continuing education and re-
> search. Only by developing an understanding of basic problems in the
> field of continuing education can we be successful in working with
> everyday problems (Daniel & Rose, 1982, p. 77).

These authors reported that three-fourths of the deans and directors who responded to the survey ranked systematic inquiry skills as significantly lower in importance than did the adult education professors who had been surveyed by Rossman and Bunning in 1978.

As has been noted earlier, the nature of the research questions asked and the methods of research employed are heavily influenced by the nature of the professors in adult education graduate programs. Similarly, the amount of time devoted to designing, conducting, and reporting research by professors is likely to influence the perceptions of their graduates. Willie, Copeland, and Williams carried out a survey of the adult education professoriat in the United States and Canada in the 1980s. They reported that the 177 professors who participated in the survey said they spent a median of 10.4% of their time in research and scholarly writing (Willie, Copeland, & Williams, 1985, p. 62). They also found that 37.5% of the Canadian professors ranked research and professional writing as their primary source of job satisfaction while only 7.2% of American professors did so (Willie, Copeland, & Williams, 1985, p. 63). Nearly 70% of the respondents claimed they would like to be able to devote more time to research and scholarly writing and, not surprisingly, more than 50% indicated they would like to spend less time on committee work and administrative tasks (Willie, Copeland, & Williams, 1985, p. 62). Even those professors who appear to have an appreciation as well as a liking for research believe that the demands on their time precludes sustained involvement in research as a major activity. The examples set by the professors in terms of setting priorities may be a more powerful influence than anything major professors claim regarding the importance of research to adult educators.

TOWARD INCREASING RESEARCH PRODUCTION IN ADULT EDUCATION

Given the evidence in the literature on research training in adult education graduate programs, any effort to improve the situation will have to address the following three obstacles.

First, the Commission of the Professors of Adult Education as well as the Adult Education Research Conference have been devoting an inordiante amount of time to the interests of some members in adult education as a social movement and to efforts to stimulate their members to devote their efforts to working to produce social change. Although there is certainly a place for such social activism in the broad field of adult education, it is unlikely that such efforts will make a positive contribution to the perception employers of graduates of adult education programs have concerning the programs and the graduates. If the commission is to become perceived as relevant to potential employers of the graduates of its programs, it will have to develop ways of relating effectively to professional groups such as the National University Continuing Education Association, the Association for Continuing Higher Education, and the American Society for Training and Development. By confining its formal working relationships to the American Association for Adult and Continuing Education, the commission maintains a dialogue with individuals who already have a broad perspective of the field, but who may not be in major administrative roles where they are in a position to hire doctoral graduates. Further, the commission must initiate collaborative work with the Coalition of Adult Education Organizations, a group who, while not embracing the full gamut of adult education organizations, provide a continuing line of communication to the executive directors and elected leaders of a considerable number of the most conspicuous ones. Until the commission achieves a higher degree of credibility with the employers of its graduates and can present the value of its research in a convincing manner, it will continue to lack support from what might be considered its natural allies. Concern for the future employers is not simply a marketing ploy; it is a vehicle for designing research of demonstrable relevance to the most influential practitioners in the field.

Second, in 1981 Griffith and Roberts (1981, pp. 3–23) observed that adult educators seem to be action oriented and attracted more strongly by opportunities to act as change agents than to advance the frontiers of knowledge. They commented that the professors of adult education seem to lack experience in writing proposals for funded research and that lack of experience is a partial explanation of why that sort of activity appears more formidable to them than to more sophisticated researchers in other sectors of education and the social sciences. Accordingly, it would seem appropriate for such organizations as the Commission of Professors, the Adult Education Research Conference, and the Canadian Association for the Study of Adult Education to sponsor workshops at which professors could strengthen existing skills and acquire new insights into the most productive ways of securing funding for their research. The increased ability to obtain financial support could not only provide released time from other university duties, but also it could result in an expansion in the number of research-oriented fellowships that could be made available within ongoing lines of research.

Third, those professors who continue to believe that the study of adult education is an appropriate academic activity and who are not obssessed with the idea that adult education must be the world's sole engine of social change will have to prevent the further growth of the perception that adult education is first of all an ideology and that political correctness is required of all who wish to work in this field. The continued existence of adult education as an evolving field of university study is threatened both within the university by those who see it as excessively ideologically laden and from without by those who believe it is unrelated with the continuing problems and tasks that working teachers and administrators face. Balance is not only desirable; it is the new imperative for our times if adult education is to continue to be a field of university study.

So the importance of the actions of professors of adult education, singly and collectively, in shaping popular perceptions of adult education graduate study and research cannot be denied. Unless the professors have a clear vision of the future, those who enter graduate programs in adult education will be left to create their own.

IMPLICATIONS FOR MENTORING AND APPRENTICESHIPS

The relationship between professors and students is of special significance in adult education graduate study and should be examined with regard to two approaches: mentoring and apprenticing. Mentoring has become such a popular word that its meaning is as diverse as the interpretations of need as it is used in the adult education literature. For the purposes of this discussion, mentoring is defined as the process in which a senior member of an organization voluntarily provides advice and guidance to a junior member of the organization, who is not administratively accountable to the senior member, regarding the unwritten customs, traditions, procedures, and understandings that are believed to influence the junior member's career success in the organization. The advice provided by a major professor or research supervisor for a doctoral student would not be considered to constitute a mentoring relationship, although it might develop into a mentoring relationship following the awarding of the doctoral degree. But so long as the senior individual is in a position of formal authority with regard to the junior, the relationship would not be considered a mentoring one. Mentoring involves a purely voluntary, nonhierarchical relationship between a veteran and a relative neophyte. The mentor has knowledge of the established ways of behaving in an organization or profession, knowledge that is not available in written form in manuals or other orientation materials. A mentoring relationship can exist between professors of adult education located at the same or different institutions, providing that if they have a common employer, the junior is not administratively accountable to the senior.

Mentoring relationships arise naturally and voluntarily. They appear when two individuals share a number of values and have a genuine interest in an organization or profession. Usually there is an age difference with the older member being the one who has the experience that can be a resource for the younger one, though it is conceivable that in some situations chronologically age and years of relevant experience in an organization or association might be reversed in that the younger individual possesses the knowledge and insights that are lacking in the older party. The relationship depends on an acknowledgement of the existence of useful knowledge possessed by one party who is willing to share that knowledge with a second party who lacks, but appreciates the value of, that knowledge.

Although some attempts have been made to create formal mentoring relationships, these are artificial and distinct from those that arise spontaneously. "Big brothers" or "big sisters" in fraternities and sororities are examples of institutionalized approaches for the transmission of the organizational folklore, mores, and procedures. Some organizations assign individual senior members to "look out for" individual new members. Such assigned caring roles may or may not be effective depending on the nature of each of the parties involved.

Within the Commission of the Professors of Adult Education and within the Adult Education Research Conference there is sometimes a perceived antagonistic attitude between the well-established senior members of the group and the newer members. New members may have a desire to overthrow what they see as the old guard, preemptorily dismissing them as out of touch and out of date. Mentoring relationships can only arise where there is a condition of mutual trust and good feeling, so those who adopt a confrontational stance are likely to eliminate any potential opportunites to benefit from the wisdom of the more experienced individuals. Overly ambitious individuals may believe they can accomplish all they desire by themselves, but most thoughtful people realize there is a high degree of interdependence within any organization or profession. So, while there is no obvious way to legislate mentoring relationships, wiser members of both the senior and the junior groups would do well to reflect on the potential benefits of mentoring relationships and the possible costs of adopting stances that make it unlikely that such relationships will arise.

Although artificially contrived mentoring relationships may be less effective than those that arise spontaneously, it is likely that an organization that espoused the view that such relationships are desirable would increase the tendency of some members to be sensitive to the opportunites for establishing such relationships. Perhaps future research will reveal that mentoring relationships have been instrumental in developing the research leadership of the field, but at present the influence of such relationships remains purely conjecture.

The professor-graduate student relationship is more accurately described as an apprenticeship model than a mentoring one. Because of the unequal power of the two parties in the relationship and because the students voluntarily place themselves under the academic control of their major professors, the obligation of the professor is assigned by the employing institution and the students choose to place themselves under the direction of the professors. Professors at other universities acquire some knowledge of the strengths, weaknesses, interests, and personalities of their counterparts and so are able to make some assumptions about the nature of students who are able to work successfully with specific professors. So there is a value assigned to having studied with Professor X over having studied with Professor Y, and that value is a reflection of the status Professor X has acquired over a period of years. One's major professor is a fact that is widely known within the profession, though one's mentors are not a matter of public record.

Through the apprenticeship process, the master provides opportunities for the apprentice to gain guided experience in carrying out all of the essential operations of the profession, craft, or skill. Grantsmanship may be taught and learned through an apprenticeship with a master grantsman and is more likely to occur than if such learning must rely on a mentor. If a research-oriented mentality is a desirable goal of adult education graduate study, then there are compelling arguments for potential students to apprentice themselves to professors who daily demonstrate those qualities that the students hope to develop in themselves. It may be that a research perspective is caught more readily than it can be taught, and if that should be the case, both professors and students could profitably invest time reflecting on how to bring that about.

In summary, it seems clear that graduate programs in adult education are not always conducive to the development of a research orientation and the acquisition of skills in conceptualizing, conducting, and reporting research. Although the obstacles to improving the situation are formidable, they are not insurmountable. What is required are cooperative efforts and dedication on the part of those who serve in leadership roles so that collectively the quality, quantity, and diversity of adult education research will be increased for the benefit of all adult learners.

REFERENCES

Brookfield, S. (1988). Graduate adult education as a sociocultural product: A cross-cultural analysis of theory and practice in the United States and Great Britain. In S. Brookfield (Ed.), *Training educators of adults: The theory and practice of graduate adult education* (pp. 279–314). London: Routledge.

Chamberlain, M. (1961). The competencies of adult educators. *Adult Education, 11*(2), 78–83.

Commission of Professors of Adult Education. (1986). *Standards for graduate programs in adult education.* Washington, DC: American Association for Adult and Continuing Education.

Commission of Professors of Adult Education. (1964). Adult edcuation: A new imperative for our times. In G. Jensen, A. A. Liveright, & W. Hallenbeck (Eds.), *Adult education: Outlines of an emerging field of university study* (pp. iv–xi). Chicago: Adult Education Association of the U.S.A..

Daniel, R., & Rose, H. (1982). Comparative study of adult education practitioners and professors on future knowledge and skills needed by adult educators. *Adult Education, 32,* 75–88.

Griffith, W. S., & Roberts, P. J. (1981). Adult education. In J. H. M. Andrews & W. T. Rogers (Eds.), *Canadian research in education: A state of the art review* (pp. 3.1–3.29). Vancouver: University of British Columbia.

Houle, C. O. (1964). The emergence of graduate study in adult education. In G. Jensen, A. A. Liveright, & W. Hallenbeck (Eds.), *Adult education: Outlines of an emerging field of university study* (pp. 69–83). Chicago: Adult Education Association of the U.S.A..

Ingham, R. J., & Hanks, G. (1981). Graduate degree programs for professional adult educators. In S. M. Grabowski (Ed.), *Preparing educators of adults* (pp. 17–38). San Francisco: Jossey-Bass.

Jensen, G. (1964). How adult education borrows and reformulates knowledge of other disciplines. In G. Jensen, A. A. Liveright, & W. Hallenbeck (Eds.), *Adult education: Outlines of an emerging field of university study* (pp. 105–111). Chicago: Adult Education Association of the U.S.A..

Jensen, G., A. A. Liveright, & Hallenbeck, W. (Eds.). (1964). *Adult education: Outlines of an emerging field of university study.* Chicago: Adult Education Association of the U.S.A..

Knowles, M. S. (1988). A general theory of the doctorate in education. In S. Brookfield (Ed.), *Training educators of adults: The theory and practice of graduate adult education* (pp. 43–49). London: Routledge.

Knox, A. B. (Ed.). (1979). *Enhancing proficiencies of continuing educators.* San Francisco: Jossey-Bass.

Liveright, A. A. (1964). The nature and aims of adult education as a field of graduate education. In G. Jensen, A. A. Liveright, & W. Hallenbeck (Eds.), *Adult education: Outlines of an emerging field of university study* (pp. 85–102). Chicago: Adult Education Association of the U.S.A.

Merriam, S. B. (1991). How research produces knowledge. In J. M. Peters & P. Jarvis (Eds.), *Adult education: Evolution and achievements in a developing field of study* (pp. 42–65). San Francisco: Jossey-Bass.

Peters, J. M., & Jarvis, P. (Eds.). (1991). *Adult education: Evolution and achievements in a developing field of study.* San Francisco: Jossey-Bass.

Peters, J. M., & Kreitlow, B. W. (1991). Growth and future of graduate programs. In J. M. Peters & P. Jarvis (Eds.), *Adult education: Evolution and achievements in a developing field of study* (pp. 145–183). San Francisco: Jossey-Bass.

Rossman, M. H., & Bunning, R. L. (1978). Knowledge and skills for the adult educator: A Delphi study. *Adult Education, 28,* 139–155.

Rubenson, K. (1989). Adult education research: General. In C. J. Titmus (Ed.), *Lifelong education for adults: An international handbook* (pp. 507–511). Toronto: Pergamon Press.

Willie, R., Copeland, H., & Williams, H. (1985). The adult education professoriate of the United States and Canada. *International Journal of Lifelong Education, 4,* 55–67.

Wiltshire, H., Taylor, J., & Jennings, B. (Eds.). *The 1919 report: The final and interim reports of the adult education committee of the ministry of reconstruction 1918–1919* (reprint). Nottingham: University of Nottingham.

CHAPTER 8

THE FUNCTIONS AND UTILIZATION OF POLICY-ORIENTED RESEARCH

Kjell Rubenson

According to Premfors (1992) policy analysis as a field of knowledge and practice is characterized by the following features:

- The object of the analysis is government actions and their effects in view of some goal or set of goals. Unintended impacts as well as deliberate non-actions are included.
- The knowledge base of policy analysis is composed of both scientific and nonscientific knowledge. While the core is made up of a limited set of social science disciplines it also draws heavily on other disciplines and fields of professional practice.
- The aim of policy analysis is to contribute to the solution of public policy problems. A policy analyst works within the constraints of specific policy processes and always works for a client. The client does not have to be a government body, much policy analysis is performed by or on behalf of private organizations.
- Policy analysis is heavily value-laden and could be regarded as a form of ideology production rather than as value-neutral expertise. (p. 1907)

Policy research in adult education explores in a normative and prescriptive mode the concepts of policy formulation, implementation, and evaluation across systems and institutions. It addresses particular policy initiatives and analyzes the strategy of planned change and the nature and sources of resistance to it. Niece (1992) argues that there are three critical value components characterizing useful policy research: (a) a commitment to issue management, (b) a desire to stimulate perceptual change, and (c) a drive to obtain predictable and structural research outputs.

With the explosion in public funding for education in the 1960s, research became a regular aspect of the educational policy process, particularly in countries with a long tradition of grounding policy recommendations in social science research. The high expectations of the usefulness of policy-oriented social research promoted by politicians, researchers, and bureaucrats alike in the early post-War years were not met, and research and policy making came to be seen as having "an uneasy relationship" (Marklund, 1981). Consequently, the use, nonuse, and abuse of social research for policy making has become a field of research in itself (Anderson & Biddle, 1991; Bulmer, 1987).

The usefulness of policy research in education as well as adult education has been questioned not only with regard to policy making but also with regard to its contribution to scholarship (Hake, 1992). With this in mind, this chapter addresses some general issues on the function of policy research in decision making and its possible role in the creation of knowledge. The analysis starts with a general look at policy research that will be followed by a discussion of the possible role of policy research in the development of adult education as a field of study.

FUNCTIONS OF POLICY RESEARCH

The functions of adult education policy research can be classified into three broader categories: instrumental, conceptual, and legitimation.

Instrumental Functions

One important reason for the emphasis on policy-oriented research is the belief that it can be directly applied to policy decisions and practice. According to this view, adult educational policy research should among other things:

- give rise to new organizational models
- give rise to administrative rules and routines
- influence the curriculum
- introduce new instructional methods
- create new teaching aids.

In each of the above cases, research provides the facts, which are then used to inform policy decisions.

Weiss (1977) has called this approach the engineering or problem-solving model; it is illustrated in Figure 8.1.

Figure 8.1: The engineering model.

Husen (1985) reminds us that this classical "philosopher-king" model, where the research provides the knowledge from which policy makers derive guidelines for action, is problematic as it tacitly assumes consensus about goals. Further, there is ample evidence that research does not get used in this direct and pointed way.

Yet the instrumental position is deeply rooted in the traditional concept of Research and Development (R & D). Instrumentalism is based on the natural sciences and assumes a linear development from basic research via applied research and development to application of new technology. It assumes a positivistic view of knowledge and a trust in quantitative methods (Torgersen, 1986). As Weiss and others have pointed out, the social sciences differ fundamentally from the natural sciences and as a result do not tend to lend themselves to a linear transformation as assumed in the R & D process (Weiss, 1977). Further, the model is subject to criticism for making naive and simplistic assumptions about how policy and practice are determined (Weiss, 1987).

Conceptual Functions

The "conceptual position" developed as a criticism against the narrow interpretation of instrumentalism. The role of research is not primarily seen as coming up with a solution and/or answer to a specific issue but rather helps develop a broader understanding of the underlying problem. This involves widening the debate, reformulating the problem, clarifying goals, and analyzing eventual conflicts between multiple goals. Instead of being of direct instrumental use, the primary function of research is conceptual. What distinguishes this kind of policy-oriented research from "free" or basic research is not its theoretical sophistication or contribution to theory but how it has been initiated. Policy-oriented adult education research is initiated in the policy arena and addresses an issue that society has defined as being of relevance. As an example, we can point to the difference in Canada between the strategic (policy-based/initiated) and regular Social Sciences Humanities Research Council (SSHRC) research grants. The conceptual approach involves a shift from shorter R & D projects in adult education to long-term, university-based research programs giving emphasis to the relations between adult education and society as a whole (Marklund, 1981).

The conceptual position is in line with the "enlightenment" model that stresses the indirect and complex process through which social research has an impact on the policy process. According to Weiss, the major impact of social research on the policy-making process is not through a direct application of research to policy but through the way it, over time, comes to shape the way policy makers and administrators come to think about social issues (Weiss, 1977). The impact is not always intentional but comes about as a result of long-term involvement with social science concepts.

Legitimation Functions

The legitimation function of research refers to the fact that a research project can be initiated, not to find evidence that will lay the foundation for future policies, but to legitimate policy decisions already taken by those in power. Politicians are open to research results that support their positions but rarely want to hear about "objective research" that contests them. Research is used to confirm an ideological position. Thus, as Taylor (1981) maintains, the continued existence of policy-oriented studies may depend less on a real commitment to the value of research than is sometimes assumed. Another way that research can be used in a more encompassing political strategy is to initiate a project with the sole purpose of delaying action.

It is important to point out that the three functions of research discussed above are not exclusive, but that one would expect to find all of them in any one project. The issue becomes the balance among the three. Although there are strong reasons to be critical of instrumental research, it also has an important role to play. Problems occur when the only form of policy-oriented research is instrumental and when little or no attention is paid to developing or broadening the underlying issues.

USE, NONUSE AND ABUSE OF RESEARCH

Much of the discussion in the literature has concentrated on the underutilization of social research in public policy making. Whether adult education research matters is a question that is often raised. John Brademas, cosponsor of the creation of the National Institute of Education in Congress, stated (cited in Kaestle, 1993) that the purpose of education research "*is to enable the taxpayer to reap greater dividends on the investment of vast sums of public moneys*" (p. 23). According to Brademas, Congress often needs good information to write good laws.

Although not specific to policy research, there is a long-standing debate within adult education circles regarding the usefulness of adult education research. Knox (1985) notes that it is frustrating that few research and evaluation reports are read and that many practitioners are unaware of relevant research available to them. It is interesting to note that a Swedish Royal Commission on educational research found that the research findings were known and used at the policy level while instructors and administrators were skeptical as to its usefulness (SOU, 1980). However, in North America with its decentralized systems of adult education, it is instructors and administrators who are seen as the primary receivers of research information.

A common criticism of policy research as well as research in general is that it has hardly measured up to the challenge of communicating its theoretical knowledge to the adult education community in an intelligible and engaging manner. A common explanation is that this is partly because research information is excessively addressed to and designed for other researchers whereas the conveyance of information to practitioners and other interest groups is neglected (The Swedish National Agency for Education, SNAE, 1993). Thus, not surprisingly, Ekholm (cited in SNAE, 1993) found that only between 2 and 4% of the editorial material in the largest union-affiliated journals in the educational sector was related to research findings. Ekholm suggests that practitioners lack regular information from which they are capable of quickly, and without people having to read too much, providing an overview of what is emerging from research. While recognizing that much of the criticism of how researchers present their findings is relevant, it is doubtful if this in any major way can explain the under-utilization of research. As the chief author of the famous What Works pamphlet, Finn (cited in Kaestle, 1993) found out that *"print and the dissemination media, no matter how skillfully done, won't work"* (p. 27). The pamphlet presented recommendations validated by quite a lot of research, was written in good English, and was widely publicized but was soon forgotten by central administrators and school principals. What often has been seen as a dissemination problem is not really a dissemination problem. Instead, there is an increased awareness that the phenomenon cannot be fully explained by technical factors, such as the form in which research is published, but that it has to be understood in terms of (a) the lack of incentives for instructors to use research to change their practice; and (b) the very nature of social science research on the one hand, and the policy-making process on the other hand. It is the second phenomenon that is of particular interest for what is being discussed here.

Social Science Research

The underlying issue is the classic question of the differences between the social and natural sciences. One often-made claim is that the inability of the social sciences to develop generalizable knowledge limits their usefulness for policy making. Thus, economics is the social science discipline that has by far had the most direct impact on public policy. This is partly explained by the fact that economics is one of the very few social sciences where law-like scientific propositions exist. In parenthesis, it is of interest to note that in the area of national economic policy, the influence has been so great that Western economics can be said to have been restructured to fit the theories and methodolgies of economists. Without dealing further with the fundamental questions relating to natural and social sciences, it should be pointed out that it is often argued that the social issues are so complex that it would be wrong and even damaging to think that the natural science ideal of knowledge production would be appropriate. Further, although economic theory seemingly comes up with clear and parsimonious answers, these are embedded in normative values that need to be deconstructed.

Another point is that the various social science disciplines have become so specialized that they cannot address broad social problems that cannot be defined within narrow conceptual frameworks. An interdisciplinary approach is often promoted as an answer to this problem. The history of the policy sciences in North America can be seen as an attempt to tackle social problems through interdisciplinary research. However, despite much rhetoric, not very much has happened. In this respect it is interesting to note that is Sweden the shift from an instrumental to conceptual position in educational policy research was accompanied by an increase in the number of disciplines involved in this kind of research (Marklund, 1981). When the narrow R & D model dominated, almost all funds went to educational research departments, but with this increase, grants were also given to other social sciences, e.g., political science and economics.

Public Policy Making

The very nature of policy making is seen as an impediment against using research. Lynn (1978) states:

Policy-making is not an event. It is a process . . . During the various stages, policy-making does not usually wait for relevant knowledge to become available. Under the pressure of events and constituencies, legislation is passed, programs are started, regulations and guidelines are written and funds are authorized, appropriated and spent, whether or not relevant analysis and research findings are available. Indeed the process is often reversed. The systematic accumulation of knowledge may not begin until policies and programs are enacted. (p. 6)

The fragmented nature of policy making in conjunction with what Weiss (1987) has called the cognitive limits of government explains some of the limits encountered in using research rationally in the policy process. Instead, research affects the policy makers in more indirect and subtle ways, through an unsystematic incorporation of concepts, data, and generalization into the policy maker's way of thinking. That is to say that research has become part of the policy maker's tacit knowledge base.

A problem with the indirect way that research results are absorbed by policy makers is that much of what is absorbed may be distorted. Thus, the ways in which research influences the policy process can result in "endarkenment" as well as enlightenment. This emphasis on the indirect effects of research on policy makers does not deny the fact that research in some instances can have a direct and calculated effect on policy decisions.

Two-Community Hypothesis

Several authors have dealt with what is perceived to be the different cultures of research and policy making. Much of the discussion departs from what Price (1965) identifies as the politically relevant spectrum that goes along the dimension truth to power. Gustavsson (1984, p. 114) presents the Price spectrum in the following way, as seen in Figure 8.2

In the scholarly community, one strong position is that engagement in policy research will result in scholars abandoning the "truth pole" and instead become involved in politics. The purist position is embedded in the view that science is the highest embodiment of human rationality. The positivist paradigm with its notion of disinterested social science has come under severe attack during the last two decades. Looking at economics, where the various school ideologies are very apparent, the notion that research is value free becomes difficult to maintain. Swedish social science policy research, which has an international reputation for successfully deploying theoretical and technical skills in developing national policies, has by and large departed from a normative view congruent with the ruling Social Democracy's ideology.

Researchers	Professionals	Administrators	Politicians

Academic con-
sent as a source
of authority

Popular con-
sent as a source
of authority

ruth $\longleftarrow$————————————————————$\longrightarrow$ Power

Legitimate
claims for
institutional
autonomy

Illegitimate
claims for
institutional
autonomy

Figure 8.2: Gustavsson's presentation of the Price spectrum.

Accepting that research, in and of itself, can express certain normative values; the fundamental issue becomes how publicly supported social criticism (a fundamental role for research) can become compatible
with the principle of political democracy. Gustavsson (1984) provided an
illuminating perspective on the issue when he asked: "*What gives researchers paid by taxpayers' money, the right to put into question, during
working hours, the correctness of democratically made decisions?*" (p.
112). The issue is normative and has to do with how to make publicly
supported social criticism compatible with the principle of political democracy. The answer, according to Gustavsson (1984), rests in a paradoxical argument that goes as follows:

1. The aim of criticism is clarification and demystification with the
   intention to promote responsible action.
2. Political and other social actions claim to be responsible action.
3. Therefore, critical activities cannot themselves be subject to the
   demand for responsible action, while at the same time they are
   themselves bound by a demand to demystify. Thus in order to
   promote responsible action, critical activities must be irresponsible
   as far as their external consequences are concerned. (p. 112)

Combining the paradoxical argument with the general principle of self
management, that citizens' participation in society's governance must be
as large as possible, Gustavsson concludes that scholars with public
financial support but without political responsibility can and should devote themselves to criticizing the ends and the means that guide public
activities. This means that researchers would have the right to question
the very premises on which a policy rests. However, he argues, not only
do scholars engaged in policy research have the right to do what the

politically responsible cannot do, they have an obligation to do so. What deserves to be defended is the freedom of scholars to choose problems and methodologies and to publish freely, not the right to avoid working with normative problems.

THE TRADITION OF POLICY RESEARCH AND THE DRAWING OF THE MAP OF THE TERRITORY

An important question has to do with what role policy research is playing and could play in the development of adult education as a field of study.

What has been said regarding the relationship between social sciences and policy making has been general and we have to remember that it may differ between countries. These differences are linked to institutional arrangements of governance and their consequences for the policy-making process as well as the scientific disciplines. It is of interest, for example, that the development of adult educational research in Sweden was closely linked to the field becoming a major topic for public policy and that the primary function of university based research has been policy oriented. This can be explained by the Swedish tradition of having large research programs connected to parliamentary commission and of equipping central authorities responsible for any sector of society with R & D resources. Further, according to this tradition, any research work that a central authority needs to have performed should be entrusted to university departments and draw on the scientific competence of the universities.

Without going into a comparative analysis, it is evident that institutional arrangements of governance and the structure of knowledge production in education differ between countries. One obvious factor in Canada is the fact that education is a provincial responsibility. Canada, or the United States for that matter, do not have the Swedish tradition of sectoral policy research carried out mainly by university departments. Instead, it is more common that the research is done within government departments and agencies. This, for example, is the case with the literacy file where the secretaries of state and statistics of Canada have been the major players. Further, and very important, adult education has until recently not been on the policy agenda in North America and, therefore, not a target for policy research. Thus, it has not been the target for any royal commissions, an important vehicle for policy research in Canada.

It is therefore not surprising that when issues like relationships between theory and practice or disseminating and using adult education knowledge are being addressed in the North American literature, one commonly uses terminology like practitioners, professionals educators, instructors, and/or adminstrators but omitting policy makers (see e.g., Brockett, 1991; Cervero, 1991; Deshler & Hagan, 1989). This reflects the historical development of adult education as a field of study where issues relating to state, structure, and macro-micro relationships largely have been absent.

The tradition, or lack thereof, of policy research has influenced knowledge production in adult education; i.e., the drawing of the map of the territory can partly explain the differences between North American and European, particularly Scandinavian, research. Despite the fact that research in North America and Western Europe is equally instrumental in nature, there are rather obvious epistemological differences. Most obvious is the stronger emphasis on psychologically oriented theories in North America and, in relative terms, the greater preoccupation with social theory in Europe. This difference should be understood in the larger context of social and cultural traditions and the impact of these on research traditions (Popkewitz, 1984).

The United States, and Canada to a lesser extent, with their decentralized political and economic systems and individual emphasis on social mobility, promote a research focus on the individual. The strong emphasis on psychologically oriented theories by North American adult education researchers is in accordance with the dominant tradition in educational research in general. To use Kuhn's concept of paradigm at the meta-level, the tradition within adult education research is part of the dominant "Weltanschauung." The same is of course true of European research, the only difference being in the Weltanschauung that governs the research tradition. When the North American literature talks about practitioners, instructors and/or administrators are the usual target groups. Consequently, the process by which adult education has become a specialized field of study in North America has been linked to the professionalization of adult education.

The accumulation of knowledge has been based almost solely on efforts to improve the practice of adult education. Jensen (1964) reflected the pervasive conception of the territory when he argued that adult education is a practical discipline. Its ultimate goal is to give to adult education practitioners better control over factors associated with the problems they face. This view, to a large extent, has determined which questions have been regarded as legitimate within the discipline. Knox (1985), reviewing the situation in the United States 20 years after Jensen's commentary, reflected the same ethos when he stated, "One major reason for adult education research is to produce findings the practitioner can use to improve practice" (p. 183).

European research, while affected by the professionalization of adult education, has to a larger extent also been influenced by the broader policy level. Consequently, in search for knowledge to inform broad social policies, scholars have focused more on the political and societal realities and their implications for adult education practice. Thus, while adult education policy research has had a major impact on the drawing of particularly the Scandinavian map of the territory, it has had little effect on the North American map. In fact, in North America educational policy research is often see as detrimental to theory development

According to Andrews and Rogers (1981), who analyzed the situation in Canada, the main problem is not policy research as such, but the fact that most policy research is contract research and usually is not intended to contribute to generalizable knowledge.

Of those who do become involved in research, many feel an obligation to undertake contract research, which usually contributes directly to policy formation for specific operating agencies, such as Ministries or Departments of Education. Such policy research activities are highly important but they generally do not contribute greatly to the growth of generalizable knowledge and the development and teaching of new practices and programs. (p. 15)

A diametrically different view on educational policy research is expressed in the following quote from a description of The Swedish National Agency for Education's research program (SNAE, 1993):

The focus of the research programme is on long term commitments and a wider scope for research aimed at the development of theory and of concepts and conceptual systems which can be used in understanding school activities and preconditions and putting them into perspective . . . The demand for a theoretical basis means that research, unlike surveys and "everyday" descriptions must convey a knowledge of everyday realities which opens up new perspectives and offers new vantage points, and this in turn gives a critical function. In this way research can be both scientifically, developmentally and practically useful.

The Swedish position, although not denying the tension between the scientific community and the practitioner community, emphasizes the interdependence of policy research and basic research and the demand that they be conducted parallel within the same organization, the university. According to this view, policy-oriented adult education research, with its clear stipulation regarding implementation, can not be conducted without a cognitive base derived from discipline-oriented adult education research. The interdependence of the two kinds of research is such that policy-oriented research is designed to help broaden the selection of research problems in discipline-oriented research. Further policy research initiated by society must carry the same weight as research initiated by science.

Despite continuing advancement in the study of adult education (see the contributions in Peters & Jarvis's 1991 book Adult education for a comprehensive review), the graduate programs in North America as well as in Europe are threatened by the academic establishment for lack of scholarly sophistication, while at the same time the practitioners are somewhat doubtful of the usefulness of the research (Rubenson, in press). I have gradually come to the view that development in adult education toward the "conceptual position" of policy research, as laid out above, would be one step to remedy some of the problems facing the knowledge production in adult education. What I see as a major obstacle for a theoretical development within adult education as well as the production of "useful knowledge" is the often sharp separation that exists between theory development and empirical (qualitative as well as quantitative) research. The call against psychological reductionism and for integrating societal aspects into theoretical frameworks and studies has, judging from Long's (1991) recent review of the formal knowledge base, had limited effect. This is not to deny the developments that have occurred in connection with the introduction of critical theory into North American adult education (see e.g., Deshler & Hagan, 1989; Merriam, 1991). The problem, with much of the so-called critical literature, however, is that it is confined to introducing social theorists to an adult education audience, or that the analyses are purely theoretical, addressing issues related to various positions of leading social theorists. Valuable as it might be, it does little to inform the empirical research and, more problematic, the knowledge production as such is hampered by lack of a fruitful interplay between empirical research and theory development. Without this interplay, the scholarly literature in our field continues to mainly put forward normative positions without an interest in or the capability to study under what conditions the ideals could be realized.

Naturally, a development towards policy-oriented research of the proposed nature will to a large extent depend on the availability of funding for this kind of critical activity. However, it will also require a willingness to partly change the way we do research in adult education departments. There would be a need for more long-term research programs, integration of empirical studies and theory development, and a willingness and capability to attack "real problems." The reward could be an evolution of the formal knowledge base and increased relevance to the community.

REFERENCES

Anderson, D., & Biddle, B. (Eds.). (1991). *Knowledge for improving education through research*. London: The Falconer Press.

Andrews, J. H. M., & Rogers, T. W. (Eds.). (1981). *Review of educational research in Canada*. Ottawa: Social Sciences and Humanities Research Council of Canada.

Brockett, R. G. (1991). Disseminating and using adult education knowledge. In J. M. Peters & P. Jarvis (Eds.), *Adult Education* (pp. 121–144). San Francisco: Jossey-Bass.

Bulmer, M. (1987). The government context: Interaction between structure and influence. In Bulmer, M. (Ed.), *Social science research and government*. Cambridge: Cambridge University Press.

Cervero, R. M. (1991). Changing relations between theory and practice. In J. M. Peters & P. Jarvis (Eds.), *Adult Education* (pp. 19–41). San Francisco: Jossey-Bass.

Deshler, D., & Hagan, N. (1989). Adult education research: Issues and directions. In S. B. Merriam & P. M. Cunningham (Eds.), *Handbook of adult and continuing education* (pp. 147–167). San Francisco: Jossey-Bass.

Gustavsson, S. (1984). Where research policy erred. In P. Baehr & B. Wittrock (Eds.), *Policy analysis and policy innovation*. London: Sage Publications.

Hake, B. J. (1992). Remaking the study of adult education: The relevance of recent developments in the Netherlands to the search for disciplinary identity. *Adult Education Quarterly, 42*(2), 63–78.

Husen, T. (1985). Education research and policy making. In T. Husen & N. T. Postlethwaite (Eds.), *The international encyclopedia of education: Vol. 3* (pp. 1582–1588). Oxford: Pergamon Press.

Jensen, G. (1964). How adult education borrows and reformulates knowledge of other disciplines. In G. Jensen, A. A. Liveright, & W. Hallenbeck (Eds.), *Adult education: Outlines of an emerging field of university study* (pp. 105–111). Washington, DC: Adult Education Association of the U.S.A.

Kaestle, C. F. (1993). The awful reputation of education research. *Educational Researcher, 22*(1), 23–31.

Knox, A. (1985). Adult education research: United States. In T. Husen & N. T. Postlethwaite (Eds.), *The international encyclopedia of education: Vol. 1* (pp. 181–184). Oxford: Pergamon Press.

Long, H. B. (1991). Evolution of a formal knowledge base. In J. M. Peters & P. Jarvis (Eds.), *Adult education* (pp. 66–96). San Francisco: Jossey-Bass.

Lynn, L. E. (1978). The question of relevance. In L. E. Lynn (Ed.), *Knowledge and policy: The uncertain connection*. Washington, DC: National Academy of Sciences.

Marklund, I. (1981). Educational research in Sweden: Reform strategies and research policy. *International Review of Education, 27,* 105–109.

Merriam, S. B. (1991). How research produces knowledge. In J. M. Peters & P. Jarvis (Eds.), *Adult education* (pp. 42–65). San Francisco: Jossey-Bass.

Niece, D. (1992). *Empirical research and public policy: The literacy file.* Ottawa: Secretary of State.

Peters, J. M., & Jarvis, P. (1991). *Adult education: Evolution and achievements in a developing field of study.* San Francisco: Jossey-Bass.

Popkewitz, T. S. (1984). *Paradigm and ideology in educational research.* London: Falmer Press.

Premfors, R. (1992). Policy analysis. In B. Clark & G. Neave (Eds.), *Encyclopedia of higher education.* Oxford: Pergamon Press.

Price, P. K. (1965). *The scientific estate.* Cambridge, MA: Harvard University Press.

Rubenson, K. (in press). Disciplinary orientations in adult education. In T. Husen & N. T. Postlethwaite (Eds.), *International encyclopedia of education: 2nd edition.* Oxford: Pergamon Press.

Swedish National Agency for Education (SNAE). (1993). *Research programme.* Stockholm: Author.

SOU (Parliamentary Committee Report). (1980). Swedish Parliamentary Commission on Educational Research (in Swedish). Stockholm: Liber.

Taylor, W. (1981). Educational research and development in the United Kingdom: Framework, impact and future prospects. *International Review of Education, 27,* 179–196.

Torgersen, D. (1986). Between knowledge and politics: Three faces of policy analysis. *Policy Sciences, 19,* 33–59.

Weiss, C. H. (Ed.). (1977). *Using social science research in public policy making.* Lexington Books.

Weiss, C. H. (1987). Congressional committee staffs (do, do not) use analysis. In M. Bulmer (Ed.), *Social science research and government.* Cambridge: Cambridge University Press.

CHAPTER 9

THE FUTURE OF ADULT
EDUCATION RESEARCH

Adrian Blunt

In the discourse of adult education the word *research* has two meanings. It can mean a careful and systematic means of study or inquiry conducted with the intention to discover new knowledge and understandings; with this connotation research is considered to be a process. The word can also be used to refer to the accumulated body of knowledge or research findings, that is, to the product of the research process. This chapter is concerned with the future of adult education research as both process and product. As a process, research will be considered from the perspective of its epistemological and methodological foundations that together determine how research is conducted. As a product, research will be considered from the perspective of a map of the territory of adult education and the proprietary rights of investigators, both of which are factors determining what research outcomes are considered to be within the legitimate boundaries of adult education as a field of academic study.

Many futurists have pointed out that there is not one future simply waiting to arrive; rather there are many possible futures, and the ones that will occur are determined by the decisions made and actions taken by persons today. We create our adult education research futures just as we construct our realities of the current world. In the literature of adult education, articles speculating on the future have appeared at regular intervals. Malcolm knowles (1991), for example, has provided a view of a future where researchers experiment with chemically enhanced learning in a society where poverty, ill health and hunger have been eliminated. He does not say how adult education contributed to the eradication of social injustice and inequity. In the same text, Deshler (1991) presents a more thoughtful discussion of major social, professional, and academic issues that have influenced, and are likely to continue to influence, the future of adult education.

This chapter, unlike Knowles's, is not a science fiction attempt to forecast an adult education nirvana. Neither is the chapter an attempt to extend Deshler's analysis of influential events and issues to make specific predictions of the future. Instead the chapter attempts to achieve two different, and more fundamental, purposes. The first is to clarify and discuss some of the currently recognizable forces that influence both the conduct of the research process and the products obtained. The second purpose is to highlight the implications of those influential forces for the future of adult education research. The chapter concludes with an argument intended to persuade readers to act, within their spheres of influence in both adult education study and practice in ways that will contribute to the shaping of a dynamic and productive future for adult education research. The goal is a research future that will be both socially responsible and pedagogically and programmatically relevant in the field of practice and also significant in developing social research theory and in building knowledge in the academic discipline of adult education.

RESEARCH AS PROCESS

In medieval Europe, university students and faculty were able to study and teach abroad in the university of their choice, without having to be fluent in several national languages, because they spoke Latin, the universal language of academe and scholarship of that time. Thirty years ago the great majority of adult education graduate students and faculty in North America, excluding only a few historians and social philosophers, also used common terms, concepts, assumptions, and technical principles in their research. They shared the ubiquitous language of the social science disciplines of that time, the language of logical positivism.

Today, meetings of adult education researchers, and their discussions about how research ought to be conducted and the results disseminated, are characterized by division, disagreement, and occasional derision. The differences of opinion also extend to disagreements over what research problems ought to be identified as priorities and the usefulness of the research results produced to date. From a largely consensual enterprise employing one dominant, relatively uncontested view of method, discussions of research have shifted over the last 30 years to become complex, fractious, and politically divisive. The reality of the research enterprise today is that there are strongly competing views based on alternative research paradigms. Today researchers must not only present evidence that their projects comply with the tenets and rules of their methodology, they must also defend their choice of methodology against the attacks of colleagues armed with the "methodologically correct" views of their alternative, chosen paradigms.

Competing Paradigms

The reasons for the dissension lie in the widespread acceptance that there are alternative paradigms from which to choose, combined with the recognition that it is the ontological and epistemological foundations of the researcher's view of the world that directly influences the following: the definition of the research problem or phenomenon to be investigated; the choice of data collection and analysis procedures to be used; and the interpretation, generalization, and dissemination of the results obtained.

The essential assumptions and characteristics of two dominant alternative research approaches, *logical positivism* and *naturalism*,[1] have been delineated and popularized, sometimes incorrectly, by many writers (see for example Lincoln & Guba, 1985; Keeves, 1988). Logical positivism is generally described as a scientific or rationalistic approach to research that uses quantitative methods based on criteria for objective measurement and statistical analysis. Naturalistic research is referred to as a humanistic approach characterized by qualitative methods that avoid instrumentation and rely on observation to gather data within a natural setting. Positivism assumes a single tangible reality, observer objectivity, and the control of interactions through experimental and statistical techniques. Naturalistic research assumes there are multiple realities, observers ascribe meanings and interpretations to their observations, and the interaction between the observer and the subjects of the study is what yields insight. Naturalistic research has understanding as its goal, while positivism's goal is prediction and control. The popular expression of the two competing paradigms in the literature has been in terms of their data collection and analysis procedures quantitative versus qualitiative.

In an article reviewing research on teaching during the 1980s, Gage (1989) used the phrase "paradigm wars" to refer to the history of struggle among researchers to establish the methodological legitimacy of, and for many researchers the dominance of, their chosen research orientation: qualitative (naturalistic) or quantitative (positivistic). In a subsequent article, Rizo (1991) provided a more complete historical overview and traced the origins of the two competing paradigms to scientific thinking in the seventeenth century.

Positivism is no longer accepted as the sole legitimate paradigmatic view within a narrowly defined conception of the social sciences. Rather, naturalistic research, or as some authorities prefer, humanism or interpretivism, has emerged to challenge the boundaries of the traditional social sciences and to establish a more broadly defined and inclusive conception of social research. In the early 1980s, two decades after becoming a major focus for debate in sociology, the work of the Frankfurt school, and Jurgen Habermans in particular, appeared, challenging the views of the positivists and humanists with a third paradigmatic view, critical social theory. While incorporating their methodologies, critical theory rejects positivism and naturalism to focus upon the study of the structures of society that oppress, control, and prevent the achievement of social equity and justice.

Epistemology and method therefore became important and seemingly inseparable as areas of social research contestation with the stakes being escalated, by some, to include the legitimacy of research as a process of investigation and inquiry. The three paradigmatic views are presented as broad categories that, while they may incorporate all of the alternative methodologies in use, do not convey the full extent of difference of view currently held by adult education researchers in terms of methodological and epistemological criteria. Such a list of categories of research methods, working within any one of which has tended to restrict collaboration with researchers working in any other category, would need to include the following: interpretivism, critical social science, action research, cultural anthropology, hermeneutics, ethnography, behaviorism, empirical positivism, historical materialism and social phenomenology, among others.[2] It is apparent from the list that many categories cannot be thought of in purely methodological terms as they connote some aspect of epistemological position. How research will be conducted in the future is therefore inextricably linked to the eventual choices made by adult education researchers on the outcomes of current debates surrounding the paradigmatic struggles. As McLuhan aptly stated, "If I hadn't believed it, I would never have seen it" (cited in Rabkin, 1976, p. 14). Any consideration of the future of adult education research needs to take into account an analysis of factors influencing the likely ways in which future researchers will choose to perceive their world. The implications of these choices for the training of researchers and the conduct of research are fundamental to any discussion of the future of adult education research as a process.

Current Thinking in Adult Education

How have adult education researchers been informed about the paradigm debate through the two most recent major adult education texts that focus on the issues and concerns of the discipline of adult education, the *Handbook of Adult and Continuing Education* (Merriam & Cunningham, 1989) and the "new black book," *Adult Education: Evolution and Achievements in a Developing Field of Study* (Peters & Jarvis, 1991)? The answer is disappointing. While acknowledging the importance of the debate and its eventual outcome, researchers pay little attention to the details of the ideas expressed in the debate. Current literature in the broad field of education and the related social science disciplines where the debate has been dramatic, vigorous, and intellectually exciting appears to have been virtually ignored. Merriam (1991) clearly states the fundamental importance of paradigmatic views in shaping research and provides a succinct overview of the three broad alternative world views, or paradigms, that currently influence the process of research in adult education. The three paradigms she identifies are based upon Habermas's theory of knowledge (1971) and are labeled "the positivist, or empirical analytic; the interpretive; and the critical" (p. 43). However, Merriam does not directly address the question of what the likely outcome of the paradigm wars will be. She does strongly reinforce Gage's view that the moral imperative of adult education ought to be a strong influence on decisions made by researchers. Her suggestion to readers is that answers to the competition or coexistence question will emerge through research practice.

Deshler (1991), writing in the same text, observed that the contributors to the "new black book" did not "agree on the best paradigm" (p. 413). Again, the question of the likely outcome of the paradigm wars was not directly considered, although Deshler cites Kemmis's view that "The dispute is not just over methods. It is fundamental, and it is unlikely to dissipate soon" (p. 413). Neither the possible outcome of the wars nor the importance of the outcome for the future of adult education research are discussed in depth. Peters (1991), in a summary perspective chapter in the new black book, devoted a section under the heading "Research Paradigms" to a reflection on the views of the contributing authors. The section acknowledges the late arrival of the interpretive and critical paradigms to adult education research and the broader field of education and concludes that the three paradigms will continue to coexist in adult education, with the two newly established views gaining influence in the future.

Deshler and Hagan (1989) contributed a chapter dealing with adult education research issues and directions in the 1989 *Handbook of Adult and Continuing Education*. The chapter presented an analysis of the differences between positivistic and naturalistic inquiry and declared the debate between the debate qualitative and quantitative research methods to have been judged to be based on a false dichotomy. In a concluding remark, the writers commented that the dailogue between the positivistic and naturalistic views "promises to be vigorous in the future" (p. 150). At the time when the most vigorous debates over the two major paradigms in education and related disciplines appeared to have reached several important conclusions about the legitimacy and demise of positivism, the dangers of relativism in naturalistic inquiry, and the compatibility of empirical and ethnographic methods within the paradigms, the debate in adult education was being predicted to become vigorous.

The two most important texts containing extensive discussions of disciplinary concerns and issues in adult education have not given adequate consideration to the paradigmatic debate that has been a central issue in research in education and related disciplines for the last decade. None of the contributors to these two texts provided a summary of the epistemological analyses and an adequate analysis of changes that occurred in the debate during the 1980s. This chapter will now focus on the rich debate that has occurred in the broad field of education—space prevents a broader discussion of literature in related disciplines—to provide an overview of the major points of view and document the major shifts that have brought the paradigm wars close to resolution. Readers are encouraged to read for themselves the articles cited; they are well written, challenging, and intellectually stimulating and reflect a sense of scholarship, humor, and critique sadly lacking in the literature of adult education. It is my hope that readers will be persuaded by this belief report that the wars have ended.

The Paradigm Wars

It is not perfectly clear what the conclusion of the paradigm wars will bring. However, significant shifts in thinking have occurred in the last 10 years. Gage (1989) outlined three potential outcomes: the death of positivism, peaceful coexistence and cooperation, or continuance of the conflict. The outcome he preferred was the second, "an honest and productive rapprochement between the paradigms." His reason for calling for a speedy resolution of the wars was based on the moral obligation that educators have to society, and the seemingly failing recognition that improvement of the education system ought to be the dominant concern of researchers, not struggle over methodology.

Perhaps the strongest voices in favor of the continuance of the struggle during the 1980s are represented by the views of Smith and Heshusius

(1986), who saw no basis for compatibility and cooperation between the two approaches. Recognizing that a shift in the literature in favor of compatibility, cooperation, and even synthesis had begun to occur in the early 1980s, they called for a return to the struggle and a continuance of the debate:

> Given the fundamental difference in the approach to disagreement, if a quantitative inquirer disagrees with a qualitative inquirer, is it even possible for them to talk to each other? The answer for the present anyway, is a qualified no. . . .In the end the two sides may be close to speaking different languages—a neutral scientific or value-free language versus a value laden language of everyday discourse. Since it is not clear what kind of *via media* could be worked out between the two languages, it is all the more important to keep the conversation open. . . .[T]o avoid the conversation is to avoid issues at the core of the research enterprise and, for that matter, at the core of our contemporary intellectual, practical, and moral lives (p. 11).

Rizo (1991), responding to Gage, argued that from his analysis of the roots of the wars, traced to the 17th century, the most likely outcome was Gage's third possibility, continuance of the conflict. Further, Rizo disagreed with Gage's gloomy prognosis for educational research should the wars continue. Rather he saw the conflict as a source of intellectual stimulation, not an obstruction to research but a means to its progress: "By learning from old discussions, we will be able not to suppress but to surpass them" (p. 9).

According to Phillips (1983), it has long been recognized in social science research that positivism could be considered to have four branches: Comtean, logical positivism, behaviorism, and a positivism synonymous, but not legitimately so, with empiricism. The first branch, Comtean, died long ago, "but others are still alive in one form or another. And because each of the four are complex positions, even the ones that have died have not departed 'holus bolus'—bits and pieces of them have managed to escape the Grim Reaper" (Phillips 1983, p. 6). Using the allegory of the execution of the Romanovs and the persistent rumor that one Romanov, Princess Anastasia, survived, Phillips argued that not all branches of the positivism family had died, and the remaining family members were owed an inquest to ensure the legacy of positivism was duly recognized. In addition to claiming that elements of positivism persisted, Phillips pointed out that many of the celebrants at positivism's wake were more positivistic than they recognized. He also warned the postpositivist celebrants against the

174 / Research Perspectives in Adult Education

dangers of relativism. Eisner (1983), in response to Phillips, acknowledged that Anastasia might still be alive, "hiding out somewhere, or even walking among us" (p. 13). "But one thing is for certain, she is no longer royalty" (p. 24).

Although positivism had been declared dead 3 years earlier by Phillips, Garrison (1986), writing in the same journal, stated that "it is unlikely that anyone would want to suggest empricism is dead, or even mortal." Garrison's (1986) paper addressed the problems of relativism in postpositivist research arguing that the potential dangers of relativism might be reduced by "practicing the pragmatic virtues of epistemological conservatism and good sense" (p. 12). The recognition of epistemological weaknesses in the qualitative armamentarium clearly contributed to a reduction in the zeal demonstrated by some naturalistic researchers for further battle, and by the late 1980s prominent qualitiative researchers appeared to be in favor of rapprochement and the search for an overarching means of unifying the research enterprise in education.

Sherman and Webb (1988a) saw unification of education research as being achievable through a theory of inquiry which would first unify the methods of qualitative research and then unite the qualitative and quantitative research approaches. The elements of such a comprehensive theory of inquiry, they claimed, are located in the collective works of Dewey (1916, 1929, 1933, 1934, 1938). Although the individual contributors to their edited text (Sherman & Webb, 1988b) reflect the full spectrum of views the naturalistic research camp holds about the dangers of, and possibilities for, cooperation and the conplementarity of the two approaches to research, Sherman and Webb insist that, "considerations that qualitative researchers raise, and the question about worth and intent posed by philosophy, are as much a part of the discussion as are measurement and analysis" (Sherman & Webb, 1988a, p. 11). To illustrate how they think of research, Sherman and Webb claim that all research is qualitative "in origin and outcome" and is connected to, or imbued with, qualitative aspects at each step in the research process (1988a, pp. 18–19). This argument is directed at graduate students in particular and is illustrated with a view of how a traditional quantitative dissertation has a qualitative context from which it originates and toward which its outcomes are directed. Citing Rorty (1982), who interpreted Dewey's position as "a middle ground" which "inspired the social sciences in America before the failure of nerve which turned them 'behavioural' " (Rorty, 1982, p. 206), the editors state that they, and the authors in their text, "hope for a return to the middle- and moral-ground" (Sherman & Webb, 1988a, p. 18).

The Shift to Complementarity

As previously acknowledged by Smith and Heshusius (1986), for several years prior to Gage's call for closure, the debate in the early 1980s had begun to shift the two sides toward resolution of the struggle by identifying common concerns and recognizing weaknesses in the epistemological arguments of both positions. In the *International Encyclopedia of Education*, Husen (1985) argued that the scientific and humanistic paradigms were complementary, and the perpetuation of arguments about their incompatibility could not be sustained. The view that the two paradigms were compatible was based on the argument that the so-called epistemological difference between them were in fact unfounded and that, in fact, the two approaches shared the same paradigm and had similar methodological problems and goals.

Keeves (1988) also reviewed the epistemological arguments and concluded that:

In educational research, the conflict between proponents of the scientific and humanistic approaches to inquiry would appear to be without sound epistemological ground. We are then left with a variety of methods available for the conduct of research and an emerging synthesis in social theory that can guide research into educational problems. The methods employed in educational theory should then be determined by the nature of the problems being considered, and the questions investigated should be those that bear most directly upon these educational problems (p. 29).

Olson (1986), from his studies on the nature and consequences of literacy, concluded that psychological and educational theory had misconstrued the distinction between the natural and human sciences and their differences were based on their objects of study rather than on their epistemologies.

[T]here are not two epistemologies, one scientific-empirical and the other interpretive-hermeneutic. There are different domains for study and analysis but there is only one epistemology. That epistemology depends upon the structure of logical arguments relating a set of facts, evidence, observations, and textual structures, on the one hand, and theories, interpretations, constructs, models, and constructions on the other. Stated most generally, it involves claim/evidence relations aimed at explanations of events ranging from mechanical process to biological ones to human behavioral ones to human intentional ones (Olson, 1986, pp. 168–169).

A major implication of this argument is that methods in the interpretive and empirical sciences are similar and the "hermeneutic circle is just a description analogous to the hypothetico-deductive method" (Olson, 1986, pp. 169). Olson argues that to claim that they are more than that is misleading.

One basis for compatibility between the two paradigms was based on a rhetorical connection. Firestone's (1987) argument is succinctly stated in the abstract of his comparative report of two case studies of educational leadership, one quantitative and one qualitative.

> Quantitative methods express the assumptions of a positivist paradigm which holds that behavior can be explained through objective facts. Design and instrumentation persuade by showing how bias and error are eliminated. Qualitative methods express the assumptions of a phenomenological paradigm that there are multiple realities that are socially defined. Rich description persuades by showing that the researcher was immersed in the setting and giving the reader enough detail to "make sense" of the situation. While rhetorically different the results of the two methodologies can be complementary. (Firestone, 1987, p. 16)

The consistency and the closeness of fit between method and paradigm were, Firestone acknowledged, uncertain and required further study. He concluded that the selection of method was not a matter of seeking truth from one direction and selecting a research technique to suit a problem. However, the choice of method according to Firestone "is not as rigorously determined by the choice of paradigm as the purists suggest" (p. 20). Brewer and Hunter (1989) claimed that multimethod research had actually become a reality during the 1980s and was "planned, and conducted as a routine matter, part and parcel of normal social science" (p. 28). The reason for the arrival of multimethod research, a synthesis of research approaches, was the recognition among social scientists that:

> . . . solutions to research problems require more and different kinds of information than any single method can provide, and also that solutions based upon multimethod findings are likely to be better solutions—that is, to have a firmer empirical base and greater theoretical scope because they are grounded in different ways of observing social reality. (p. 28)

Transcending the Dichotomy

A further argument for the complementarity of application of the two research approaches has been provided by Salomon (1991), who identified a distinction between two approaches to educational research that transcend the qualitative and quantitative research paradigms. Beginning with an acceptance of the appropriateness of the two major research approaches, quantitative and qualitative, Salomon asks the question, "What is the deeper difference between the two kinds of research?" He argues for consideration of two new paradigms that distinguish between "research that suits best the study of casual relations among selected variables [analytic] and the study of complex learning environments undergoing change [systemic]." Then he attempts to determine what each approach contributed to a study of classroom learning.

> The systemic study . . . could not support the formulation of any clear functional relations, except in the most general and inexact way, but it could tell us how the *Pattern of interrelations* among classroom events changes over time. . . . [and] . . . studies which are based on the analytic approach fail to capture the richness, complexity, and *interdependence* of events and actions in the real classroom. (p. 16)

Salomon observed that the two approaches complemented each other in the sense that each approach informed and was able to provide guidance to the other. He concluded that, "As with the case of quantitative and qualitative research in education, cohabitation is not a luxury; it is a necessity if any fruitful outcomes are ever expected to emerge" (p. 17).

Critical theory has also been seen as a potentially unifying force of great relevance for education (Keeves, 1988). Because critical theory's processes are participatory, culminate in action, and focus social action on the achievement of equity and justice, Keeves thought that critical theory provided an alternative to the neutral scientific approach and the implicit relativism and conservatism of the humanistic or interpretive approach (p. 23). Keeves (1988) also refers educators to the work of Giddens (1984), whose detailed analysis of epistemological currents in four areas of social theory may provide a unifying framework for social inquiry in the future.

Giddens's theory of structuration, according to Keeves, recognized that four important advances had been made to change traditional views in research regarding the natures of the human agent, language, social action, and the double hermeneutic. Structuration theory allows the use of empirical methods by researchers and practitioners not to explain and control, but to describe and interpret. According to Giddens (1984), social research has "a necessarily cultural, ehtnographic or 'anthropological' aspect" (p. 284); needs to be "sensitive to the complex skills which actors have in co-ordinating the contexts of their day-to-day behavior"

(p. 285); and must "also be sensitive to the time-space constitution of social life" (p. 286). In addition, structuration theory is incomplete if not directly linked to critical theory (p. 287). The quantitative—qualitative debate is seen from Giddens's perspective as a nonissue; the two approaches experience similar epistemological problems and should be seen as complementary rather than in opposition. Giddens distances his project from positivism and avoids the epistemological debates by focusing on ontological concerns, the subject matter of social scientific knowledge (Cohen, 1987).

Also recognizing the possibility to move beyond complementarity and cooperation, House (1991) raised the prospect of a synthesis of all three "paradigms" to be achieved through a new philosophy of science he identified as scientific realism. According to House, the nature of science itself has been misunderstood and a new understanding may allow for an approach to educational research that incorporates the essential elements of all three current paradigms, "an approach that is scientific, the incorporates the perspectives of participants, and that leads to social justice—but which is superior to any of these positions."

Yet another proposal for "getting over the quantitative-qualitative debate" has been presented by Howe (1992), who sought to expand the debate by referring to perspectives on human nature and on the relationship between theory and practice. Howe's views are instructive as he commences his argument by noting that educators have accepted the practice of combining quantitative and qualitative techniques and procedures, although the combining of the epistemological paradigms "remains incoherent." Howe argues not for the combining of the two perceived epistemologies, but for their dismissal and replacement by a critical social science research model, a model not to be equated with the critical theory of the Frankfurt school. Howe illustrates his interpretation of the critical science research model from the work of Apple (1988) and of Smith and Shepard (1987) and argues that the model demonstrates compatibilism, or the borrowing of the essential features of positivism and interpretivism:

[C]ompatibilism borrows from the natural model by acknowledging the uneliminable role of *mechanistic* explanations (explanations in terms of unwitting, unseen, and unplanned causes) of social structures and individual behavior, like the working of the economic system: compatibilism borrows from interpretivism by acknowledging the uneliminable role of *intentional* explanations of social structures and individual behavior, like the reasons parents might give for sending their children to a fundamentalist school (Howe, 1992, p. 243).

The Future for Research as Process

The purposes for the preceding sections of the chapter were first to illustrate how social science researchers constructed the two major paradigms of logical positivism and naturalism and engaged in adversarial relationships based on their choice of paradigm, and the related quantitative or qualitative research methods, in order to achieve dominance for their particular paradigmatic view. Second, by referring directly to literature from the paradigm debate, the chapter sought to persuade readers that there is sufficient evidence to warrant the abandonment of the belief that researchers must continue to commit themselves to conduct their research from only one paradigmatic view, a commitment that requires slavish adherence to a few prescribed research methods. Readers who at this stage may wish to persist in their belief that the paradigms are, and must ever be, in opposition and that positivism remains a threat to naturalistic inquiry and "correct" research are urged to read Phillips's (1992) *The Social Scientist's Bestiary: A Guide to Fabled Threats to, and Defenses of, Naturalistic Social Science.* The following quotations from that text are presented as final rhetorical volleys to persuade readers that an honorable peace is at hand if we choose to observe it.

Nowadays the term "positivist" is widely used as a generalized term of abuse. As a literal designator it has ceased to have any useful function—since those philosophers to whom the term accurately applies have long since shuffled off this mortal coil, while any living social scientists who either bandy the term around, or are the recipients of it as an abusive label, are so confused about what it means that, while the word is full of sound and fury, it signifies nothing. (Phillips, 1992, p. 95)

As for those researchers who persist in tilting at the imagined dragons of positivism, Phillips dismisses them as being delirious and their concerns as delusions.

(When one is confused, or suffering from delirium, it is possible to see *anything.*) Displaying what often amounts to an embarrassing degree of philosophical literacy, the [anti-positivist] vigilantes rarely bother to distinguish between classical (or Comtean) positivists on the one hand, and the even more nefarious logical positivists on the other; furthermore, they use a number of faulty criteria, either singly or in combination, to identify their illusory foe. The general fantasy is that anyone who is impressed by the sciences as a pinnacle of achievement of human knowledge, anyone who uses statistics or numerical data, anyone who believes that hypotheses need to be substantially warranted, anyone who is a realist . . . is thereby a positivist. (Phillips, 1992, p. 95)

Researchers have been reminded that it is essential that the purpose of research in an applied field of study not be forgotten, As Gage (1989) has stated for education broadly, and Merriam (1991) has stated for adult education in particular, the question of whether paradigms must be competitive or whether they can co-exist, fades in importance when set against the larger moral imperative of practice. While this is a compelling argument to motivate many adult education researchers to abandon, or ignore, the paradigm wars, it is important to recognize that the adult education literature has not provided an insightful analysis of the opportunities that have been identified to close the debate nor has it identified potentially valuable directions for research in the future.

Issues in the "paradigm wars" have become fundamental concerns in the intellectual work of researchers and, whether they wished to or not, each researcher has to some extent become engaged in the struggle, or been disarmed and immobilized by it. Practitioners, on the other hand, influenced by the essential pragmatism of their work, have remained dismayed and unsympathetic observers. Widespread dissatisfaction now exists among practitioners about the seeming distraction of researchers with the demands of methodological issues (methodological correctness) while pressing problems in the field of practice are ignored or unrecognized.

Brewer and Hunter (1989) consider it to be no accident, nor the result of objective logical analysis, that the current generation of researchers have held such partisan beliefs about research and acted in such adversarial ways:

Research styles are not simply the result of individual choice or idiosyncratic aesthetics. Rather they are socially embedded in intellectual communities, networks of like-minded practitioners. The selective socialization, training, and proselytizing within these communities gives mutual support but at the same time it perpetuates structural cleavages and conflicts among practitioners of different styles; or at best, differentiated indifference. (p. 26)

Since the research process reflects the skills, value orientations, and beliefs of researchers acquired in adult graduate training programs, decisions made today about the training of graduates are decisions that will shape the conduct of tomorrow's research. To develop graduate training programs for the future, we need to think about ways of moving beyond the unnecessarily confining perspectives of the current monoparadigmatic views that typify the approach of most researchers in adult education today.

It ought also now to be obvious that a focus on the technical aspects of research, the dominant focus in most graduate research classes, does not lead directly to the construction of theory or the solution of problems of practice. It needs to be recognized that an understanding of the ontological and epistemological foundations of adult education research are required if we are to extricate ourselves from the current snares of method and tangles of paradigmatic purity. How ought departments to provide research training that will enable adult education researchers in the future to acquire state-of-the-art skills in social science research methods and to think clearly about how adult education research questions are embedded in the ways in which we view our world? Who will train the next generation of researchers when much of the expertise required lies in the related disciplines and adult education maintains such a strong isolationist stance?

Four conclusions can be drawn from this brief and selective review of the literature addressing the debate over paradigmatic issues and its influence on research processes:

1. A consensus has emerged in education and related disciplines that the debate over the epistemological distinctions between quantitative and qualitative research can now be left to social research philosophers.
2. Methodology need no longer be a site of struggle when the paradigmatic assumptions underlying the statement of the research question and the selection of techniques for data collection, analysis, and reporting are recognized and respected.
3. The adult education research literature has not adequately informed readers on the conduct of the paradigm debate, its outcomes, and the emerging opportunities for new research directions.
4. The future of adult education research as a process hinges on how the next generation of researchers will be socialized into the discipline and trained to conduct research. Preferably that training will feature interparadigmatic views and multimethod approaches.

RESEARCH AS PRODUCT

Tornebohm (cited in Rubenson, 1989) used the metaphor of cartography to demonstrate how the epistemology of a discipline can be used to define its territory. As research is linked with aspects of the real world, the cumulative knowledge produced by research may be regarded as "an authorized map of the territory." Applying Tornebohm's notion of episte-mological mapping, Rubenson (1982, 1989) has drawn attention to the focus that influence the drawing of the map of adult education's terri-tory. By considering the question of what forces influence the napping of a field of study, it is possible to reflect on what may need to be done if future cartographers of "terra adult education" are to more clearly de-fine its political borders, better depict the topography, accurately locate its residents, sketch the distribution of resources, and trace its communi-cation networks.

This section of the chapter will briefly review Rubenson's work to consider the criteria he identified and his assessments of how they have influenced the mapping of adult education. The criteria are then revis-ited to consider more recent evidence, which in turn is used as a basis to discuss the potential of the criteria to influence the mapping of adult education's knowledge base in the future.

Rubenson (1989) poses two questions to assist in identifying the deter-minants of adult education's epistemological map:

a) Which assumptions and perceptions of the territory govern the efforts to accumulate knowledge within adult education, that is, which questions are regarded as legitimate within the field?
b) Which research traditions (scientific ideals and perspectives) gov-ern research in adult education? (Rubenson, 1989, p. 508)

With regard to the first question, Rubenson concluded that three factors needed to be considered: adult education as a field of practice, adult education as an eclectic interdisciplinary field of study, and the disciplinary focus of the research questions posed. Rubenson observed that the pragmatism of adult education as an applied field of social practice has been a major determinant of the legitimacy of research activities and products. Between the late 1950s and the mid-1970s adult education in North America experienced a rapid growth of participation in programs and a strong commitment toward professionalization. These forces resulted in early adult education research efforts being focused on program needs and pedagogical concerns. Applied research, that is re-search directed toward resolving problems of practice, has dominated adult education research efforts, and the agenda of the field of practice has determined the legitimacy of the intellectual work of researchers and the products of the research enterprise.

As for the early eclecticism of adult education research, Rubenson considers it to have been displaced by a strong intradisciplinary focus. Particularly in North America, the products of adult education research have reflected an isolationism from other social science disciplines.

Regarding the third factor, the disciplinary focus of the research questions posed, Rubenson observed that in North America the dominant influence has been psychology, while in Europe it has been sociology. The governing research traditions in adult education, Rubenson noted, had become more firmly established due to increases in research productivity and the use of more sophisticated empirical techniques. The increase in productivity, however, was achieved without the quality of research having been sustained at levels equivalent to that of research in the related disciplines.

In summary, Rubenson concluded that the development of the map of the territory of adult education had been: limited by a focus on practicality and an attitude of anti-intellectualism; defined, in North America, by a psychological emphasis on the individual learner; validated by an increasingly intraspective focus; and developed in a climate of international isolationism.

Since Rubenson's analysis, originally conducted in the late 1970s (Rubenson, 1979), there have been developments that need to be considered and incorporated into the current assessment of the state of the mapping enterprise. This review is needed to provide the basis for a consideration of the possible futures for research as product.

Adult Education as a Field of Practice.

Rubenson's observation (1979, 1982, 1989) that research in adult education has largely been applied research focusing on program and administrative problems has been widely shared for some years (Copeland & Grabowski, 1971; Dickinson & Rusnell, 1971; Long & Agyekum, 1974; Long, 1980; Deshler & Hagan, 1989). The question remains, therefore, whether pragmatism will continue to be the dominant determinant of the legitimacy of adult education research questions.

Rapid social, technological, and economic change continues to sustain and extend the need for adults to learn throughout their lives. Increasingly, societies are moving to provide more formal and informal opportunities for adults to continue to learn. Lifelong learning is widely expected to become ubiquitous, with the home, community, and workplace environments experiencing technological and social changes that make them more effective learning environments. In addition to the "work force" as a labor market category, there is now an emerging "learning force" comprised of adults engaged in full-time and part-time study while on leave from, or deferring entry into, employment.

Professionalization of adult education also appears to be continuing, and while funding pressures on universities may serve to limit the expansion of adult education graduate programs, community colleges and other institutions have the capability to extend their training programs to meet the needs of society to train adult educators, should that become necessary. With a continuing expansion of participation in adult, continuing, and postsecondary education, it is unlikely that demands from the field of adult education practice for research to continue addressing its concerns will diminish.

Often, graduate students are people who have returned to a university to obtain a degree after several years of experience in the work force. Many hold jobs and wish to study part time; others have taken leave from positions in adult education and related fields to which they intend to return. In their graduate programs students frequently choose to study problems or questions they had originally identified in the work place. With the continuance of a strong field of practice focus, it is higly likely that graduate research, particularly at the master's level, will continue to be characterized by practice relevance and pragmatism. Interest in basic research among graduate students is more likely to be located among doctoral students, yet even here it is likely that applied research will continue to predominate.

However, a gradual decline of applied research conducted by faculty may occur as the next generation of university-based researchers start their careers. University adult education researchers have traditionally experienced a "Catch 22" situation, with practitioners holding a negative attitude toward research as they have judged the results to have contributed little of value to practice, and at the same time the reputation of adult education researchers in the university community has suffered because of their focus on applied research.

Should university reward systems continue to place a greater emphasis on research and scholarly writing as the main criteria for promotion and tenure, it is likely that the research interests of new faculty will focus accordingly on the research that is most highly valued in academe—that is, on basic research, the search for knowledge without regard to immediate and apparent utility. Although governments are urging universities to focus on teaching and research to achieve national economic goals, it is not likely that there will be any greater shift to the adoption of government research agendas unless additional funds are contributed. Yet as the ongoing review of the role of the university in the 21st century proceeds in both North America and Europe, there is growing recognition that governments do not wish to continue funding universities to the extent they have done so previously and new postsecondary institutions have the capability to perform, at lower cost, some of the less traditional and less scholarly functions of the academy. Under these circumstances, the responsibility for training adult educators may begin to shift toward community colleges and new, smaller universities specializing in professional programs for human service workers. This move could result in a two-tiered system, with new institutions focusing on applied research and the traditional university programs of adult education perhaps focusing more directly on basic research.

Graduated with research skills who return to the field of practice may in the future choose morre frequently to be continuing producers of applied research rather than simply consumers of research, as they presently tend to be. Several writers have drawn attention to the interests of graduates in conducting research in the adult education workplace and the need to support that activity in adult education institutions (Ostrowski & Bartel, 1985; Thomas, 1989). Workplace research may also become more widespread if university graduate programs begin to consider more carefully the processes through which knowledge is produced and disseminated. A catalyst may be recognition of the value of teaching applied research skills with the intention of achieving similar applied outcomes as the skills that are currently taught in needs analysis, program planning, teaching, and evaluation courses. The academic thesis, for some students, may legitimately be replaced by more contemporary forms of research report appropriate for dissemination by electronic means or desktop publishing.

It would appear likely, therefore, that the current state of imbalance within the adult education research enterprise with regard to applied versus basic research will not change. Applied research can be expected to continue to be the dominant force in shaping the product of adult education graduate research for the foreseeable future.

Adult Education as an Interdisciplinary Field of Study.

In 1959, Brunner and his associates (Brunner, Wilder, Kirchner & Newberry, 1959) observed that most of the research in adult education had been conducted by social scientists. Jensen (1964) recognized the importance of the research conducted in other disciplines and argued that the borrowing and reformulation of knowledge from related disciplines was an important strategy for the development of a knowledge base for the emerging discipline of adult education. In part Jensen made this argument because he recognized the pressure that was placed on adult education researchers by the field of practice to contribute to the solution of problems experienced by practitioners. He referred to the professional fields of engineering, social work, public health, and law, among others, to highlight their experiences as recently established fields of academic study engaged in building a disciplinary knowledge base. Twelve years after the comments of Brunner and his colleagues, Copeland and Grabowski (1971) reported that an increase in the number of adult education graduate programs had contributed to an increase in the number of adult education researchers as well as the quantity and quality of adult education research. With regard to the future role of other social science disciplines in the further development of adult education knowledge, the writers were unequivocal in recognizing the value of an interdisciplinary research focus:

> While the proportion of adult education research conducted by adult educators is increasing, researchers in the social sciences continue to make important contributions. In our opinion, these contributions should be encouraged because of the social science foundation on which much of the practice in the field is based. Providing adult education problems and settings for social scientists to investigate and forming teams of adult education researchers offer two ways whereby the quality of research in adult education will steadily improve. (Copeland & Grabowski, 1971, p. 25)

It appears that as the number of adult education researchers and the quantity of research produced continued to increase, university departments of adult education sought to strengthen their claim for academic recognition and status and to strengthen the professional status of the adult education practitioner by focusing attention on the uniqueness of adult education research and the importance of acknowledging independence from the other disciplines of those who produced it. Long (1980) traced the discussion of the competing needs for adult educators to conduct both basic and applied research through the literature to the 1950s, when the proposal was first made by Whipple to "separate adult education from the graduate school and make it a professional element in the university structure similar to schools of medicine and law" (Long, 1980, p. 12).

Long (1980) also documents the views of the Commission of Professors of Adult Education and some of its individual members during the 1960s regarding the reduction of dependence of adult education on research produced by other social scientists. The commission's official strategy was to promote the discovery of new knowledge by adult educa-tion researchers, and, in addition, to continue the testing and interpret-ing of knowledge developed by othere social scientists.

During the 1970s and 1980s, the argument to separate adult education knowledge production from its origins and maintain an independent status for adult education researchers was strongly sustained. Boyd and Apps (1980), in their conceptual model of adult education, sought to redefine adult education as a field of academic study and prescribed a process for knowledge production within it that (a) commenced with adult educators developing the conceptual bases for the field; (b) later, incorporated knowledge from the social sciences within the conceptual frameworks; and (c) throughout, resisted the possible definition of adult education by other disciplines. Their position was based on four errone-ous assumptions they believed were made by Jensen (1964) in his pro-posal that adult education borrow and reformulate knowledge from other disciplines.

The four erroneous assumptions made by Jensen, according to Boyd and Apps (1980), were "First, that concepts from other disciplines can be applied directly to adult education without specifying situational vari-ables. Direct appropriation is an error because the disciplines, usually seen as sources of concepts for adult education, developed their con-cepts without concern for adult education" (p.3). The second erroneous assumption was that concepts can stand alone. Boyd and Apps wrote: "But concepts do not have an existence independent of the theoretical framework in which they were developed" (p. 4). Third, it is erroneous to believe that concepts can be combined. "Unless one is fully versed in the basic assumptions that structure the theoretical frameworks, one may be trying to combine assumptions that directly contradict one an-other" (p. 4). "The fourth erroneous assumption, probably the most serious, is that disciplines can define adult education. By borrowing heavily from other fields of study to define and solve problems faced in adult education, we are allowing those disciplines to define adult educa-tion for us" (p. 4).

It must be difficult for researchers with backgrounds from the more rigorous disciplines of sociology, psychology, philosophy, economics, and history to take seriously Boyd and Apps's use of these so-called erroneous assumptions as a basis for proposing disciplinary isolationism. Failing to recognize assumptions, applying concepts inappropriately, and fearing that the work of other social scientists may contribute, in some negative manner, to the definition of one's discipline are facets of bad social science research practice. Certainly there is an important point to be made that Jensen (1964) did not alert readers to the potential problems of interdisciplinary misappropriation of knowledge. However, Boyd and Apps did not cite one example from 50 years of adult education research to demonstrate an example of an error that had actually occurred, and which they were so afraid might, and were so convinced would, occur in the future. Instead they presented a hypothetical case of what might occur at some time if adult educators persisted with the idea of adopting and adapting knowledge from the more rigorous disciplines before adult education had fully conceptualized and defined itself as a discipline.

Boyd and Apps (1980) moved beyond pointing out the potential for error and based their rationale for distancing adult education as an emerging discipline from other established disciplines solely on fear of bad social science practices. Their argument was that Jensen did not recognize the dangers of misappropriating knowledge from other disciplines and errors could be made through ignorance or lack of vigilance, so it is best not to encourage attempts to appropriate knowledge from other disciplines. This argument does a disservice to adult education research and serves to suggest that an antiintellectual culture may have pervaded the post-black-book period of disciplinary expansion.

Rubenson (1989) also has challenged Boyd and Apps's view, pointing out that "it is in the effort to understand the structure, the function and the problems of adult education that help from a number of disciplines is needed" (p. 509) That Boyd and Apps's argument is still taken very seriously by Peters (1991), among others, serves to illustrate the depth and extent of the conviction held by some, that adult education's best interests are served by isolationism. In the "new black book" edited by Peters among others (Peters, Jarvis, & Associates, 1991) six authors each contribute a chapter addressing the multidisciplinary dimensions of adult education. Not one of the six authors refers to Boyd and Apps's objections to disciplinary borrowing. Tennant (1991) documents how psychology has been a source of knowledge to "inform, guide and justify" adult education practice (p193). He argues for psychology to be accepted, not uncritically, and afforded a prominent but not pre-eminent position in adult education. Knox's (1991) chapter dealing with educational leadership and program administration promotes the incorporation of "generic ideas from related fields with pertinent ideas from adult education". The lack of influence from sociology, according to Griffin (1991), has limited the development of adult education. Sociology he claims is essential for an understanding of the significance of adult education in the lives of people. Philosophy according to Lawson (1991) is foundational to adult education, "In my view, the most influential ideas are those drawn from outside adult education, since, I believe adult education knowledge cannot develop without reference to them" (p 297). Political science and adult education have a mutual relationship in Thomas' (1991) view, and Stubblefield (1991) offers a rationale for the inclusion of history in adult education graduate programs based on "the nature of history as a discipline and its value as a way of learning" (p. 323). It is quite interesting therefore that Peters (1991) chooses in a concluding chapter to balance the views of these authors by reminding readers of alternative positions and concluding that adult education's scholars remain ambivalent about the most desirable relationship with the related disciplines.

Plecas and Sork (1986) have referred to adult education as an "undisciplined discipline" and have argued that, to effectively build a discipline, adult education researchers must first agree on a central focus for adult education and second, must conduct research cumulatively to build a theoretical foundation in relation to that focus. The focus for adult education they proposed be accepted was stated as:

[T]he primary phenomenon under study would be organized learning, with the goal of the discipline being to develop a body of knowledge relating to how learning can be best facilitated given various adult learner populations and various social and political conditions. (pp. 58–59)

For Plecas and Sork, the question of an interdisciplinary or intradisciplinary focus then becomes the pragmatic problem of considering the extent to which adult education researchers can reasonably expect to have a thorough understanding of the intellectual property of other disciplines.

Should adult educators be dabbling in questions about what individuals and organizations can or ought to do to effect social and political conditions when the expertise on social and political theory and research is more likely to be found in the disciplines of sociology and political science and their respective literatures? (p. 54)

Unless research contributed to an understanding of the interactive relationship between adult learning and instruction, Plecas and Sork would consider it to be beyond the boundaries of adult education research. Their call for disciplinary focus is a call for goal conformity that, if it does not become an imposed orthodoxy, is more intellectually acceptable than the call for isolationism as it serves to be less exclusionary. Researchers can argue their claims to interdisciplinary expertise and the interdisciplinary legitimacy of their work within Plecas and Sork's focused framework, while the exclusionary framework of isolationism serves to silence or deny a voice to outsiders and to insiders attempting to see outside. Unfortunately, I suspect that a significant number of adult educators would wish to pursue Plecas and Sork's proposal to the point of establishing it as an orthodoxy to serve the purposes of a hegemonic "disciplinary cleansing" in the pursuit of professionalism.

Assuming a more consensual adoption, Plecas and Sork's proposal might assist the discipline's cartographers to develop a useful map of the "safe terrain"—a map of "terra adult education" that has been settled, developed, and defended. It may also serve to be the basis for a smaller scale map of the surrounding frontier regions, "terra nova" where disciplinary access has been established, claims have been staked, jurisdictions are shared, the rights of others are respected, and rugged intellectual individualism is accepted. The preferred reading of researchers in these regions would more likely be, for example, Gramsci (1971) and Freire (1973; see 1993) than Boyd and Apps (1980b) or Houle (1992).

Opposition to the goal of disciplinary isolation has frequently been voiced by prominent adult education researchers. There are two broad bases for their arguments that adult education research needs to maintain strong ties with its interdisciplinary origins. First, the development of theory, which is urgently needed, will be enhanced by linkages with the existing conceptual frameworks and theories of the traditional, stronger social research disciplines. Second, methodological rigor can best be achieved, and maintained, by close interdisciplinary relations with other social scientists. Nordhaug (1987) has captured the extent of, and the unequivocal dissatisfaction with, the atheoretical nature of adult education research in general by succinctly quoting the cryptic views of others:

The theoretical basis of adult education research has been characterized as "a conceptual desert" (Boshier, 1971, p. 3); as "almost non-existing" (Cross, 1982, p. 109); as "having a crippling effect on adult education research through decades" (Boshier, 1973, p. 255); as "ill-equipped to serve as a framework for looking at the questions that range from macro- to micro-aspects" (Rubenson, 1980, p. 14); as "resting upon rather shaky theoretical-scientific foundations" (Alanen, 1978, p. 4); and as "purported theory which is not theory" (Boshier & Picard, 1979, p. 44). (Nordhaug, 1987, p. 2)

While there is widespread agreement about the atheoretical nature of adult education research, there are two competing views about how to improve the situation. One group including Apps (1979), Mezirow (1971), Boyd and Apps (1980a and others) argue that intradisciplinary efforts can best provide it, while a second group, including Bright (1989), Boshier (1973), Rubenson (1989), and Nordhaug (1987) among others argue that the advancement of theory building is more likely to be achieved through interdisciplinary efforts. It is interesting to observe that Mezirow (1971) argued for a "research based body of theory, indigenous to adult education" because the mainstream social and educational research methodologies had yielded only "banal generalities" (pp. 135–136). Yet the arguments he used to support his point of view and the alternative approaches he proposed be adopted at that time originated in the discipline of sociology with Blumer's (1969) critique of mainstream sociology and the introduction to sociology of grounded theory by Glaser and Strauss (1967). Further, Mezirow is more recently credited with the introduction of aspects of critical theory into adult education research (Collard & Law, 1989) so his support for an intradisciplinary approach to knowledge building does not extend to the adoption of methodology and social analysis from those same disciplines whose interests he wishes to divert away from a focus on adult education issues. Is it reasonable to borrow methodology developed to advance research in another social science discipline and argue that knowledge relevant to adult education contributed by that methodology, from within the other discipline, ought to be ignored or excluded?

One problem that arises when adult education researchers are isolated from the more rigorous research traditions of other disciplines is that they do not have the opportunity to acquire a thorough grounding in contemporary social research methods and techniques that are accessible, almost without exception, only through other disciplines. The current controversy surrounding the validity of the Self Directed Learning Readiness Scale (SDLRS)[3], for example, has arisen because the sociopsychological scale development and validation procedures used have been questioned and the evidence for the instrument's validity is now being recognized to be weak. This questioning of the validity of the SDLRS is occurring after the scale has been used by many adult education researchers who failed to critically analyze the instrument's construction procedures and claims of validity. Evidence of a serious lack of understanding of multivariate research analysis tools in one research report critiqued by Boshier (1976) also serves to demonstrate the potential for methodological error in adult education research to pass unnoticed. In a published study of motivational orientations that claimed to have found a normal distribution of factor scores, Boshier showed that in fact the distribution was simply an artifact of the computer analysis program selected by the researcher. Almost one decade later Dickinson and Blunt (1980) observed that, while survey research was then the most common method of research in adult education and was anticipated to remain so, its application was characterized by a lack of rigor and sophistication and the training of adult education researchers in survey methodology was quite inappropriate. In direct reference to the means of improving the quality of survey research, they further commented that:

> The integration of empirical and theoretical elements found in other social sciences, such as sociology, which are more advanced than education with respect to the state of survey research, may be more appropriate to the needs of adult education. (Dickinson & Blunt, 1980, p. 62)

Writing in the same book, Grabowski (1980) commented on improvements in the quality and quantity of graduate research and the increase in numbers of graduate students during the 1970s. His view was one of optimism for the future as other disciplines granted increased recognition to the emerging distinctiveness of adult education as a field of study, and self-assurance replaced defensiveness among adult education researchers.

> Adult education drawing as it does from related disciplines such as anthropology, psychology, sociology, and even economics, political science, and history, must always share research endeavors with these fields. This limitation, if it be one, is also the glory and strength of adult education research even on the graduate level. (Grabowski, 1980, p. 128)

There is little evidence that the recommendations for closer links with the social science disciplines, where the most current expertise in research methodology resides, have been acted upon. Peters, writing in the "new black book," the most recent in-depth consideration of the state of adult education as a field of study, concluded:

> It seems that, even as the field of study has evolved from a position of being so strongly dependent on the disciplines during its first forty years or so to a less dependent status over the last twenty years, leading scholars are still ambivalent about what ought to be the proper relationship between adult education and the related disciplines. (Peters, 1991, p. 428)

Peters expressed skepticism about the likelihood that adult educators might work cooperatively on projects with researchers from other disciplines. He doubted that adult educators had a contribution to make that would be recognized by other social scientists, and asked the question, "We need the disciplines, but do they need us?" (p. 428). The extent to which adult education researchers need the other disciplines is made clear by Houle's (1992) bibliography of 1,241 adult education books, which lists only eight references under the category of research.

The opposition has been clear and consistent, but the drive toward disciplinary separation and the minimization of interdisciplinary cooperation has been strong, has prevailed, has been dominant, and has been shown to be irreversible to date. It is possible that the project of Houle et al. to build a body of literature that would meet the need of the discipline to achieve a satisfactory level of status and respectability in academe has now been sufficiently successful to allow for a return to an interdisciplinary focus. There is a pressing need for adult education research to achieve higher standards, and the need for research in support of theory construction remains as great as ever. The direction that holds most promise is toward greater interdisciplinary work.

It is likely that one or more of the following may be needed to trigger changes in the current practice of training adult education researchers solely within departments of adult education and their larger host faculties of education: (1) a concerted effort by the Commission of Professors of Adult Education to persuade members to improve the quality of research through interdisciplinary linkages; (2) a greater effort by researchers to publish adult education research texts that promote change, as this text attempts; (3) a major critical review of the state of the art of research methods in adult education, conducted by an outside group such as the U.S. Department of Education; (4) a commitment by leading adult education graduate departments to train researchers through interdisciplinary courses, which might persuade others to follow suit; and/or (5) explicit threats to the existence of adult education departments by traditional social science scholars, on the basis of the atheoretical work of adult education researchers.

Disciplinary Focus of the Research Questions Asked

What is the influence of other social science disciplines on the questions asked in adult education research? As previously stated, for some years it has been recognized that adult education research in North America has largely been conducted within the disciplinary realm of psychology. The psychological orientation, in fact, has been so strong that one observer described the effect as having established a "scientific monoculture" (Nordhaug, 1987). In European adult education research, sociology has tended to be the dominant influential discipline, resulting in what Rubenson (1989) has referred to as a "people-in-society" research orientation as compared to a "people-over-society" orientation in North America.

Recent literature illustrates the growing argument in favor of disciplinary diversity in both North America and Europe. Nordhaug (1987) argues for an interdisciplinary organization of the discipline, with a sociology of adult education, a psychology of adult education, and a history of adult education, etc. "[I]nfluences from traditional disciplines must not only be clearly recognized and openly acknowledged but also ought to be a cornerstone for theoretical development" (p. 3). Rubenson (1989) saw the range and complexity of questions faced by adult education as too complex for the application of unidisciplinary theories. He also warned against the undesirable possibility that, as North American adult education research shifted to incorporate sociological theory, it might move from psychological reductionism to sociological deductionism.

Bright (1989) complied the views of several adult educators in one of the few in-depth discussions of the epistemological foundations of adult education. The contributors to *The Epistemological Debate* (Bright, 1989), as might be anticipated, did not agree on the relationship of other disciplines with, and the value of their contributions to, adult education in the future. However, the contributors did agree that the epistemological foundations of adult education were insecure, and lacked rigor relative to the other disciplines, and that adult educators needed to be better informed about the epistemological debate. In summary, Bright concluded that the "necessity for a change in orientation in adult education, and the logic of establishing it upon firmer epistemological and methodological grounds than is currently the case appears to be inevitable" (p. 218).

As argued earlier, training adult educators solely within graduate departments of adult education reduces the likelihood that the more rigorous and sophisticated methodological approaches in use in related disciplines will be adopted in adult education in a timely manner. It is simply not possible to raise research standards and achieve methodological diversity by distancing training programs and research projects from other stronger social research disciplines. The choices to be made to ensure the future health of research are between increased cultural and scientific conformity in a closed community relying on less than current research methods and distancing itself from historically related groups, and increased cultural diversity in an open research community that uses current research methods and strategies and that maintains its roots and strong links with the larger social research enterprise.

A conundrum for adult education lies in the problem of how the discipline might become more multidisciplinary to avoid scientific monoculturalism while achieving the kind of disciplinary independence in the university as a professional program that Houle, Boyd, Apps, and others argue for. Certainly Plecas and Sork (1986) state that legitimate adult education problems (within their consensual focus) can be investigated from different perspectives—sociology or psychology, for example—but it is not very likely that the training of adult education researchers from an increasingly intradisciplinary basis is the best means to achieve that goal. If critical adult education is to remain a major focus in adult education research in the future, what literature will support its interpretation, justification, and application? Surely it is not possible to work in critical adult education without reading literature from sociology. The current work of feminists in adult education is informed by the increasingly strong body of knowledge and the advances in methodology made by feminists in several social science disciplines. Has the introduction of a vigorous debate on women's issues in adult education detracted from the building of adult education as a scholarly discipline? In my view, the substantive issues raised, and the quality of the research contributed by, feminist adult educators has greatly enhanced the discipline of adult education. Can that work be continued without a strong linkage to the feminist literature in other disciplines? An increased intradisciplinary focus will perpetuate the ethnic-, gender-, and class-based disciplinary conservatism of adult education. That conservatism is the target of vigorous attacks from adult education feminists and critical adult educators whose work has demonstrated its potential to maintain the relevance and vitality of the field of practice and the discipline.

Certainly feminists and critical adult educators have demonstrated no higher levels of scholarly virtue than those whose works they have critiqued, and the missionary zeal of graduate students to displace the old guard from their positions of privilege have been strident, confrontational, and politically correct. However, the benefits for adult education from having these issues placed on the discipline's agenda outweigh the negative effects experienced to date. The reintroduction of critical reflection and analysis on the role of adult education in society and the questioning of the achievements of the discipline over the last two decades is a sign of a healthy intellectual community and augurs well for the commitment of the next generation of researchers. That a more balanced, open, and less confrontational discussion is now needed is probably a view shared by most attendees of the Adult Education Research Conference and members of the Commission of Professors.

Governing Research Traditions

As judged by the number of adult education books and research articles published, the literature of adult education continues to expand, further strengthening the claim that adult education has a distinct body of knowledge on which to base an academic discipline. A recent and most significant marker in the history of adult education as a field of study is Houle's (1992) bibliographic essay, which cites 1,241 books written for adult educators, largely by adult educators. The publication of *The Literature of Adult Education* was the culmination of a 15-year project to identify the world's English-language adult education texts. Houle's work will likely serve to strengthen teaching and assist future researchers in countless ways. However, the work raises concerns for adult education researchers as it avoids critical analysis, serves the goals of professionalization possibly to the detriment of scholarly inquiry, and reveals disturbing gaps in the literature of adult education (Blunt, 1992).

The terms *feminist, gender, social class,* and *ethnic status* do not appear in the subject index of Houle's book. Under "Women" are cited one text that indentifies the advantages that distance education offers women, seven texts in the broad area of women's education, and one book on worker's education for women. Houle acknowledges that the literature on the women's movement is extensive and that the topic has been expressed as an area of interest in the adult education literature since the 1930s, but there has not yet been a single volume that has linked the women's movement and adult education. Under the subject heading "Research, for body of adult education knowledge," Houle lists seven books. One by Long and Hiemstra, (Eds.) (1980) was part of the 1980 Handbook series, which if only one volume had been produced as in previous and subsequent practice, would have reduced the number of citations to six. The dearth of books in these latter two categories serves to highlight the lack of social relevance and currency of scholarly writing in adult education research. In large part this is attributable to adult education's atheoretical research focus, failure to build knowledge cumulatively, and increasing disciplinary isolation. It is interesting to note that currently the research section of the American Association for Adult and Continuing Education (AAACE) is on the verge of collapse as too few papers have been submitted to the section for presentation to the association's annual conference in recent years. This may be further evidence that the divide between researchers and practitioners in the United States continues to grow wider and deeper. However, as Brockett (1991) points out, overall the production of research continues and new means of disseminating findings are being introduced.

Further intradisciplinary strengthening of the field of adult education in North America since Rubenson's observations (1979, 1989) can be observed in the continuing support for the Adult Education Research Conference (AERC), an increase in the number of manuscripts published in *Adult Education Quarterly,* the contribution of *The International Journal of Lifelong Education* since its establishment in 1982, and the more recent arrival of *The Canadian Journal for the Study of Adult Education* in 1987. The publication of the *Handbook of Adult and Continuing Education* (Merriam & Cunningham, 1989) and the controversial *Adult Education: Evolution and Achievements in a Developing Field of Study* (Peters & Jarvis, (Eds.), 1991) have also served to focus attention on, and to strengthen, adult education as a field of study. It is noteworthy that the United Nations Educational, Scientific, and Cultural Organization (UNESCO) appears to have survived its scandals of profligate spending and mismanagement during the 1980s and will continue to provide international leadership for adult education research and knowledge dissemination.

The critical mass of faculty and graduate students required to establish a strong research culture is lacking in the majority of adult education departments. The building of collaborative networks and closer connections with departments that have a strong tradition and commitment to research may be one strategy to strengthen the research and training capability of smaller departments. In western Canadian universities, for example, the deans of graduate studies have established an agreement that enables and encourages graduate students to study at other western universities. Under this agreement adult education students at the Universities of British Columbia, Calgary, Alberta, and Saskatchewan may attend classes and study with faculty from the other participating institutions. The agreement holds promise for the strengthening of the adult education departments at these universities.

The Future of Research as Product

Rubenson's application of Tonnenbohm's concept of disciplinary mapping has served as a useful device for thinking about the forces that have shaped and will continue to shape adult education's research future. It would appear that while adult education's map continues to be redrawn, the changes being introduced today have been brought about by almost exactly the same forces that Rubenson observed as contributing to the development of the map of adult education 20 years ago. Unless in the immediate future unanticipated shifts in external social and economic forces occur, or the members of the adult education community engineer a shift in their individual and collective priorities, the product of the adult education research enterprise in the future will be little different from today's product.

Pragmatism is likely to continue to be the major influence in determining the focus of graduate research as the great number of students will continue to bring with them research questions and problems they identified in their workplaces. It is possible, however, that as universities face economic pressures arising from global restructuring, faculty researchers might choose to strengthen their positions by focusing to a greater extent on basic research. New postsecondary institutions may also move to establish training programs to meet the increased demand for adult educators, and these programs would maintain a focus on applied research.

Resistance among many leading adult education scholars continues to prevent a noticeable return to an interdisciplinary research orientation, yet while the views of supporters of the intradisciplinary focus prevail, research continues to be atheoretical and knowledge building remains an unsatisfactory, noncumulative exercise. However, opportunities for researchers to overcome continental isolationism continue to expand as trans-Atlantic visits and exchanges increase, more researchers collaborate on scholarly writing projects, and the dissemination of research through new journals and books continues to grow globally.

The influence of feminsts and critical theorists has continued to expand the research boundaries of adult education and to provide the most noticeable incursions of interdisciplinary influences into the otherwise closed culture of the adult education research community.

An examination of the forces likely to shape the product of research in the future leaves one with the realization that the product most likely to be produced in the future will be as unsatisfying as the current product. It is possible, however, that a shift in thinking about the state of the adult education research enterprise can change the current dynamics to enable an alternative future to emerge.

TOWARD AN ALTERNATIVE RESEARCH FUTURE

It is from a position of dissatisfaction with the most likely anticipated future for adult education research, assuming no major change to the status quo, that I propose an alternative future. The future envisaged for adult education research in the closing sections of this chapter is a future characterized by pluralism of paradigmatic view, research method, and disciplinary research purpose and priority. What is proposed is not an ivory tower vision but a realistic future that is shaped with respect to "town and gown" priorities and that is achievable if adult educators within their personal spheres of influence in the fields of adult education study and practice decide to work toward achieving it. The future that I propose requires that four elements of change be introduced into today's research enterprise. The first element needed is acceptance of the legitimacy and desirability of a multiparadigm research culture and concurrent acceptance of multimethod research strategies. Second, more researchers will need to adopt a long-term orientation to their intellectual work that would reflect openness to interdisciplinary research, focus on important rather than trivial research questions, contribute to theory building in addition to the solution of problems in the field of practice, and recognize the importance of research traditions and cumulative knowledge building for constructing a more precise map of the territory of adult education. Third, a new orientation toward the traditional related academic disciplines is required to support the renewal of graduate training programs for developing the skills required by the next generation of researchers. More collaborative interdisciplinary knowledge building is required to ensure a healthy, socially and pedagogically relevant adult education research community in the 21st century. Last, a commitment to the democratization of the intellectual work of adult education researchers is needed. The great majority of the graduates of academic departments of adult education do not contribute to knowledge production after completing the thesis and dissertation requirements of their degree programs. Further, there is evidence that knowledge production in adult education is concentrated in a small number of universities (see Blunt & Lee, 1993). A healthier and more dynamic adult education research culture, one that reduces the impact of social structures that perpetuate the distinction between theory and practice, can emerge from a more egalitarian and cooperative future research enterprise.

A sufficient argument in favor of abandonment of adversarial interpretations of the three major paradigmatic views that currently guide research has been presented earlier. Here all that needs to be said is that in the adult education research future proposed, there is little space for those who wish to perpetuate beliefs that prevent researchers from integrating pardigmatic views and adopting multimethod research. It will be necessary for the Commission of Professors, the Adult Education Research Conference, and leading departments of adult education to provide leadership to identify the knowledge and skills needed to better reflect the contemporary reality of social research. One essential requirement for doctoral level study, if not at the masters level, will be the study of the ontological and epistemological foundations of adult education research. It will be essential that the technical capabilities required to conduct applied research projects no longer be regarded as more important than the additional intellectual capabilities and understandings required for the conduct of basic research and theory building. Current faculty will need to attend meetings of researchers in related disciplines to begin to enhance their research perspectives. This may be easier for Canadian researchers as the Canadian Association for the Study of Adult Education (CASAE) is one of The Learned Societies that meet together in one location each year. Faculty in U.S. institutions will need to attend the American Education Research Association meetings and meetings of their related disciplines in addition to their adult education meetings.

To move toward the development of a more detailed map of the territory of adult education, a means of assessing and categorizing the knowledge base in terms other than research content is required. Becher (1987), writing about the cultures of academic disciplines, has presented a simple analytic framework to reveal how disciplines differ in their actions and behaviors, based on whether their intellectual work involves "hard" or "soft" subjects and "pure" or "applied" fields. Adult education as a field of study has now reached the point where research will soon be more clearly differentiated. Research will be judged to be "hard" or "soft" in terms of its relationship with other social science disciplines and "basic" or "applied" in terms of its contribution to adult education as a discipline (field of academic study) or to adult education as an applied field of social practice.

Research can be judged to be "hard" or "soft" by the extent to which it is linked with conceptual, theoretical, and methodological sources from the "harder" social science disciplines, including philosophy, sociology, psychology, anthropology, and history, as compared to the "softer" disciplines of community development, social work, public health, public administration, training and development, and education generally. Basic research within this model will be that which develops theory; the potential to contribute to adult education as a field of academic study is its primary focus. Applied research, on the other hand, will have the solution of problems and the improvement of practice as its primary focus. Basic research, for example, might address the development of explanatory models, conceptual frameworks, and theory in areas such as adult learning, perspective transformation, motivational orientation, participation, policy development, critical adult education, ethical practice, and historical analysis of adult education as

Discipline Focus

		Hard	Soft
	Applied	Applied Hard	Applied Soft
Field Focus			
	Basic	Basic Hard	Basic Soft

Figure 9.1: Discipline and focus categories of adult education research.

an agent of social change. Applied research might directly address problems such as the improvement of adult education practices in adult pedagogy, program planning, needs analysis, program evaluation, marketing, administration, adoption of innovations, and the identification of skills to be learned through human resource development and specific training programs.

Figure 9.1 shows the relationships between the two variables, discipline focus and field focus, in terms of four cells that are combinations of the two discipline and the two research focus categories. Applied hard research (cell 1) would use theoretical and methodological primary resources from related hard disciplines while aiming to resolve a particular problem in, or to improve some aspect of, adult education practice. Applied soft research (cell 2) would use primary conceptual and methodological resources largely from adult education and the related soft disciplines to answer questions or solve problems from the field of practice. Basic hard research (cell 3) would use theoretical and methodological resources that are primarily from related hard social science disciplines and focus on building adult education theory. Basic soft research (cell 4) would use primary resources from the related soft disciplines and adult education with the aim of expanding adult education's theoretical and conceptual base.

The figure illustrates ways in which adult education research can be viewed from new perspectives. An alternative and practical means of mapping the territory is provided. Research in adult education through this strategy can be mapped: (1) in terms of linkages with related disciplines and chronicled in terms of shifts from one disciplinary focus to another; (2) in terms of the contributions of individuals, university departments, and organizations; (3) from the perspective of the dissemination roles of journals; (4) to assess the contribution of graduate student thesis and dissertation studies; and (5) comparatively to identify more precisely the differences between research in Canada and the United States and between North American and European research. The framework might enable Plecas and Sork's sought-after body of core, or centrally focused, research to be delineated. It might also serve to identify and select studies for inclusion in future meta-analyses, an emerging need if the current body of research is to be integrated and synthesized.

With regard to the future of the discipline of adult education, Peters (1991) cites Clark's (1987) observation that academic disciplines, faculties, and universities serve as mediating institutions that connect individuals and groups to the whole academic system. Peters (1991) then builds on this observation to propose a future relationship between adult education and the related disciplines that is posited upon scholars in adult education being "first and foremost members of the education profession, not members of the disciplines. This locates the field alongside the related disciplines, not in them" (p. 434). However, the analogy originally proposed by Clark, in a study of the American professoriate's institutional and disciplinary differentiation, is in my opinion preferable to that subsequently proposed by Peters. Clark (1987) referenced the works of Polanyi (1967), who observed that modern science was "constructed like chains of overlapping neighborhoods"; of Campbell (1969), who used the metaphor that the "multiple specialties overlap nuch like the scales of a fish"; and of Crane (1982), who stated that science and academia had "interlocking cultural communities."

It was the notion of overlapping and interlocking disciplines that Clark chose to adopt and that I consider to be the more valuable means of representing the preferred future relationship between adult education and the related social science disciplines. Peters's notion of "location alongside, not within" conveys the idea that we should respect our neighbors' property lines; that is, we should mutually respect the ownership rights of our disciplinary neighbors. This basis for relating with our neighbors will appeal to many adult education researchers, some of whom live in the suburbs and never speak to their neighbors. The view is typical of adult education's position in academe: traditional, largely uninvolved with epistemological struggle and change, socially conservative, atheoretical, and methodologically outmoded. Clark's notion, on the other hand, is more appropriate for adult education in the postmodern period. Instead of the white picket fence, the property line, and distant neighbors, Clark proposes a living arrangement best represented by the modern condominium; that is, a living arrangement that recognizes private space, public space, and a common interest in jointly owned space. Rather than an arrangement that may lead to isolation, alienation, and a perpetuation of individual interest, the condominium operates on a collective agreement and a commitment to mutually beneficial cooperation that respects the rights of both the individual and the community. In Clark's words:

> *The* analytical handle is the idea of integration through overlap. Then we no longer need to think, as observers or participants, that integration can come about only by means of some combination of identical socialization, similarity of task, commonly held values, and united membership in a grand corps or association. Academics need not think that they must somehow pull themselves together around a top-down pronouncement of a fixed set of values swimming against the tides of history and seeking a return to a golden age that never was. As we probe the nature of the modern academic life, especially in America, it is much more fruitful to grasp that integration can come from the bit-by-bit overlap of narrow memberships and specific identities. (Clark, 1989, p. 8)

Clark's analysis serves as a thoroughly pragmatic basis for the future adult education research community envisioned in this chapter. This future is compatible with the origins, traditions, values, and goals of adult education research in North America. The value of diversity is recognized and valued rather than the overarching conformity of professionalization and research orthodoxy. A return to an inter-disciplinary focus is made possible without the destructing of those intradisciplinary gains that have been made. Academic unity and the notion of a grand unifying plan for discipline building is recognized as utopian, instead space and opportunities are created for the ad hoc creation of interest groups and alliances. This proposed future holds promise for the current and future generation of researchers and respects the contributions of prior generations. Can the same be said of our more likely future, which will be a reproduction of the increasingly intraspective research enterprise of today, if we choose not to act to implement changes needed to build a future we might prefer?

ENDNOTES

1. Naturalistic inquiry, naturalistic research, and naturalism are used in the sense intended by Denzin (1971), who coined the terms, to categorize all research that is not concerned with variables and their measurement. Naturalistic research is used throughout the chapter as a label for an entire knowledge

paradigm that has evolved in response to, and with some proponents in opposition to, positivism (Tesch 1990).

2. Tesch (1990) lists 46 "brands" of qualitative research. Some of the terms listed describe perspectives qualitative researchers adopt, such as interpretive or naturalistic; others are based on disciplinary research traditions such as ethnography or symbolic interactionism; others refer to research approaches such as case study or discourse analysis; and yet others refer to types of data or research methods such as participant observation or document study. It is extremely difficult to differentiate between these terms solely on the basis of epistemology and research method. One common element among the qualitative methods, in terms of the paradigm wars, has been the firmly held belief that qualitative research is oppositional to quantitative research.

3. See Field, 1989 & 1990; Bonham, 1991; Guglielmino, 1989; Long, 1989; McCure, 1989.

REFERENCES

Alanen, A. (1978). Adult education and pedagogy. *Adult Education in Finland, 15*, 3–17.

Apple, M. W. (1988). *Teachers and texts: A political economy of class and gender relations in education.* New York: Routledge.

Apps, J. W. (1979). *Problems in continuing education.* New York: McGraw-Hill.

Becher, T. (1987). The disciplinary shaping of the profession. In B. R. Clark (Ed.), *The academic profession: National, disciplinary, and institutional settings* (pp. 271–303). Berkeley: University of California Press.

Blumer, H. (1969). *Symbolic interactionism, perspective and method.* Englewood Cliffs, NJ: Prentice-Hall.

Blunt, A. (in press). A deckhand's view at the lauching of *The literature of adult education. Proceedings of the Commission of Professors of Adult Education* Anaheim, CA, November 1–3, 1992.

Blunt, A., & Lee, J. (1994). The contribution of graduate student research, *Adult Education Quarterly, 44*, 125–144.

Bonhan, A. (1991). Guglielmino's Self Directed Learning Readiness Scale: What does it measure? *Adult Education Quarterly, 41* (2), 92–99.

Boshier, R. (1971). Motivational orientations of adult education participants: A factor analytic exploration of Houle's typology. *Adult Education, 21*, 3–26.

Boshier, R. (1973). Educational participation and drop-out: A theoretical model. *Adult Education, 23*, 255–282.

Boshier, R. (1976). Factor analysts at large: A critical review of the motivational orientation literature. *Adult Education Quarterly, 27* (1), 24–47.

Boshier, R., & Picard, L. (1979). Citation patterns of articles published in *Adult Education. Adult Education, 30*(1), 34–51.

Boyd, R. D., & Apps, J. W. (1980a). A conceptual model for adult education. In R. D. Boyd, J. W. Apps, & Associates (Eds.), *Redefining the discipline of adult education* (pp. 1–13). San Francisco: Jossey-Bass.

Boyd, R. D., Apps, J. W., & Associates. (Eds.). (1980b). *Redefining the discipline of adult education.* San Francisco: Jossey-Bass.

Brewer, J., & Hunter, A. (1989). *Multimethod research: A synthesis of styles.* Newbury Park, CA: Sage.

Bright, B. P. (Ed.). (1989). *Theory and practice in the study of adult education: The epistemological debate.* London: Routledge.

Brockett, R. G. (1991). Disseminating and using adult education knowledge. In J. M. Peters, P. Jarvis, & Associates (Eds.), *Adult education: Evolution and achievements in a developing field of study* (pp. 121–144). San Francisco: Jossey-Bass.

Brunner, E. de S., Wilder, D. S., Kirchner, C., & Newberry, J. S. (1959). *An overview of adult education research.* Chicago: Adult Education Association of the U.S.A.

Campbell, D. T. (1969). Ethnocentrism of disciplines and the fish-scale model of omniscience. In M. Sherif & C. Sherif (Eds.), *Interdisciplinary relationships in the social sciences* (pp. 328–348). Chicago: Aldine.

Clark, B. R. (Ed.). (1987). *The academic profession: National, disciplinary, and institutional settings.* Berkeley: University of California Press.

Clark, B. R. (1989). The academic life: Small worlds, different worlds. *Educational Researcher, 18*(5), 4–8.

Cohen, I. J. (1987). Structuration theory and social praxis. In A. Giddens & J. Turner (Eds.), *Social theory today* (pp. 273–307). Stanford, CA: Stanford University Press.

Collard, S., & Law, M. (1989). The limits of perspective transformation: A critique of Mezirow's theory. *Adult Education Quarterly, 39* (2), 99–107.

Copeland, H. G., & Grabowski, S. M. (1971). Research and investigation in the United States. *Convergence, 4* (4), 23–30.

Crane, D. (1982). Cultural differentiation, cultural integration, and social control. In J. P. Gibbs (Ed.), *Social control: Views from the social sciences* (pp. 229–244). Beverley Hills, CA: Sage.

Cross, K. P. (1982). *Adults as learners.* San Francisco: Jossey-Bass.

Deshler, D. (1991). Social, professional and academic issues. In J. M. Peters, P. Jarvis, & Associates (Eds.), *Adult education: Evolution and achievements in a developing field of study* (pp. 384–420). San Francisco: Jossey-Bass.

Deshler, D. with Hagan, N. (1989). Adult education research: Issues and directions. In S. B. Merriam & P. M. Cunningham (Eds.), *Handbook of adult and continuing education* (pp. 147–167). San Francisco: Jossey-Bass.

Denzin, N. K. (1971). The logic of naturalistic inquiry. *Social Forces, 50,* 166–182.

Dewey, J. (1916). *Essays in experimental logic.* Chicago: University of Chicago Press.

Dewey, J. (1929). *Experience and nature.* New York: Norton.

Dewey, J. (1933). *How we think*. Boston: Heath (Gateway Edition, 1971).

Dewey, J. (1934). *Art as experience*. New York: Minton, Balch.

Dewey, J. (1938). *Logic: The theory of inquiry*. New York: Holt.

Dickinson, G., & Rusnell, D. (1971). A content analysis of *Adult Education*. *Adult Education, 21* (3), 177–185.

Dickinson, G., & Blunt, A. (1980). Survey Research. In H. B. Long, R. Hiemstra, & Associates (Eds.), *Changing approaches to studying adult education* (pp. 50–62). San Francisco: Jossey-Bass.

Eisner, E. W. (1983). Anastasia might still be alive, but the monarchy is dead. *Educational Researcher, 12* (5), 13–14, 23–24.

Field, L. (1989). An investigation into the structure, validity, and reliability of Guglielmino's Self Directed Learning Readiness Scale. *Adult Education Quarterly, 39* (3), 125–129.

Field, L. (1990). Guglielmino's Self Directed Learning Readiness Scale: Should it continue to be used? *Adult Education Quarterly, 41* (2), 100–103.

Firestone, W. A. (1987). Meaning in method: The rhetoric of quantitative and qualitative rsearch. *Educational Researcher, 16* (7), 16–21.

Freire, P. (1993). *Pedagogy of the oppressed:* Twentieth anniversary edition. New York: Continuum Publishing Co.

Gage, N. L. (1989). The paradigm wars and their aftermath: A "historical sketch" of research on teaching since 1989. *Educational Researcher, 18* (7), 4–10.

Garrison, J. W. (1986). Some principles of postpositivistic philosophy of science. *Educational Researcher, 15* (9), 12–18.

Giddens, A. (1984). *The constitution of society*. Berkeley: University of California Press.

Giddens, A., & Turner, J. (Eds.). (1987). *Social Theory today*. Stanford, CA: Stanford University Press.

Glaser, B., & Strauss, A. (1967). *The discovery of grounded theory*. Chicago: Aldine.

Grabowski, S. (1980). Trends in graduate research. In H. B. Long, R. Hiemstra, & Associates (Eds.), *Changing approaches to studying adult education* (pp. 119–128). San Francisco: Jossey-Bass.

Gramsci, A. (1971). *Selections from the prison notebooks*. (Q. Hoare & G. Smith, Eds. & Trans.). New York: International Publishers.

Griffin, C. (1991). A critical perspective on sociology and adult education. In J. M. Peters, P. Jarvis, & Associates (Eds.), *Adult education: Evolution and achievements in a developing field of study* (pp. 259–281). San Francisco: Jossey-Bass.

Guglielmino, L. M. (1989). Guglielmino responds to Field's investigation. *Adult Education Quarterly, 39* (4), 235–240.

Habermas, J. (1971). *Knowledge and human interests*. (J. Shapiro, trans.). Boston: Beacon Press.

Hoghielm, R., & Rubenson, K. (Eds.). (1980). *Adult education for social change: Research on the Swedish allocation policy*. Stockholm: Liber.

Houle, C. O. (1992). *The Literature of adult education: A bibliographic essay.* San Francisco: Jossey-Bass.

House, E. R. (1991). Realism in research. *Educational Researcher, 20* (6), 2–9.

Howe, K. R. (1992). Getting over the quantitative-qualitative debate. *American Journal of Education, 100* (2), 236–256.

Husen, T. (1985). Research paradigms in education. In T. Husen & T. N. Postlethwaite (Eds.), *International encyclopedia of education.* Vol. 7 (pp. 4335–4338). Oxford: Pergamon.

Husen, T., & Postlethwaite, T. N. (Eds.). (1985). *International encyclopedia of education.* Oxford: Pergamon.

Jensen, G. (1964). How about education borrows and reformulates knowledge of other disciplines. In G. Jensen, A. A. Liveright, & W. Hallenbeck (Eds.), *Adult education: Outlines of an emerging field of university study* (pp. 105–111). Washington, DC: Adult Education Association of the U.S.A.

Keeves, J. (1988). The unity of educational research, *Interchange, 19* (1), 14–30.

Knowles, M. S. (1991). Epilogue. In J. M. Peters, P. Jarvis, & Associates (Eds.), *Adult education: Evolution and achievements in a developing field of study* (pp. 421–445). San Francisco: Jossey-Bass.

Knox, A. B. (1991). Educational leadership and program administration. In J. M. Peters, P. Jarvis & Associates (Eds.), *Adult education: Evolution and achievements in a developing field of study* (pp. 217–258). San Francisco: Jossey-Bass.

Lawson, K. H. (1991). Philosophical foundations. In J. M. Peters, P. Jarvis & Associates (Eds.), *Adult education: Evolution and achievements in a developing field of study* (pp. 282–300). San Francisco: Jossey-Bass.

Lincoln, Y. S., & Guba, E. G. (1985). *Naturalistic inquiry.* Newbury Park, CA: Sage.

Long, H. B., & Agyekum, S. K. (1974). *Adult Education* 1964–1973: Reflections of a changing discipline. *Adult Education, 24* (2), 99–120.

Long, H. B. (1980). A perspective on adult education research. In H. B. Long, R. Hiemstra, & Associates (Eds.), *Changing approaches to studying adult education* (pp. 1–21). San Francisco: Jossey-Bass.

Long, H. B., Hiemstra, R., & Associates. (Eds.). (1980). *Changing approaches to studying adult education.* San Francisco: Jossey-Bass.

Long, H. B. (1989). Some additional criticisms of Field's investigation. *Adult Education Quarterly, 39* (4), 240–243.

McCune, S. K. (1989). A statistical critique of Field's investigation. *Adult Education Quarterly, 39* (4), 243–245.

Merriam, S. B. (1991). How research produces knowledge, In J. M. Peters, P. Jarvis & Associates. *Adult Education: Evolution and achievements in a developing field of study* (pp. 42–65). San Francisco: Jossey-Bass.

Merriam, S. B., & Cunningham P. M. (Eds.). (1989). *Handbook of adult and continuing education.* San Francisco: Jossey-Bass.

Nordhaug, O. (1987). Adult education and social science: A theoretical framework. *Adult Education Quarterly, 38* (1), 1–13.

Olson, D. R. (1986). Mining the human sciences: Some relations between hermeneutics and epistemology. *Interchange, 17* (2), 159–171.

Ostrowski, P. M., & Bartel, S. (1985). Assisting practitioners to publish through
the use of support groups. *Journal of Counselling and Development, 63,* 510–511.

Peters, J. M. (1991). Advancing the study of adult education: A summary per-
spective. In J. M. Peters, P. Jarvis, & Associates (Eds.), *Adult education:
Evolution and achievements in a developing field of study* (pp. 421–445). San
Francisco: Jossey-Bass.

Peters, J. M., Jarvis P., & Associates. (Eds.). (1991). *Adult education: Evolution
and achievements in a developing field of study.* San Francisco: Jossey-Bass.

Phillips, D. C. (1983). After the wake: Postpositivistic educational thought.
Educational Researcher, 12 (5), 4–12.

Phillips, D. C. (1992). *The social scientist's bestiary: A guide to fabled threats to,
and defenses of, naturalistic social science.* New York: Pergamon Press.

Plecas, D. B., & Sork, T. J. (1986). Adult education: Curing the ills of an
undisciplined discipline. *Adult Education, 37* (1), 48–62.

Polanyi, M. (1967). *The tacit dimension.* Garden City, N.J.: Doubleday.

Rabkin, E. S. (1976). *The fantastic in literature.* Princeton, NJ: Princeton University Press.

Rizo, F. M. (1991). The controversy about quantification in social research: An
extension of Gage's "historical sketch." *Educational Researcher, 20* (12), 9–12.

Rorty, R. (1982). *Consequences of pragmatism.* Minneapolis: University of Minnesota Press.

Rubenson, K. (1979). *Adult education research: In quest of a map of the territory.*
A paper presented to the Commission of Professors of Adult Education,
Boston, November 4–5.

Rubenson, K. (1980). Background and theoretical context. In R. Hoghielm &
K. Rubenson (Eds.), *Adult education for social change: Research on the Swedish allocation policy* (pp. 1–45). Stockholm: Liber.

Rubenson, K. (1982). Adult education research: In quest of a map of the territory. *Adult Education, 32* (2), 57–74.

Rubenson, K. (1989). Adult education research: General. In C. J. Titmus (Ed.),
Lifelong education for adults: An international handbook (pp. 507–511). Toronto: Pergamon Press.

Salomon, G. (1991). Transcending the qualitative-quantitative debate: The analytic and systemic approaches to educational research. *Educational Researcher, 20* (6), 10–18.

Sherman. R. R., & Webb, R. B. (1988a). Qualitative research in education: A
focus. In R. R. Sherman & R. B. Webb (Eds.), *Qualitative research in education: Focus and methods* (pp. 2–21). London: Falmer Press.

Sherman. R. R., & Webb, R. B. (Eds.) (1988b). *Qualitative research in education: Focus and methods.* London: Falmer Press.

Smith, J. K., & Heshusius, L. (1986). Closing down the conversation: The end
of the quantitative qualitative debate among educational inquirers. *Educational Researcher, 15* (1), 4–12.

Smith, M. L., & Shepard, L. (1987). What doesn't work: Explaining policies of retention in the early grades. *Phi Delta Kappan, 68,* 129–134.

Stubblefield, H. W. (1991). Learning from the discipline of history. In J. M. Peters, P. Jarvis, & Associates (Eds.), *Adult education: Evolution and achievements in a developing field of study* (pp. 322–343). San Francisco: Jossey-Bass.

Tennant, M. (1991). The psychology of adult teaching and learning. In J. M. Peters, P. Jarvis, & Associates (Eds.), *Adult education: Evolution and achievements in a developing field of study* (pp. 191–216). San Francisco: Jossey-Bass.

Tesch, R. (1990). *Qualitative research: Analysis types and software tools.* New York: Falmer Press.

Thomas, A. M. (1991). Relationships with political science. In J. M. Peters, P. Jarvis, & Associates (Eds.), *Adult education: Evolution and achievements in a developing field of study* (pp. 301–321). San Francisco: Jossey-Bass.

Thomas, M. B. (1989). Writing links research and practice. *Lifelong learning: An omnibus of practice and research, 12* (8), 4–7.

CHAPTER 10

CONCLUSION

D. Randy Garrison

The first doctoral programs specializing in adult education were established in the 1930s. Notwithstanding this fact, it has only been in the last 30 years that we have begun to see a systematic approach to the study of adult education. Despite considerable progress in establishing adult education as a credible field of study, we find ourselves at a crossroad. The reality and fundamental concern is that adult education does not possess a readily identifiable coherent and distinctive theoretical framework. As a consequence, most of the important issues discussed in previous chapters are directed toward this concern. It would seem that a serious threat to the epistemological development and identity of adult education as a field of study is a fragmentation of its aims. If this premise is accepted, the question then becomes how to address this diffusion of aims and construct the necessary theoretical coherence and distinctiveness that will ensure its continued identity and development.

Previous discussions suggest there is a fragmentation of theoretical, practical, and policy interests that presents a serious challenge to establishing research priorities for a relatively small and emerging field of study. A basic question is, should research continue to proceed capriciously or can the field establish and address important and legitimate concerns? To complicate matters further, there appears to be a growing concern as to the primacy or balance of sociopolitical (policy) aims and basic research. Finally, there is the issue of the training of future researchers—particularly with regards to research methodology.

It would seem imperative that adult education establish an epistemological foundation if it is to be more than a loose collection of theories with questionable distinctiveness. To do so, adult education researchers and practitioners must clarify the defining assumptions of the field. The fact that adult education is a pragmatic interdisciplinary field of study does not preclude the possibility of identifying the field's essence and developing a coherent and distinctive theoretical framework. However, this will necessitate an elevation of the importance and attention given to basic research.

The issue surrounding applied and basic research is not an either/or choice. We must come to accept different ways of knowing for different purposes. Adult education has always focused upon issues and questions relevant to practitioners. The reality is, however, that adult education is in desperate need for coherent and distinctive theoretical frameworks that reflect the essence of the phenomenon called adult education. Collaborative research findings have the potential to be immediately useful to practitioners as well as ultimately to the study of the field as a whole. Rubenson (chapter 8) makes a strong argument for conceptually based policy-initiated research that could provide adult education with a theoretical base while addressing practical and socially relevant problems. This interdisciplinary approach to adult education research has much appeal in conjoining the practical, empirical, and theoretical.

As difficult and discomforting as it may be, an issue that needs to be addressed head-on is the balance between sociopolitical activism and the establishment of an epistemological foundation for the field. This issue has been addressed obliquely through discussions of applied and basic research in previous chapters. The assumptions of sociopolitical activism need to be examined in terms of the essential activities of the field of adult education. In particular, the ideological nature of some perspectives need to be examined (see chapters 5 and 7). The issue is balancing the adult education agenda between the practical interests of social change and the scholarly interests of establishing the field's knowledge base. Here again Rubenson provides a vision of conceptual research not involved in power politics yet initiated by relevant practical social problems. In the final analysis, however, our continued existence as a legitimate field of study and practice will be dependent upon the credibility of its epistemological foundation.

Another important issue is the relationship of adult education to the larger field of education. It would seem futile to attempt to establish adult education as a unique field of study in some way independent of the genus EDUCATION. Adult education must embrace the concepts and knowledge of other fields and disciplines as many in this volume advocate. However, we should pay particular attention to, and participate in, knowledge development in the larger field of education. Most of the distinctions made to distinguish adult education from other educational fields are a question of degree not kind. For example, concepts such as self-directed learning and critical thinking are key concepts in most educational fields. Not only must we be interdisciplinary in our study of adult education, but we must critically connect with the larger field of education. By not doing so we risk simply becoming irrelevant—an anachronism. It is imperative that we establish our place in the larger field of education. We are not well served by isolating ourselves conceptually or in practice.

One very important way to prevent continuing marginality is to attend and present at conferences such as the American Educational Research Association Conference. The premise is that adult education is not unique and, therefore, the issues and theories of the larger field of education are directly applicable. In fact, less reformulation and testing are likely to be required than when borrowing from the generic disciplines. As suggested previously, concepts such as self-directed/regulated learning have been rigorously developed in fields of education other than adult education. As such, we do not have exclusive ownership of this and other concepts. Traditional adult education approaches to learning are being adopted by other fields of education. It would appear to be irresponsible for adult educators not to build upon this research while recognizing important distinctions of context. Adult educators must open themselves to all educational literature and research forums. It is not enough to read only adult education research and attend adult education research conferences.

The final broad issue is facilitating the production and dissemination of all forms of research. The point has been made strongly and repeatedly that it is essential to recognize and value the complementarity and diversity of perspectives with regard to research methodologies. It is futile to continue the methodological wars. Research questions determine methodology. Most important, all research methods have standards that must be addressed within a critical community of researchers regarding the validity of a study's findings. All methodologies use similar intellectual methods. With regard to qualitative and quantitative inquiry, Phillips (1992) states:

Bad work of either kind is still—at best—only tentative. But good work in both cases will be objective, in the sense that it has been opened up to criticism, and reasons and evidence offered in both cases will have withstood serious scrutiny. (p. 78)

It is the role of journals to provide the forum for critical scrutiny of research results. It is critical that adult educators not only conduct research but contribute to the knowledge base by submitting manuscripts for publication. As Merriam (chapter 6) notes, the process of writing and getting published is not a mysterious one. If the field of adult education is to establish itself as a credible field of study, it will need the contributions of many more researchers than those presently contributing to the field. Sadly, a vast warehouse of quality research by graduate students remains unpublished and, therefore, does not have the opportunity of contributing to the field's knowledge base. This results in an absence of cumulative inquiry. Passing the final oral exam should not be the end of the research process. Concerted attempts to publish the findings should be made with the assistance of the student's supervisor, while recognizing ethical considerations (see chapter 4).

Training of competent and committed adult education researchers through graduate work is of paramount importance to the field. As argued in chapter 1, without the critical mass of adult education researchers in key areas of interest, there will not be the quantity and quality of research and discourse to establish the epistemological foundation of the field. Unfortunately, the majority of graduate programs emphasize applied research skills to the detriment of basic research skills (Blunt, chapter 9). Professors of adult education must develop a commitment to research and publishing in their students, particularly those in doctoral programs. In addition, adult education's gatekeepers must welcome novice researchers into the research community and provide the guidance and support needed to ensure their continued contribution to the knowledge base of the field. As a research community, we must develop priorities similar to those of the Social Sciences and Humanities Research Council of Canada Strategic Grants Program which plan "to increase investment in the training of the next generation of researchers; to develop and promote research structures to enhance research quality, productivity and relevance; and to ensure that research results are more widely disseminated" (Annual Report, 1991, pp. 26–27).

The future holds many serious challenges to adult education researchers. One vision worthy of serious consideration with the potential of identifying and developing distinct and coherent theory relevant to the practice of adult education is through interdisciplinary research teams. Such an approach would assemble the critical mass of researchers as well as the sustained critical scrutiny necessary for the field to establish itself in the long term. This approach is consistent with the interdisciplinary, conceptual, and long-term commitment to major research programs advocated by Rubenson (chapter 8). A theoretical and interdisciplinary team approach provides a wider scope to research problems which, in turn, provides increased opportunities for critical scrutiny. If funding limitations do not allow research teams to be assembled at one site, then collaborative networking strategies should be employed (see Hiemstra & Brockett, chapter 4).

In conclusion, the epistemological foundations of the field of adult education have not been established. The theories and concepts that adult educators covet are being usurped by the larger educational field. If we are to become more than a diffuse field of practice and sociopolitical activism, then the development of a coherent and distinctive epistemological foundation is a necessity. This, in turn, will require concerted efforts to train future adult education researchers and support their research efforts. We must recognize and address the fundamental choices and decisions that face us. As we emerge from the transition we are experiencing, we will hopefully put aside our methodological differences, develop an interdisciplinary focus, and become an integral presence in the larger educational community through major research and scholarly graduate programs. While there is room for all interests and agendas in adult education, we must maintain an open and critical discourse and keep in sight the need to establish an epistemological foundation.

REFERENCES

Annual Report. (1991). Social Science and Humanities Research Council of Canada. Ottawa: Communications Division.
Phillips, D. C. (1992). *The social scientist's bestiary.* New York: Pergamon.